Track of the Grizzly

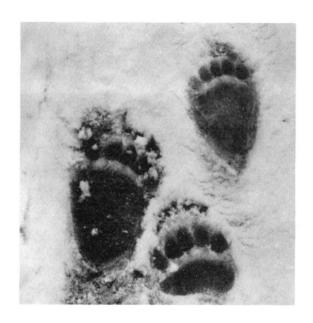

Track of the Grizzly

Frank C. Craighead, Jr., Ph.D.

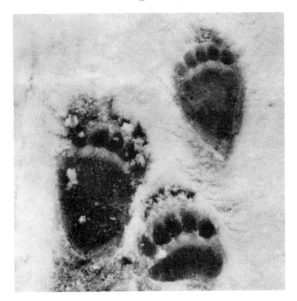

Sierra Club Books / San Francisco

Copyright © 1979 by Frank C. Craighead, Jr.

Track of the Grizzly *was first published in hardcover by Sierra Club Books in 1979. First softcover edition, 1982.*

Line drawings and cover design by Bill Wells
Maps by Chris Wenner
Book design by Dare Porter

Printed in the United States of America on acid-free paper containing a minimum of 50% recovered waste paper, of which at least 10% of the fiber content is post-consumer waste.

Library of Congress Cataloging in Publication Data

Craighead, Frank Cooper, 1916–
    Track of the grizzly.

    Bibliography: p. 248
    Includes index.
        1. Grizzly bear.   2. Mammals—Yellowstone National
Park.   3. Yellowstone National Park.   I. Title.
QL737.C27C7   599'.74446   78-8563
ISBN 0-87156-322-3

10   9   8   7   6

This book is dedicated to kindred traits —
the inquisitive nature of the grizzly
and the imaginative spirit of man.

Contents

Preface

This book is about grizzly bears — and incidentally about the people who study them. The bears are the subject of a research project, the people are primarily scientists or students of wildlife. Both the grizzlies and the scientists are affected by the acts and decisions of other individuals and groups. All the people are real, not fictitious; so are the bears. The events of the narrative all occurred and are described as I and others experienced them. In short, this is a true story of bears and humans.

The book is documentary in nature; its contents are based on field notes and journals, records, previously published papers, memorable incidents, and accumulated observations. The facts are reported as found by our research team. Field biology has its shortcomings, compared with more precise scientific disciplines, particularly in the difficulty of obtaining quantitative data; still, I believe the information presented here is the best of its kind available. Occasionally, events have been inferred from established knowledge and physical clues. Occasionally, too, the author has taken the liberty of attributing certain activities of one grizzly to another, or of combining a number of separate incidents into a sequence of events. The purpose of this was to help give continuity and coherence to the narrative; it in no way detracts from the validity of the information.

One of the objectives of this work is to present the results of a scientific study of the grizzly in a readable, informative, and, I hope, somewhat entertaining form. I have always felt that the scientist has an obligation to explain his work and findings to the general public as well as to other scientists. Another, more indirect, aim is to offer some insight into the work, lives, joys, and trials of wildlife biologists. But my primary goal throughout is to provide a far more complete and detailed profile of the grizzly bear than has previously been available. I have tried to show the great bears as I learned to know them, because it is crucial that many others learn to know them better. These magnificent creatures are in many ways the epitome of evolutionary adaptation, but in order to survive in today's world they need our understanding. Without it they are doomed. Some may ask: "So what?" This book is my reply.

Acknowledgment is due to many who helped make possible our study of the grizzly bear, and thus this book. First and foremost, I recognize the tremendous contribution of my brother, John Craighead, who directed many aspects of the work. The years of research during which we worked closely together were a labor of love for us both. The present treatment, however, is solely mine; John is writing his own book and I suspect the approach will be quite different.

At one time or another in our technical papers, John and I have tried to acknowledge the contributions of all who participated in the grizzly bear study or encouraged us in this enterprise. I wish to thank all these again but will not attempt to enumerate. However, I would like to express my appreciation to several people in particular: Lemuel Garrison, former superintendent of Yellowstone National Park; Dr. Melvin M. Payne, Chairman of the Board, the National Geographic Society; Dr. Vincent J. Schaefer, Director, Atmospheric Sciences Research Center, State University of New York at Albany; Donald Ozmun, a longtime friend and supporter; and Paul Buser, Frank Goodyear, Charles Pihl, Samuel Scrivener, and Dr. Jerry Stout, all directors of the Environmental Research Institute. Special recognition is due to Dr. Lawrence M. Gould, who helped us initially to obtain research funds and later through his efforts to inform scientific colleagues of attempts to hinder research in Yellowstone. I especially thank Harry Reynolds, Jr., a former Park Service employee, for having had the courage to state his convictions in writing, and I thank Diana Landau for her excellent editorial help.

The research was supported by the National Geographic Society and by grants from the National Science Foundation. Both gave us a free hand in our work and publications. Other support came from the Atomic Energy Commission, the U.S. Fish and Wildlife Service, Aeronutronic Ford Corporation, the Arthur T. Erickson Foundation, the National Park Service, and the Yellowstone Park Company. Contributing organizations included the Wildlife Management Institute, the Boone and Crockett Club, the New York Zoological Society, the American Museum of Natural History, the University of Montana, the State University of New York at Albany, and the fish and game departments of Wyoming, Montana, and Idaho.

Frank C. Craighead, Jr.
Moose, Wyoming

Introduction

The grizzly bear once roamed the North American continent as a coequal of primitive man. Each made use of the same habitat and competed for many of the same foods—tubers, leaves, berries, the seeds of plants, and the flesh of animals. The bear respected man, who had the advantage of his primitive weapons, but did not fear him. Man in turn respected and in some cases even revered the bear; there is paleontological evidence from cave paintings and preserved skulls of a bear cult dating back some 40,000 years to Neanderthal times. Later, the grizzly bear would be held sacred by some western Indian tribes. Others, as a test of courage, would challenge the bear to mortal combat in the hope of obtaining a bearclaw necklace, a token of bravery and tribal status. The mystique of the bear persists even in our own time; many big game hunters regard a grizzly trophy as the ultimate proof of strength and courage.

Much of the bear's fascination for early peoples probably had to do with the more obvious similarities between the two creatures. Both were omnivorous; in fact, bears may well have indicated potential food sources to roving hunters and gatherers. The bear's ability to rise on its hind legs in a manlike posture also suggested a kinship with human beings, and the track of its hind foot, while large, resembles man's. A skinned bear has an exceptionally human appearance. And the bear can rotate its forearm and grasp and hold objects with its dexterous front claws, almost as if they were fingers.

In physical feats, the bear could outdo its human competitor, who held in awe the animal's tremendous strength, its astounding speed and agility, and its ferocity when aroused. The bear could run faster and swim better, its reflexes were faster, it could tolerate and survive serious wounds, and could travel in uncanny silence and stealth. While man struggled to feed himself and keep warm during the long, severe winter, the bear slept and lived off its fat, which supplies about 3500 calories per pound. The food that produced this fat was obtained by a hunter and forager more efficient than the best of the human variety. Too, the grizzly's hard muscular structure and its vascular system, with an unusually large heart and thick-walled aorta, would have made it a creature very difficult to kill with crude weapons. It was in every way a worthy opponent of primitive man. The grizzly had little reason to flee from its human competitor, or from any other species, for that matter. The great bears, numbering in the hundreds of thousands, lived largely unchallenged in a vast pristine wilderness, their range extending from the Mississippi to the Pacific and from Mexico to the Arctic Circle.

The grizzly bear has been known to the white man for over four hundred years. Coronado was probably the first of the early explorers of the New World to see a grizzly, in what is now west-central New Mexico in the year 1540. In 1602 another Spaniard, Sebastian Viscaino, described grizzlies feeding on a whale carcass near Monterey, California.* The first reference to the killing of a grizzly by a white man was in 1690. In a journal entry dated September 1690, Henry Kelsey, who was exploring the Canadian prairies for the Hudson's Bay Company, mentions a bear that provided good meat but whose hide the Indians discouraged him from keeping because "they said it was God."†

Lewis and Clark, on their transcontinental expedition of 1804–1806, observed and collected specimens of grizzly bears. Meriwether Lewis noted in his journal the grizzly's qualities of strength and fearlessness: "The Indians give a very formidable account of this animal, which they never dare to attack, but in parties of six, eight or ten persons; and are even then frequently defeated with the loss of one or more of their party." A few weeks later he described an encounter with a grizzly:

> *The river rising and the current strong, and in the evening we saw a brown or grizzly bear on a sand beach. I went out with one man, George Drewyer, and killed the bear, which was very large and a "turrible" looking animal, which we found very hard to kill. We shot ten balls into him before we killed him and five of those balls through his lights. This animal was the largest of the carnivorous kind I ever saw. . . . Notwithstanding he had*

---

*This would likely have been the California subspecies *(californicus)* or ecotype, depending on the classifier. An ecotype is not a subspecies but a population living in and adapted to an environment separate and different from that of others of its species.

†This was apparently the plains grizzly, an ecotype about which little is known.

*five balls through his lungs and five others in various parts, he
swam more than half the distance across the river to a sandbar,
and it was at least 20 minutes before he died; he did not attempt
to attack, but fled and made the most tremendous roaring from
the moment he was shot.*

Lewis and Clark also wrote a scientific description of the grizzly
that was reasonably accurate for the time. This and a specimen they
obtained in 1805 were used by George Ord of Philadelphia in 1815 as
the basis for the scientific name he gave to the species, *Ursus arctos
horribilis* Ord. *Ursus arctos* was the name given to the European
brown bear in the eighteenth century by Linnaeus. This species was
recognized as holarctic—that is, ranging around the world in the arctic latitudes—by von Middendorf as early as 1851. From time to time
since then, depending on the data available to them, various
taxonomists have added to or subtracted from the number of species
and subspecies distinguishing these northern hemisphere bears. In
1963, after extensive study, Robert L. Rausch published a paper on
geographic variation in the size of North American brown bears as
indicated by skull measurements. He concluded that the Kodiak
brown bear, the type found on islands off the coast of Alaska, possessed sufficiently unique characteristics to be considered a distinct subspecies, *Ursus arctos middendorffi.* He also proposed that, because it
had priority, the name *Ursus arctos horribilis* be used for all other
brown bears, including the grizzly, inhabiting the greater part of the
species' range in North America. These two are the only subspecies
of brown bear currently recognized in North America. The black bear
(Ursus americana) and the polar bear *(Ursus maritimus)* are of
course entirely different species. The subspecies *horribilis* is often
referred to in the vernacular as the silvertip grizzly because of its
distinctive silver-tipped guard hairs.

There are numerous accounts and stories of grizzlies from the
trappers and explorers of the first half of the nineteenth century, but
from about this period on, grizzly numbers steadily declined throughout their range. Clearly, it was not until the advent of the repeating
rifle that human beings became a serious threat to the grizzly bear.
This weapon, which perhaps gave the decisive advantage to the white
settlers in their struggle against the Native Americans for control of
the continent, was also quickly put to use in reducing the numbers of

wild animals, particularly predator species, viewed as a threat to the progress of civilization.

In their thoughtless determination to control the environment of both the Indian and the bear, the newcomers were not long in eliminating the grizzly from much of its former range. In California, where there had been an estimated ten thousand grizzlies before the settlers arrived, the species had been completely exterminated by 1924. A remnant population in Mexico appears about to follow the California grizzly. Within the contiguous forty-eight states, aside from rare exceptions, grizzlies are now found only in Montana, Wyoming, and Idaho. Here they live in the high mountain country and in wilderness areas of large national parks and forests. These lands support a total of perhaps 600–700 animals.*

In 1959, my brother John and I and a number of colleagues began a long-range study of the grizzly bear in Yellowstone National Park and parts of four adjacent national forests. This area comprises some 5 million acres, and in terms of its natural character and the life forms (specifically, the grizzly) it supports can be considered the greater Yellowstone ecosystem (see map on page 5). As a result of the protection afforded by Yellowstone National Park, these lands are home to one of the largest remnant populations of grizzlies in the lower forty-eight states. (Until recently, the hunting of grizzlies was permitted in the surrounding national forests of Wyoming and Montana—Idaho closed its season in 1946—but at the time our study began the grizzly was not overhunted.)

The Yellowstone Ecosystem *The heavy white line indicates the extent of the grizzly bear's range in the region surrounding Yellowstone National Park. The points connected by this line represent bear sightings, kills, or radio fixes. (Portions of the national forests outside the park officially designated as wilderness or primitive areas currently include the Teton Wilderness, the North Absaroka Wilderness, and the Beartooth Primitive Area. Such designations place restrictions on the manner and extent to which these lands can be used. They aid in the preservation of the grizzly and grizzly habitat.)*

---

*This figure is based on our own studies in Yellowstone and various estimates by bear biologists and managers.

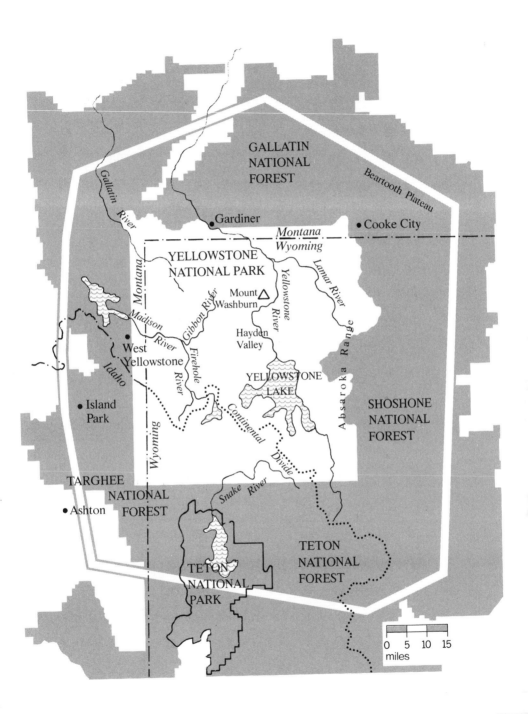

The ecosystem is a predominantly timbered region lying at altitudes of from seven to eight thousand feet, above which thrust many high ridges and peaks. Astride the Continental Divide, the backbone of the Rocky Mountains, lies this last stronghold of the grizzly, a region of bare rocks and spires descending to alpine meadows (the favorite summer foraging areas of the grizzly), and timbered slopes and ridges. Here small rivulets develop into streams which pick up runoff and underground water to become rivers draining vast watersheds. The two major drainage systems are those of the Snake–Columbia and the Yellowstone–Missouri rivers and their tributaries.

Most of the timber lies within the montane zone of spruce and fir, but about three-quarters of it consists of lodgepole pine in the gradual process of replacement by the spruce–fir climax vegetation. Interspersed in the timber are small sagebrush–grass meadows, dry areas with rich soil. These open areas are important to the grizzly bears because of the food they provide, and perhaps also because they approximate the once preferred habitat of grizzlies: stream-bottom grassland bordered with streamside thickets of willow and cottonwood. Although open country provides the bulk of the bear's food, timbered areas give them such sustenance as huckleberries, pine nuts, and elk sedge, and provide essential daytime retreats and concealed denning sites. Thanks to the dynamic process of plant succession, the grizzly in the Yellowstone region has access to a variety of plant habitats and the animal communities they sustain. Throughout vast stretches of the transitional lodgepole pine, seedlings of whitebark and limber pine are growing into young trees. These five-needle pines, when mature, produce tremendous nut crops approximately every five years. If not interfered with, this replacement of lodgepole with five-needle pines will eventually provide a much greater source of fall food for the grizzlies. In addition, both localized and extensive fires have produced shrub growth which includes huckleberries for the bears.

The population of grizzlies inhabiting this ecosystem appeared to be holding its own at the time our study began, at least according to the sparse information available, and probably actually represented less than the total carrying capacity of this vast land. At the same time, the human demands on the land were growing by leaps and bounds; all sorts of recreationists, including hikers, backpackers, car-campers, big game hunters, and fishermen were visiting Yellowstone National Park and environs in ever greater numbers. More visitors meant more development and a greater potential for disruption of grizzly bear ecology. It also meant an increased chance of unexpected and mutually hazardous encounters between people and grizzlies.

History and lore are replete with tales of grizzly bears (most emphasizing their ferocity). In the early part of the twentieth century a few pioneer wildlife students such as William H. Wright and Enos A. Mills spent considerable time observing grizzlies, their writings making a valuable contribution to the meager body of knowledge about the great bears. But prior to our study, reliable scientific information on the grizzly was extremely limited. There are good reasons why this was so: the grizzly's essential shyness, its tendency to be nocturnal, its wild and rugged habitat, and the obvious dangers and difficulties of getting close enough to study or handle the bears. Among the key unknowns were how much territory and privacy the grizzlies needed, how the presence of greater numbers of humans in the ecosystem might affect them, and how large a viable population is. Estimates of population size in those days relied heavily on guesswork and scattered sightings, so any effort at management then was bound to be highly problematic. In order for the Yellowstone ecosystem to continue to function as a refuge for grizzlies, it was imperative to know much more about the bears — their nature, numbers, and needs. This was the raison d'etre of our research project.

Our study, which was launched with the financial support of a number of private and public agencies, was a wide-ranging one aimed at filling in gaps in the scientific knowledge of the grizzly. From the very beginning we realized that in order to derive a complete picture of grizzly ecology and to relate our findings to the management of the bears, it would be essential to know the size of the population and extent of the area over which it roamed. We needed to know whether its numbers were increasing, decreasing, or remaining more or less stable from year to year. In order to detect trends and measure changes in the population, we needed to know not just the total number of bears but also the composition of the population by age and sex. To this end, we systematically gathered data on the numbers of adults, sub-adults, two-year-olds, yearlings, and cubs that composed the total population each year. The information we gathered on sex ratios (that is, the number of females, both young and adult, as compared to males in the population) would help us obtain statistics on differential death rates and reproduction. And as we began to learn the answers to some of these questions, still others would present themselves — the whys and hows.

We also hoped to learn as much as possible about the grizzly's social organization, feeding habits, seasonal movements, the extent of individual ranges, breeding age and frequency of breeding, size of litters, and causes of mortality. We wanted to try to calculate longevity, observe hibernation and prehibernation behavior, and record data on man — bear confrontations. We were apprehensive that as more people made use of the bears' shrinking domain, an increase in bear attacks or maulings might precipitate a reaction that could result in wholesale destruction of the animals.

To gather the various kinds of data outlined above, we would need to be able to precisely recognize individual bears year after year, and this in turn required that we mark them in some way. We needed, first of all, a practical technique for capturing and immobilizing such a large and powerful animal long enough to do this. Most of the grizzlies we handled were first captured in a culvert trap, consisting essentially of a large metal cylinder mounted on a trailer. Like a rabbit box trap, it had a drop-door at the entrance which was released by a baited trigger at the rear. Once trapped, the bear could be immobilized. Other grizzlies were shot, while free-roaming, with darts containing a drug (usually sucostrin, which acts through the central nervous system to relax the animal's muscles, or sernylan, which functions as a sedative or tranquilizer).

Once a bear was immobilized, we clamped a small numbered metal tag in each ear and inserted plastic rope markers of various distinctive color combinations. These markers enabled us to recognize individual bears from a distance of up to a quarter mile. At the time of capture each bear was assigned a number on the basis of the sequence in which it was captured. This number was tattooed under the right armpit or on the lip, ensuring positive identification if the bear should be killed, even if its markers were missing. In a few cases we were fortunate enough to capture and mark a whole family, that is, a mother with cubs or yearlings. Information on a particular individual or family was filed in a folder under the appropriate number, and in this way we began to accumulate life histories. Many of the bears also acquired names in the course of our acquaintance with them.

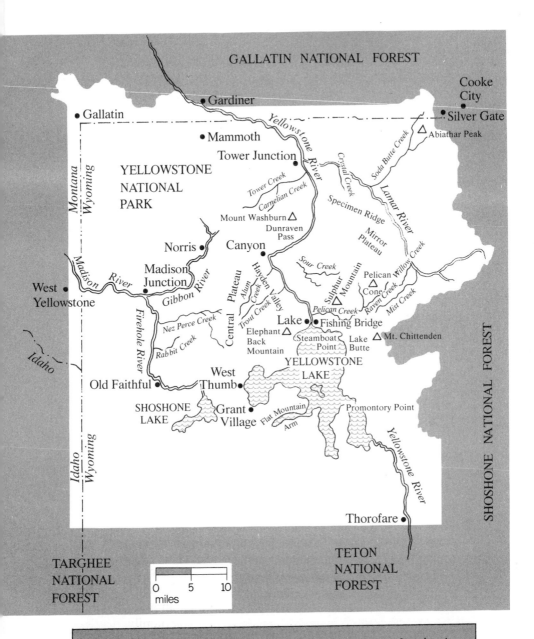

Yellowstone National Park *This map locates place names referred to in the text. It is not a definitive map of the park, as many features and landmarks have been omitted for clarity.*

Quite early in our work it became evident that we needed a research technique that would permit us to readily locate and observe grizzlies at night, when they are most active, and to do so over extensive areas of timbered terrain. Similarly, to locate them in their daytime beds, secluded in dense timber and windfall, required something other than conventional methods of research. We turned to the field of electronics. In collaboration with engineers (Dick Davies and Joel Varney of Aeronutronic Ford Corporation, and Hoke Franciscus, a friend and ham operator), we drew up specifications for a system of tracking by the use of miniature radio transmitters. Step by step we tested prototype models, until the day came when, thanks to the technology of the space age, we succeeded in tracking a grizzly bear through her daily wanderings—and later to her winter den. This was Number 40, the bear we called Marian. (We instrumented her for eight consecutive years. Usually she and the other instrumented grizzlies lost their collar in late spring when down in weight. If not, we recaptured them, and removed and replaced the radio.) By degrees our own lives became sufficiently entwined with Marian's that we thought of her with affection and were shaken by her eventual fate.

Our research project on the grizzly bear was conducted under agreements of understanding between the National Park Service, my brother John Craighead, as leader of the Montana Cooperative Wildlife Research Unit at the University of Montana, and me, representing the Environmental Research Institute of Moose, Wyoming. From 1959, the first year of the study, through 1967, our collaboration with the Park Service was close and amicable. We enjoyed the support and encouragement of Lemuel Garrison, who served as Park Superintendent until 1964, and his interim successor John S. McLaughlin. Park rangers and other personnel supplied us with helpful information, and we regularly assisted them in capturing, handling, and relocating troublesome bears. Naturally, such cooperation took many other mutually beneficial forms.

The research we were involved in was by nature long-range: following the careers of individual bears from year to year, keeping track of changes in the social organization of the bear community, and in particular trying to determine the size, composition, and growth trends of the population and the diverse factors, both natural and imposed, that influenced it. We planned and hoped to remain at work in the park for as long as was necessary to complete a thorough ecological study of the grizzly.

In 1968, however, changes in Park Service policy with regard to grizzly bear management, instituted by a new Yellowstone Park administration in response to external pressures and in complete disregard of scientific information we had made available, placed us in the position of opposing the official line on management. In the ensuing few years, the climate for independent scientific research in Yellowstone steadily worsened, and our work was in various ways impeded, misrepresented, and publicly disparaged by park officials because its results did not conform to the changed position of management. More important, the new policies were very nearly disastrous to the grizzly community. The events of this period and the controversy that lingers even today are fully documented in Chapter 10; for now, let it suffice to note that they resulted in the untimely termination of our field work in Yellowstone in 1971.

The Craighead grizzly bear study was a team effort, both in the accumulation of data and in its later interpretation. While I focused my energies on radio-tracking, John was planning, supervising, and participating in research aimed at gathering demographic information: the data that would eventually give us all the vital statistics of the grizzly population. Maurice Hornocker, working at first as a graduate student and then as an assistant, placed special emphasis on behavioral studies. Maurice, Jay Sumner, Bob Ruff, Jim Claar, Henry McCutcheon, Jerry McGahan, Charlie Ridenour, Henry Tomingas, Dick Ellis, and Jack Seidensticker, and others, all at one time or another participated in most of the activities which comprised our field research. Most started as graduate students, and some subsequently became field assistants; it was thanks to their help that we were able to build up a large body of information on the grizzly bear.

Others who made vital contributions include Joel Varney and Hoke Franciscus, who developed our system of biotelemetry, and Harry Reynolds, Jr., who helped us at first in his capacity as a park ranger, then served briefly as a field assistant after leaving the Park Service, and later publicly supported our work when it was under attack. Dr. Morgan Berthrong, a longtime friend and associate of

John and myself, worked closely with us in studying grizzly bear physiology and analyzing blood and tissue samples from bears we autopsied after they had been killed.

Much of the scientific data presented in this book has been previously published (in some cases in greater detail) in technical papers and popular articles. Many of these, together with other literature on the grizzly, are listed in the Bibliography. Readers seeking more information on any particular aspect of the subject will find these informative.

1

The Bear
Marian

Summer had left the high country of Yellowstone National Park; bison, elk, and mule deer were on the move. Under the sleek coats of the grizzlies were thick layers of fat stored for winter use. The gray-streaked skies belching snow flurries behind 10,240-foot Mount Washburn emphasized the change in seasons. From our vantage point overlooking Hayden Valley we could hear the howling of coyotes and the challenging bugle of bull elk. Canada geese honked upriver, and the distinctive calls of sandhill cranes and ravens carried across the valley.

Normally we would have been attuned to these wildland voices, but on September 22, 1961, my brother John, Maurice Hornocker, and I were listening instead for a sophisticated manmade sound, a high-pitched, pulsing signal. Beep, beep, beep, full of portent and meaning, the repetitive metallic pulse came in loud and clear on the crisp fall air. The sound had nothing of wildness about it. No deep primitive instinct of the chase stirred in us at the sound, nor did it evoke a feeling of oneness with nature. Yet this beeping coming to us in the vastness of Hayden Valley thrilled us as few sounds ever had. The vibrant pulsing signal, though new to the Yellowstone wilderness, told us that we were in communication with the grizzly we identified as bear Number 40, just as surely as the distant honking told us that the Canada geese were on the wing. But the beep was more specific than the honk of the goose or the gutteral caw of the raven, for it emanated from one particular grizzly bear somewhere within the three thousand square miles of the park. Hearing this sound meant that we were monitoring the first free-roaming grizzly sow to be tracked by radio.

Number 40's debut as a free-roaming electronic instrument of science took place that day. We had captured her on the previous night, and then the next morning, September 22, we immobilized her. The drug, succinylcholine chloride (sucostrin), that Maurice measured out in a syringe and John administered, kept her inert for about fifteen minutes. But putting a radio on her—our first attempt on a bear—required nearly an hour.

"I think she's coming out of it," Maurice said.

"O.K., the anesthesia is ready," said John, who then knelt over Number 40 and injected the drug. The grizzly coughed, and in ten minutes was fully anesthetized.

We quickly began the systematic procedures we had used since 1959 on all the bears we immobilized. Number 40 was first weighed while suspended in a nylon rope net. She tipped the scales at 300 pounds, having gained 125 pounds since the first time she was captured, in 1960. Next we checked the colored ear markers and numbered ear tags that we had placed on her on that earlier occasion, noting that the left ear marker was missing. We recorded other general information: total length sixty-five inches, neck circumference twenty-eight inches, general condition excellent, age three and a half years, never borne cubs. Harry Reynolds and Mike Stephens helped to take dental casts and a blood sample.

The previous night we had worked late to finish assembling the radio collar. The battery pack had been dipped in silastic rubber to waterproof it. The two-ounce transmitter, the fourteen-ounce, seven-cell battery pack, and a section of the loop antenna had been wrapped in fiberglass cloth and coated with resin. The battery terminal had been soldered and then coated with orthodontic acrylic. The entire assembly was then sanded and wrapped with colored tape. The brightly colored collar that John handed me as I knelt by grizzly Number 40 weighed about two pounds and was as waterproof, shockproof, and bearproof as we could make it. Still, Harry voiced the skepticism we all felt: "Do you really think a grizzly will keep that thing on?" We had gambled time, money, and two years of work on the premise that this powerful carnivore would tolerate a collar. An initial experiment with a rope collar had proved successful, but a bear's tolerance for a fully rigged radio collar was yet to be tested.

In the course of our radio-tracking research, from 1961 to 1969, we were to place radios on forty-eight grizzlies, twenty-four of them different individuals (some were instrumented a number of times). Gradually, one instrumentation procedure blended with another so that recall of individual events is difficult. However, the memories of that first instrumenting are still crystal clear. There were a few tense moments when we thought it was a failure. I had pulled the antenna loop over Number 40's head and saw that it fitted snugly. Mike Stephens carried the receiver up the valley to test the strength of the radio signal. We checked all our procedures. Mike called in by walkie-talkie to say that the signal was very weak, so we rechecked the acrylic sealing, the connection of the loop antenna, and the tuning of the transmitter. Number 40 raised her head slightly. Her respiration rate had more than doubled, signalling that she would soon come out from under the effects of the anesthesia. We had been working for a long time, oblivious to the weather, but our hands were cold and blowing snow was turning the ground white. The bear would soon be up and away, but would our radio transmitter work? Mike called in, "It's colder than hell out here. . . . What's holding things up?" I ignored the query and asked if the signal was any stronger. "No good," came in loud and clear. Number 40 again raised her head, this time a little higher. "We'll have to give it up," John said, for we all knew the signs of the rousing grizzly and had experienced our share of close calls already. As we withdrew, our subject rose unsteadily to her feet. What had gone wrong? Dejectedly we watched our experimental bear head south for the nearest timber. And then Mike's voice boomed in on the walkie-talkie. "We've got it now! The signal's great!" While lying on her side, the grizzly's body had partially shielded the signal, but when she was up and moving, increasing the elevation of the transmitter, the signal strength improved. We had already learned one lesson of many that only experience could teach.

Now, as we listed to the steady beep, we had the answer to the question that had haunted us. The signal started as an invisible, soundless radio wave that spread in all directions from the tiny transistorized transmitter embedded in the newly affixed collar. The radio frequency was transformed into an audible frequency in the receiver beside me. This pulsed beeping, spilling into the afternoon air at seventy beeps per minute, could lead us across the sage–grass valley and through heavy lodgepole timber to grizzly sow Number 40 some miles distant, and could inform us of the exact location of the bear at any moment, day or night, for ninety days or more.

As the signal came in, I slowly rotated the loop antenna of the receiver to obtain first the strongest signal, then the weakest, or null. The position of the loop antenna indicated the direction of the signal source and thus the bear. "She's nearly due west," commented John, "but can we home in on her?" "It's a good start just being able to hear her." Indeed it was, for everything now depended on our keeping this signal. The next step in our experiment was to actually track down the bear by following the signal. From now on we intended not just to cross paths with a grizzly bear but to confront a particular grizzly at a specific time and place, the meeting to be determined by how fast and accurately our electronic equipment would lead us to her.

We climbed a long, sloping hill in the indicated direction, checking the receiver as we went. John and Maurice followed closely behind, carrying cameras, binoculars, and a telescope. Following the contour of the hill, we passed through lodgepole pines into open parkland, then ascended another hill, and yet another, in a beeline course. Before we topped the last rise the strength of the signal increased. Was the grizzly still some distance away? It was not just an academic question. For the first time in our study of the grizzly, we had the advantage of surprise on our side, especially when we were moving into the wind. Grizzlies are short-sighted and cannot readily discern a man beyond a hundred yards or so, but their sense of smell is extremely keen. Though we carried a firearm, we had yet to use it for defense and hoped we never would. But our purpose was not to avoid the grizzlies; the point was to get close and observe them without being detected. It had been and would be dangerous, for if jumped or startled at close range a grizzly might charge as readily as run. Thus we felt relief along with excitement when we cautiously peered over the hill and saw Number 40, head lowered, plodding along the valley floor unaware of our presence.

"There she is," we exclaimed in unison. John said that he could see the colored collar, and Maurice confirmed his observation as he followed the bear's movements with the scope.

All through the evening of 22 September the beep from our portable receiver told us where Number 40 was in the swirling snowstorm. From then on through the next month it kept us informed as to her whereabouts. We located her feeding on an elk carcass, followed her on a short foraging trip after pine nuts, and watched her associating with other bears. We tracked her from a day bed to the Trout Creek dump, where she foraged for scraps left over from tourists' tables. At that early point in our study the maximum distance at which we were able to pick up the bear's signal was about a mile, but later we modified and greatly improved the capability of our wildlife telemetry system. However, the system's early limitations in no way detracted from that first thrill when we followed the signal to the crest of the hill and saw the collared grizzly plodding along completely unaware of our presence. At that moment we proved that we had acquired the capability of arranging a meeting between bear and man at times and places of our own choosing. Also, we now had the means to obtain information on free-roaming animals continuously and from afar with a minimum of time, effort, and manpower. Inherent in this prototype system was the potential of gathering physiological information simultaneously with ecological data.

Regardless of what fate had in store for Number 40, she had made history as the first grizzly bear to be instrumented and tracked by radio. We felt she deserved a name. Dick Davies of Philco Corporation had designed this first small transmitter, and he and his wife had visited us in Yellowstone to help test the equipment. We thought it appropriate to name the bear after Dick's wife, so with her consent, Number 40 became the bear Marian.

For two years before the time Marian and the radio collar came on the scene, we had been at work gathering data. Our study began in 1959, and on June 26 of that year, through the peephole of a culvert trap, we had our first close-up look at a wild grizzly. As my eyes adjusted from the bright sunlight outside to the darkness within the trap, I saw an angry face lunging toward me, and I reared back just in time to avoid the long, lethal claws that flashed through the tiny opening. "Wow," I said, "he looks pretty big." Maurice Hornocker and John agreed, though we soon discovered that, as grizzlies go, this bear was not particularly large. By weighing trap and bear at once, we found that he tipped the scale at two hundred pounds.

On the basis of his weight we computed the amount of sucostrin that would immobilize without harming him. With a graduated syringe John measured out one milligram of the drug for every 3.5 pounds of body weight, or a total of about 57 milligrams. (We subsequently learned that we had used a larger dose than was needed; 1 milligram to each 5 pounds of body weight turned out to be sufficient.) He carefully squeezed the sucostrin from the syringe into a hollow projectile dart along with some sterile water, then placed the dart in the chamber of a CO_2 gun set at low compression. Poking the gun through an opening in the trap, I pulled the trigger, aiming the hollow needle at the base of the bear's neck. Within eight minutes the drug had begun to take effect, starting with a slackness in jaws and neck, followed by the relaxation of shoulder, limbs, abdomen, rib muscles, and finally the diaphragm. After the grizzly failed to bite a stick placed in his mouth, we opened the trapdoor, pulled him out, and got to work on the routine that would become so familiar in time. First we attached markers to the ears. Next we recorded the number 1 on the form we had prepared, and set down the measurements of foot, claw, neck, and total body length. Grizzly Number 1 turned out to be a typical animal. He had the silver-tipped guard hairs from which the species derives one of its common names, was of moderate size, and showed no peculiarities worthy of comment. But trapping and marking our first grizzly was no less momentous for that. Our long-range ecological project was now truly under way.

During that first year of study, 1959, we captured and marked with ear tags thirty grizzlies, some in culvert traps and others by immobilizing them with drug-filled syringe darts fired from a gun. Most of these animals were trapped in Hayden Valley but dispersed widely in fall. The following spring many of the marked bears reappeared, along with others. By the fall of 1960 an additional thirty-seven bears were sporting markers, bringing the total of tagged bears to sixty-seven. By observing both marked bears and a few others readily recognized due to specific physical traits, we were learning to identify a growing number of the grizzlies that constituted the Yellowstone community. Some bears, both marked and unmarked, became old acquaintances. To those with unusual physical and character traits we naturally gave names as well as numbers in order to differentiate them more readily from the less distinctive animals.

One of the bears marked in 1960 was Marian, whom we first trapped on July 1. At this time she was a young bear, two and a half years old and weighing 175 pounds. She was a small female and not particularly aggressive. At the time that we fitted Marian with her radio, she undoubtedly recognized most of the bears within this population, but her means of identification were different from ours. Scent alone probably played an important role.

The grizzlies that Marian foraged with at night or joined in secluded timbered retreats for rest were gradually taking shape as individuals in our minds. Number 76 was Pegleg, who had a stiff walk and was eventually destined to be tracked by radio. Also conspicuous were Scarface, with his battle scars, and Cutlip, with his lower lip hanging permanently askew, a scar from a battle with another large bear. Number 26 was named the Fifty-pound Cub (to distinguish him from another cub trapped about the same time that weighed ninety pounds), and could only be identified by his ear markers or through association with his mother. She was unnumbered, but we called her G.I. because of the strictness with which she disciplined her cubs. Bigfoot was another of Marian's companions, as was the Sucostrin Kid, a yearling who for some inexplicable reason required far more than the normal dosage of sucostrin to immobilize him. Then there were the prominent Rip-nose Sow and Number 88 with his white claws. The latter was named Loverboy and was recognizable without his markers from his cropped left ear and the scar below his right eye.

Bruno, Number 14, was later to lead us over the mountainous country of eastern Yellowstone, while we followed his beeping radio signal.

Another particularly conspicuous bear was the Owl-faced Sow, whose facial disc reminded us of a short-eared owl. She was one of the first mothers we observed to adopt the cubs of another sow. Shorty, Notch-ear, and Old Short-ears were unnumbered grizzlies whose names described the characteristics that enabled us to identify them, at least throughout one season. And the Grizzled Sow, Number 65, was a large, powerful female who had confidence to match her size. She produced a litter of four cubs in 1962, and one of her later offspring, Number 202, when fitted with a radio, taught us about the relationship of a yearling's home range to that of its mother.

In 1961, Marian became well acquainted with another young bear, Number 37, since both often sought daytime retreats in the same wooded area of upper Trout Creek. Number 37, later named Beep, was also a pioneer in our radio-tracking research but had even more seniority than Marian. Throughout 1960 and part of 1961 he wore an adjustable rope collar, thereby assuring us that a grizzly would tolerate a collar—the best method, we thought, of attaching a radio to a bear. Number 37 also had the distinction of becoming the second grizzly to be instrumented with a radio, hence his nickname.

Our acquaintance with Beep and his family began in 1960, when we trapped his mother and one yearling and immobilized another with a drug-filled dart. This latter yearling became Number 37. His littermate was Number 38, and his mother, a very aggressive bear, Number 39. Thus in a single day we had added a complete family to a growing list of marked bears. The family as a whole bore the unlucky number 13. It lived up to the superstition, for it was short-lived but nevertheless interesting and scientifically informative.

On July 3, 1961, Number 39 weaned her yearlings and thereafter they were on their own. This was an early weaning; mother and yearlings usually travel, forage, and sleep together throughout the second summer, but Number 37 and his brother were not to know so secure a family life. After their mother weaned them, she left them to fend for themselves. However, they had each other and remained inseparable during 1960, relying on one another for companionship and mutual protection.

When initially captured in late June, the yearlings weighed within five pounds of one another: 145 and 140 pounds respectively. When

Number 37 was retrapped late in August of the same summer, he had gained exactly 100 pounds in a period of almost two months. This was a 69 percent increase over his June 29 weight. It was at this time that we put a self-adjusting braided rope collar containing a mock-up radio transmitter around his neck. The purpose of this experiment was to see if a collar might prove suitable for eventually attaching a radio to a grizzly bear. The answer came about a year later when we retrapped Number 37, still wearing the collar, which was in good condition. Apparently he had made no serious effort to remove it.

In the meantime, both he and his brother were providing us with some interesting information as they grew and developed. As a fall yearling, Beep weighed 245 pounds, but he lost weight during the spring months, as most bears do. However, in less than three summer months he had recovered his loss and increased to 315 pounds. A year later, as a three-year-old, he tipped the scales at 440 pounds, about 150 pounds more than the average fall weight we had so far determined for male three-year-olds. Though Beep and his brother, Number 38, weighed the same as yearlings, there was a difference of 100 pounds between them as fall two-year-olds, illustrating the tremendous variability in growth rate that can occur in young bears.

When we retrapped Number 38 as a two-year-old, we transported him across Yellowstone Lake, leaving him on Promontory Point. Three days later he was back at Pelican Creek, having taken a circuitous shoreline route covering a minimum of thirty-one miles. Number 38 was revealing to us the homing instinct in grizzlies. Late in the fall of 1961, we captured his littermate near a construction camp south of West Thumb and released him forty airline miles to the north near Crystal Creek, in the hope that he would adjust to his new environment and remain away from campgrounds or developed areas. The next spring he was back near West Thumb and from there he wandered over to Old Faithful. In learning to fend for themselves after weaning, Numbers 37 and 38 were developing traits that indicated that they would be troublesome adult grizzlies — approaching too close to humans and even entering campgrounds. We hoped that by putting a radio on Number 37, we might learn more about the activities of problem bears. We also hoped we could help prevent his being killed by a bullet, which was bound to happen if he continued to cause trouble.

There was a light covering of snow on the ground, and the wind was cold and gusty on the day we adjusted the radio around the neck of Number 37, our second radioed bear. The rays of the wintry sun, gold behind black clouds, were disappearing, and it was dark before he ambled off. After a few days we lost his radio signal, but soon we relocated him a considerable distance away at West Thumb. Here he attempted to enter a trailer belonging to construction workers. He was retrapped — when his collar was seen to be missing — transported to the northwestern portion of the park, and released. When he was again fitted with a radio in 1962, he led us up over the Trout Creek divide, down the Nez Percé drainage, and over to the developed region of Old Faithful, thus increasing his chances of getting into trouble.

Had we learned nothing else from Number 37, I would still remember him because of one particular incident. One night I was waiting inside the closed culvert trap, hoping to take pictures of this radio-instrumented grizzly lured from a distance to a bait. It was drizzling slightly when John and Maurice lowered the steel door, effectively sealing me in and the bears out. I had my sleeping bag, flashlight, directional receiver, walkie-talkie, camera, chocolate bars, and a box of crackers, and was armed with a .357 revolver just in case of trouble. I planned to photograph out of an open window cut in the metal side of the trap. The window was large enough for my camera when fitted with long focal lenses, which meant that it could readily accommodate a bear's head as well.

The steady rain, now bordering on snow, increased after I entered the blind, and an early darkness soon enveloped me. Without a light I could see nothing, not even the trees nearby. After I had pulled on a heavy parka, removed my boots, and slipped my feet into a warm sleeping bag, I checked for Number 37 by holding the directional receiver out the window. (This was necessary because the surrounding metal attenuated the signals.) A loud and clear beeping indicated that the grizzly was moving in fast. We had left bait for him the night before, and now he was accustomed to it and heading for it purposefully. He came into view and for some time I observed him, the silvery gleam of raindrops on his guard hairs shining jewel-like in the beam of the flashlight. Although this momentary flashing of my light at first frightened him, he gradually became accustomed to it.

One by one, a few other bears silently joined in the feast, and I decided to attempt a few flash pictures. Very, very slowly I eased the camera and flash rig out the open window, having previously set the exposure and estimated the distance. When growls and muffled noises told me that a grizzly was tugging at the staked-down meat close to the trap, I pushed the shutter release. Instead of the instantaneous, white flash I anticipated, I was blinded by a rapid succession of all-engulfing bursts of light. A flood of intense illumination bounced back and forth off the shiny steel walls of the culvert trap. It was as though I were looking at the sun through binoculars. My eyes soon adjusted somewhat, but a pulsating golden glow still so blinded me that I was unable to see the nearby window or even the camera in my hand.

Startled, confused, and temporarily blinded, I felt completely helpless. I could imagine a grizzly flailing with his long claws through the open window, even though I knew it was unlikely. The accumulating water from the steady rain must have shorted out my equipment; I groped for the flash battery case, trying to turn off the power. I felt the wire leading to the camera and ripped it loose. The flashing stopped but instead of being clothed in darkness, I was still enveloped in a golden aftervision, a result of the intense light my eyes had been exposed to. When I could make out the shape of objects in the light of my flashlight, I was able to relocate the window and release the prop that held the hinged door open. Gradually my sight returned to normal and my heart rate dropped. With the aid of the flashlight I dried off my flash equipment, reassembled it, and crawled into my sleeping bag. With the sound of the rain splattering on the metal trap I slept until 2 A.M., when I was awakened by a growl. Again I cautiously opened the window, and during the next half hour took several flash pictures of Number 37, along with another, unidentified grizzly, tearing and tugging at the bait. Satisfied that I had a few good pictures, I dozed restlessly until morning, when John and Maurice arrived to release me from my metal cage.

Throughout our years of study, there were numerous times when we found ourselves in close proximity to free-roaming grizzlies without a radio to pinpoint their locations or a trap for protection, and these occasions provided many of the more dramatic moments in our work. The first time we were charged by a grizzly in the course of our work—an inevitable occurrence that each of us privately imagined many times—the bear did not make contact, but this in no way detracted from the excitement of the event. Naturally we had wondered how we would react to the bear, and the bear to us, upon meeting suddenly and at close quarters.

The pattern of such face-on confrontations was revealed early in our research. One day in September 1959, the lookout on Mount Washburn called our lab by phone to tell me that through his scope he was watching a grizzly feeding on an elk carcass. I drove to the lookout, verified the sighting during lulls between snow flurries, and plotted the bear's position on my map. Deciding to investigate, I asked Bob Howe, a subdistrict ranger, if he would like to accompany me. We hiked through the lodgepole forest, keeping downwind and just uphill of the grizzly. As we arrived near the spot where I thought we might see the bear, a large bull elk arose, walked ahead into a meadow, and trotted off. His course to the south was directly in line with the grizzly, which I could now see at the far end of the meadow.

The bear's front paws were resting protectively atop an elk carcass. From that distance he was unable to see us and the wind was toward us, so he wouldn't scent us, at least for the time being. Though we were concerned that the running elk might alert him, we began a cautious stalk, using terrain and trees to keep out of sight. Leaving the unbroken timber, we crawled out to scattered trees in the open. As yet the grizzly gave no sign of alarm. From a distance I snapped a few pictures of him. He may have caught the light reflecting from my moving camera, for he became restless and began to investigate, moving toward the timber in a circling maneuver, sniffing and trying to pick up a scent. It was our turn to become nervous. We were unable to see the bear after he entered the timber, through which he would be able to approach us quite closely. We debated whether to climb a tree where we were, but decided to sprint back across the open space to a spot where we could still climb trees if necessary, but where the grizzly could not approach us unseen.

During this brief sighting we had observed the grizzly protecting his kill from ravens and several coyotes, and had seen a smaller grizzly approach. The latter appeared to be intimidated by the obviously more dominant bear and had not yet tested to see if he could feed peacefully with the larger animal. Now this second grizzly was also nearby and out of sight. I was observing one of our first grizzly "kills," and I was not at all certain how the bears might react to each other, let alone to human intruders.

From our new refuge, Bob and I observed the larger grizzly's return from his reconnaissance. Apparently satisfied that all was well, he once more spread himself over his kill protectively, and we approached closer while he dozed. Our vision was obscured due to a rise in the ground, and the sun was in our eyes, so we moved back and tried a circuitous stalk, this time getting close enough to see that the bear did not have ear markers and thus was not one with which we were familiar. The bear was now alerted to our presence and moved toward us. We were again in the predicament of having the grizzly nearby and moving toward us through dense timber, so we quickly chose a lodgepole with low limbs and climbed it, waiting in our uncomfortable perches to see what might happen next. As the grizzly neither returned to the carcass nor appeared close by, we concluded that he had picked up our scent and left. Cautiously, we dropped out of the tree and approached the dead elk in the middle of the meadow. The grizzly had buried all but the head and antlers with dirt and grass; we wondered why but were not to find out until later. The elk, a huge one, must have weighed eight hundred pounds, perhaps more, and its antlers measured fifty-two inches from the skull to the tip of the far tine and forty inches across from tip to tip. We tried to roll the dead animal to see if he had been gored by another elk during a mating season fight, but our utmost efforts were inadequate. The animal's size, weight, and apparent good condition made me suspect that it had first been injured by another bull elk, then finished off by the grizzly.

Struggling to turn the elk, I looked up and saw the grizzly jogging out of the shadows to our west. "Bob!" I shouted. "The grizzly—he's coming!" I started backing in the opposite direction, abandoning my lens, tripod, and pack. I slung my camera over my shoulder, readied my .38, and yelled to Bob to throw a shell in the chamber of the rifle he was carrying, just in case. I glanced quickly at the nearest tree a quarter mile away. The grizzly was still moving rapidly toward us, occasionally stopping to rise up on his hind legs in an attempt to scent or see us. He would then drop on all fours, charge closer, and again rear up only to rush on. Was he attacking? What else? I thought as we continued to back off. As the distance between us dwindled, the grizzly rose and dropped to the ground once more, then increased his speed in a final attack—or was it a rush to the elk? We didn't stop to ponder the question but turned and ran in desperation, though even as we sprinted for the trees I knew we couldn't reach and climb one before the grizzly was upon us. I turned to face him just as he reached the elk carcass, where he picked up our scent, apparently for the first time.

Only now did he identify us as humans, and only now was I sure that he had not been attacking. He paused for a microsecond in surprise before making a rippling, rhythmic turn and running for the far timber. Still running, he disappeared. We were more than surprised; we were scared. But fortunately we had been saved from an encounter, perhaps a disaster, by the grizzly's natural inclination to avoid man. It was not the last time that our human scent would send a large, aggressive grizzly running. We were not misled; the grizzlies did not fear us, but if given an option usually chose to avoid us, even to the extent of temporarily abandoning food.

Our initial success in tracking Marian with a radio collar left us with high hopes for this particular research technique, and we worked continually to improve the dependability and capabilities of our radio-tracking system. With the help of Joel Varney, a very talented and enthusiastic electronics engineer, we developed and tested tracking receivers weighing only two and one-half pounds. Joel miniaturized our fully transistorized transmitters to 1.8 ounces. Our laboratory at Canyon became our base station, equipped with receivers that could quickly be connected to a five-element directional antenna. From the laboratory we monitored the instrumented grizzlies day and night, regularly picking up their signals from ten, twelve, and even twenty miles away under favorable conditions. Supplementing this system was a three-element antenna at our field station, located on a treeless hill eight miles to the south. We used two radio-equipped vehicles to locate and follow grizzlies that wandered to distant parts of the park. From a high point such as Mount Washburn we could readily monitor a thousand square miles of territory and determine whether or not our radio-tagged grizzlies were present. When our bears wandered out of our range, we occasionally resorted to taping our loop antennas to the strut of a fixed-wing plane. The additional altitude permitted us to readily pick up wandering bears from a distance. After locating them by air, we would then take off on foot with our portable directional receivers and follow the pulsed signals to their transmitter source, where we would either sight or jump the bears, usually at a distance of less than a hundred yards. The water- and shock-proof transmitters sent out differently pulsed signals, and these rhythms served to identify each instrumented grizzly. With improved equipment and techniques the inevitable day arrived when we first monitored the signals from a number of instrumented grizzlies simultaneously. We were receiving signals from Marian, at seventy-four beeps per minute; Pegleg, a roaming boar, at ninety-four pulses per minute; Number 75, a belligerent sow, at sixty-two per minute; and Number 7, the Sour Creek Sow, at the slower rate of fifty per minute. In this situation we were receiving more information than we could assimilate.

Telemetry allowed us to gather general information by inference on the location, behavior, and movement of the animals from a distance. A signal that periodically varied in loudness or strength indicated that a grizzly was active and moving about. One of constant loudness, especially during the daylight hours, often meant that the transmitting bear was resting or sleeping. An intermittent signal usually denoted that a grizzly was active, perhaps traveling; the signal varying when a ridge, a hill, or dense timber came between the bear and our receiver, or when the bear changed directions. In this way we learned that Marian's daily eating and sleeping habits were quite regular. After determining the basic pattern of her day's activities by radio-tracking, corroborated by visual observation, we could infer certain activities from the character of the signals we received. At times Number 40 slept in a foot-deep excavation in a low swale among the lodgepole pines nine miles from base. It was her practice to curl up in bed with her entire body below ground level. When she rested in this manner, the signal emanating from her collar antenna only came in loud and clear on our base receiver when she raised her head. When she lowered it, the shielding effect of the ground at this distance was sufficient to prevent or greatly reduce signal reception. Thus in the course of the day we heard or lost Marian's signal, depending on whether she slept with her head low, raised it to look around, or stood up to move about.

This type of monitoring also helped us determine when it might be informative to move in and observe. We learned early that, since the signal grew louder the closer we approached to a bear, the receiver volume had to be turned down to prevent alerting the bear to our presence. With practice we became quite expert at estimating our distance from a grizzly merely by observing the position of the volume control knob. However, situations arose when the signal fooled us. On one such occasion Joel Verney and Hoke Franciscus, our electronics collaborators, along with Maurice and me, were closing in on Marian when the rather loud signal began to fade. We assumed that she had arisen from her day bed and was moving away, so we continued to follow the weak signal rapidly. Suddenly the signal boomed out loud and clear even after I turned the volume down, an indication that the bear was dangerously close. At this instant, when we were almost on top of her, Marian suddenly rose up from her day bed and glared at us from only forty feet away. A larger, more aggressive grizzly would almost surely have charged us if we had jumped it in this manner. Marian appeared to be even more surprised than we were. She sprinted away, and then stopped to turn her head and looked menacingly back — or was that merely a glance of curiosity? We stood motionless and tense while she assessed the situation, perhaps even deciding whether to return to defend her daytime retreat. When her dark rippling form disappeared into the still darker timber, we broke the silence of the Yellowstone wilderness with a sigh of relief.

While our adrenalin-stimulated hearts returned to normal, we figured out what had caused the near catastrophe. Marian had dug her bed at the base of a fallen tree whose earth-cluttered roots shielded the radio signals as we approached from the east. From the greatly attenuated signals we assumed that the bear was much farther away than she actually was. As we moved past the earth barrier, the signal again loudly boomed in on our receiver. At this moment the startled grizzly had bolted from her bed while we stood petrified.

This incident served to intensify our fondness for Marian. We realized that there were undoubtedly two studies underway: she was learning about us just as we were discovering things about her. Apparently Marian had decided that these human beings that persistently appeared in unexpected and out-of-the-way places were not going to harm her. A relationship of mutual trust, and perhaps respect, was developing. At the very least she was showing a tolerance of our strange actions.

Already our studies were revealing that the grizzly did not fear man but preferred to avoid him when possible and, as other bear— man confrontations showed, to combat him if necessary. Constant experience in handling trapped and drugged bears and in observing others at close range demonstrated the tremendous power, speed, and ferociousness of an enraged grizzly bear, and we took precautions accordingly. But we also had ample opportunity to observe its intelligence and its essentially gentle and inquisitive nature. Although we carried firearms, we were never to use them in the course of a decade of intimate association with the grizzly in its own habitat.

2

Social Studies: The Grizzly Hierarchy

Each spring, most of the grizzlies inhabiting some five thousand square miles of Yellowstone and surrounding country move to or migrate toward the high central plateau portions of the park—the open and lush meadows of Hayden Valley and Pelican Creek. Some move north from the distant shores of Jackson Lake in Grand Teton National Park and the Thorofare country of the Teton Wilderness. Others come from the high jagged wilderness to the northeast surrounding Cooke City, Montana, or from the Gallatin big game country to the west.

This general pattern of movement and the resulting concentration of grizzlies is definitely influenced by the availability of food, both natural and man-supplied. Marian and many of the other grizzlies that gradually assembled in Hayden Valley in the spring of 1960 had moved into this open-meadow, grass-sage habitat in search of new green grass, sedge shoots, bulbs, tubers, and the roots of various plants. Here also the bears could scavenge tidbits from the nearby Park Service garbage dump. The first of such dumps were established over eighty years ago, and the grizzlies very quickly incorporated them into their annual foraging activities.

The bears' annual movement or migration is initiated by the coming of the vernal equinox. The sun gradually warms the high Yellowstone country and triggers a new surge of energy and activity in the biota. The adult boar (male) grizzlies begin to stir, emerging from hibernation in late March. They are the first of the grizzlies to greet the spring, traveling for miles over the still deep but crusted snow. Later, mothers emerge from snug winter quarters with tiny cubs born in late January and early February. Sows with energetic yearlings at their sides make snow tracks telling of wrestling matches and playful tussles. The six-month sleep of winter is over. For a time, the bears wander, forage, and rest in the general vicinity of their winter dens. They seek the damp sedge meadows for tender shoots, dig the soft soil of the drier meadows and mountain slopes for bulbs of the early-blooming wildflowers, spring beauty and yellow-bell; eat the tender seed pods of dogtooth violet; and graze the clovers, docks, and other greens—the shapely, rose-purple flowers of the shooting star, and perhaps even the young, tender leaves of the stinging nettle. The ripening meat of a bison or elk that has succumbed to the rigors of winter will attract and hold the bears until the flesh is consumed. Then the converging grizzly tracks in the snow will be replaced by emerging greenery around the scattered bones and dried, twisted sections of hide—all that remains of the carcass.

The buildup of the grizzly population in the high plateau country is well advanced by June and early July when the grizzlies mate. Over the years, the summer concentration of grizzlies in this rather limited area has resulted in the development of a complex social hierarchy which serves to diminish competition. Each bear, from the aggressive male who dominates the grizzly society down to the insecure orphan cub or yearling, finds a place in the social organization. The degree of aggressive behavior or assertion of dominance determines the individual's position, and relative positions change from year to year. Sows with cubs are more aggressive than barren ones and thus obtain a temporarily high social status. Large sows with cubs defer only to the large, aggressive males. Males and females associate only during the breeding season.

When we first trapped and marked Marian in 1960, she was a barren small sow, low in the social structure and readily showing deference to the older and larger bears of both sexes. In those days Marian appeared to take little heed of the shifting positions of the dominant and subdominant boars within the social structure. It seemed unlikely that this small, timid bear could aspire to mate with the powerful, aggressive bear dominating the Yellowstone ecosystem, and at the time we never gave a thought to such a possibility.

In the summer of 1959, the first year of our study, the dominant male in the Hayden Valley area was one we called Old Scarface. He weighed around a thousand pounds and was a veteran of numerous battles with other huge males. His face bore the marks of those battles, and one particular scar, resembling a giant dollar sign, made him easily recognizable. When we began observing him, the obvious challenger to his position was the bear we named Cutlip. At one point in the summer, Cutlip had finally launched a challenge from which John and Maurice saw Old Scarface walk away defeated. (Maurice Hornocker was the team member most involved in studying the grizzly hierarchy.) But Cutlip did not remain long at the top of the social pyramid. His reign lasted just a week.

The new contender was Number 12, whom we had released in Hayden Valley after marking. Within a few days he had met Old Scarface and Cutlip and had fought them both. He began with a challenge to Cutlip, who tried to scare him off by bluffing. When this failed, Cutlip retreated on the run from the aggressive dark-colored newcomer. Then Old Scarface elected to take on the challenger, facing him stiff-legged with his neck stretched and head forward, as he had so many contenders in the past. The fight was short and furious, with Scarface going down in defeat. The respect and deference of the bear community was immediately transferred to the new champion. We named him Inge after the current champion in heavyweight boxing, Ingemar Johansson.

Perhaps the emotional effects of dethronement have a more subtle effect on the loser than his purely physical injuries. Fundamentally, Inge's defeat of the two dominant bears seemed to be psychological, for after 1960 we did not see Scarface again and presumed him to be dead, and Cutlip in his turn disappeared the year after. Though past his prime, Cutlip was not really an old bear, but having briefly reached the top, apparently he had found no way to go but down. The loss in prestige and status may have initiated psychological changes that accelerated aging.

The social hierarchy in which Inge had become the dominant boar, the "alpha animal," was not unlike that of the chief and high-ranking warriors in certain Indian tribes — a society where rank was determined by courage, fighting skill, and physical superiority along with age, intelligence, imagination, and other factors. Undoubtedly, subtle traits not evident to human observers were at work in determining the status of bears who appeared to be equals in aggressiveness. The positions of aggressive males, such as one we called Scar Chest, were recognizable because these bears hesitated before retreating from the dominant male, and in some instances initiated combat with him.

Over that first year, we observed a number of subdominant grizzlies contending for the dominant position in the social structure. The males below them showed gradations of behavior, down through those who avoided the dominant and subdominant bears altogether and fought them only when surprised, cornered, or attacked. The degrees of dominance were easiest to observe when the bears congregated at a dump or around a carcass, and combat was most frequent during the mating season. But when bear met bear even at the far limits of their habitat, each knew where it stood in relation to the other — unless this was a first meeting, in which case some mutual understanding on relative status was soon reached. Recognition was based on scent and to a lesser degree on sight. At close range opposing bears communicated their mood or intent through head, body, and mouth movements as well as ear position and nature of walk. Low growls, roars, and a variety of sounds often accompanied these movements, but communication related to status was largely visual.

From season to season the position of adult males in the hierarchy did not change drastically, but over a longer period we could observe the vigorous young animals moving upward as they grew in size, strength, and combativeness. In the course of his climb, each bear gave and received painful wounds on the head and neck which healed as scars. Ears and jowls were often mutilated or even destroyed. Most of the wounds were bites from powerful jaws armed with canine teeth strong enough to puncture heavy metal. Boars who won fights appeared to acquire increased confidence, which in turn made them still better fighters. This pattern was unmistakable in the career of Inge, Number 12, which we began to follow in the summer of 1959.

Another animal whose climb we observed was a young adult male we trapped in the summer of 1959. At the time of his capture he weighed 505 pounds. While he was still in the trap, we attached a green-tailed plastic loop to each ear, and tattooed the number 14 in his armpit. Then we began pulling him out of the trap feet first, and young Harry Reynolds exclaimed, "Look at the size of that foot!" The back pad measured close to eleven inches long, or near the record length for much older and larger bears. So we called Number 14 Bigfoot—a nickname we later changed to Bruno. He eventually became a radio bear, one of the few very large boars we were able to track for any length of time.

In contrast to that of a male, a female's social rank was temporary, depending to a large extent on whether or not she had a family. Females with young cubs usually deferred only to the dominant male and those immediately under him. Although they tried to avoid confrontation, they would readily attack any male, including the dominant ones, who approached them or their offspring too closely. A strong maternal instinct meant that they watched their cubs carefully, constantly tending them while any other bears were in the vicinity. Any overstepping of the boundary within which the mother felt secure would trigger aggressive action. This violation of what the sow considered a safe distance applied to man as well as other bears, and these females constituted the greatest potential hazard for visitors to the park.

We saw many examples of this protective behavior in the sow we nicknamed G.I., or the Disciplinarian, the unmarked mother of Number 26, the Fifty-pound Cub. Always unusually solicitous of her cubs, she became still more apprehensive when other bears, particularly boars, were close by. When she joined other bears to feed, she unfailingly placed her two cubs where she could keep a watchful eye on them, growling in bear language, "Stay there!" Obediently, her cubs would often remain like statues for long periods. Once, after a stretch of such enforced immobility, one cub grew restless and wandered a short distance away. Almost simultaneously a big boar appeared from out of the brush. The sow, neck outstretched, streaked toward her cubs, picked up the errant bundle of fur in her jaws, and plopped him roughly back into place. Then with mouth open and incisors bared she wheeled to take on the intruder, who prudently altered his course. The mother had communicated her message. Later, when we captured the Fifty-pound Cub and fitted him with yellow plastic ear markers, his brief absence from his mother only made the sow more vigilant thereafter. It also appeared that these cubs were learning combativeness from their mother.

In general, females with yearlings tended to be less combative than those with cubs. One whom we dubbed the Lean Sow was in 1960 the aggressive mother of three cubs and thus high in the social hierarchy; we ranked her just under the subdominant male bears. By the time her cubs were yearlings she had become less aggressive, and when she released her two-year-olds and was again without a family, she reverted to the more cautious behavior of a barren adult female. Females with no offspring to protect were generally cautious and retiring; however, they might at times be quite aggressive toward bears of lower rank, particularly subadults. Before Marian had her first litter she seemed to us to be extremely jealous of other sows with cubs and even resentful of the cubs themselves. On one occasion I watched her chase a thoroughly scared cub in circles in and out of clumps of sagebrush. Twice she nearly caught the terrified cub and her antagonistic behavior boded no good for the cub had she succeeded. Earlier she had backed down before the aggressive, warning behavior of the cub's mother. Chasing the cub may have been a redirection of her own aggression influenced by frustration.

A lactating mother grizzly with cubs does not act like a sow without cubs, nor will her behavior be the same after the cubs are weaned. Moreover, individual mothers vary in temperament. As a result of the numerous and intricate changes that accompany lactation, some appear to be in a constant state of anxiety, and others, such as the Disciplinarian, to be rigidly overbearing. In still others, the maternal instinct may actually cause a mother to appear docile and friendly, at least until disturbed or provoked. It was this trait that led to trouble for Number 31, whom we called Sylvia, a sow with three cubs. During the summer of 1960, she brought her offspring out into the open meadows near the Old Faithful geyser, where she could graze the new green grass. Here they were on display to all early-season visitors. These were still relatively few, but those who drove by would jam on their brakes, grab their cameras, and leave car doors ajar while they photographed the friendly bear and her cubs. Most did not recognize her as a grizzly, and few understood the danger of the situation. The odds for disaster were too great, and Sylvia had to go. At the request of the Park Service we immobilized her with a drug-laden dart and then noosed two of the three cubs (the third got away). Sylvia was shipped off to a New York zoo, and the cubs were marked and released as an experiment, to learn whether they could survive on their own and, if so, how. One of them, Number 78, weighed a mere twenty pounds at the time. We nicknamed him Ignatz.

After a month we caught up with Ignatz and snared him a second time. He had gained eight pounds, which was not a lot, but he was managing to get along. During the interval he had learned that tourists were a soft touch. Whenever he or his littermate showed up along a highway, visitors would stop and feed the lonely little cub, even though this was against park regulations. Many of the foodgivers seemed to want him to take the tidbits out of their hands, but fortunately he had enough natural caution to keep his distance. Possibly his two encounters with a noose had something to do with his reserve. He found, however, that he could obtain food without getting too close to his benefactors by making a sudden, short, bluffing charge. Usually the food would be dropped as the startled visitor backed off. Ignatz was learning to live by his wits, in a way that reminded me of the precocious orphans I had seen begging on the streets of Hong Kong.

Unlike black bears, grizzlies rarely become "roadside bums," but when one does, his life is soon cut short, so we were concerned over what lay ahead for Ignatz. Hoping to save him from the otherwise inevitable while continuing to learn what we could from observing him, we removed him from the source of temptation. We transported him across Yellowstone Lake and left him on isolated Promontory Point, far from his usual haunts and human influence. A week later he appeared along the highway near Steamboat Point at the northern end of the lake about six miles east of Fishing Bridge. He had traveled about thirty miles along the eastern shoreline, through country completely strange to him, his early life having been spent entirely in the vicinity of Old Faithful far to the west. How had he been able to find his way back to the region he associated with food? Whatever accounted for the strong homing instinct he thus revealed, it would very soon lead to serious problems. And in time that same instinct would become a liability to the entire grizzly population. On July 19 we located Ignatz at a picnic table close to the highway. He had by now discovered that large trash and garbage containers could be a source of food; when we caught up with him, he was busily feeding on the remains of a cantaloupe. It was evident that Ignatz was developing bad habits, but at least he was no longer approaching sightseers directly. His littermate had developed this trait, so rare in a grizzly, to the point where he was shipped off to a zoo in Mexico.

Was there any chance that Ignatz might still mend his ways? He was a larger bear than his brother, he was in good condition, and there was some reason to assume that as the fall season came on and the number of visitors decreased, he might still become self-sufficient. With respect to the hierarchical society of grizzly bears, the term "omega animal" refers to one that wins no fights and tends to avoid others of his kind—but not human beings. It may be that such young, insecure animals tend to relate to people as a result of shunning other bears (particularly large boars, who have been known to attack and kill them). Ignatz's brother had been such an animal. Ignatz, though also very low on the social scale, exhibited a certain aggressive cunning that gave him status, at least from our point of view. Once when he entered the Lake campground, rangers tried to rope him rather than wait until he could be lured into a trap. Once roped, he abandoned all the traits of an omega animal and charged the rangers, scattering them in every direction and tearing one would-be captor's trousers. He then turned and ran off dragging the rope, which he was later able to remove. We could not help chuckling over the way the young grizzly had terrorized his human antagonists. But we could also sympathize with the rangers. In our own work, we occasionally had to hold an immobilized cub or yearling while we tried to finish our work after the effects of the drug had worn off, and we had learned to respect the steely muscles and needle-like teeth and claws of a cub grizzly.

On September 1, 1960, our research team received a call for help from two park rangers, Lee Robinson and Riley McClellan. The third cub in Ignatz's litter, the one we had failed to noose, was in the Old Faithful campground, rearing up and making lunges at visitors who approached him too closely. Some of them had been foolish enough to try to pet him. In addition, a large marked grizzly had roamed through the campground the night before. Could we help them capture and move the two problem bears before trouble developed?

It was already dark when we arrived at the campground and began patrolling the area in search of the miscreants. Finally I spotted the adult grizzly, a large one. Estimating its weight at well over 400 pounds, by flashlight we filled each of two darts with a 90-milligram dose of sucostrin. In the process we temporarily lost sight of the grizzly, and when we picked it up again in the beam of the flashlight it appeared still larger; we would have supposed it to be a different bear had we not seen the metal ear tags. There was no time now to prepare a larger drug dose. The grizzly was moving, and we had to act without delay. I aimed from the patrol car and hit the bear in the neck from a distance of about forty feet. With the impact of the dart, the bear swung round and vanished into the darkness.

After a period of silent waiting, we left the car, nearly stumbling over some campers. The bear, wherever he was now, must have passed within a few feet of the sleeping men. In order not to excite him before the drug could fully take effect, we drove to the other side of the campground loop and once again started out on foot toward where we thought the bear should be. We found him about a hundred feet from the road, struggling to get to his feet. He had traveled less than a hundred yards from the spot where I had hit him. Evidently the drug had entered a neck vein, since it had taken effect in about two minutes, instead of the usual fifteen. The grizzly was still raising his head and snapping his jaws when Maurice and I grabbed him by the hind legs and started dragging him toward the road. We knew we had to get him into a trap quickly, before the drug began to wear off. Although the average recovery time was about a half-hour, we might have as little as five more minutes' time with this particular drug dose. We shouted for more help but got no response; there were no rangers within earshot just then. Struggling to keep a grip on his thick ankles, we dragged the huge animal toward the waiting culvert trap. He growled as we strained to raise his head and front feet to the level of the elevated floor of the trap. By the time Riley and another ranger showed up to help, we had the bear about halfway inside. With hearts pounding and breath coming hard, we were all too vividly aware that if we didn't get the door shut behind him very quickly, he would be loose among us. I was giving a final push to the captive's rear haunches when someone yelled, "Drop the gate!" I barely got my hands out of the way before the door whistled down like a guillotine. By the time I managed to stagger around to the back of the trap and flash a light on him, the bear was raging and roaring, already almost entirely revived. Maurice and I were still gasping; our lungs burned from the exertion for hours afterward.

By the time we left the trap and began our hunt for Ignatz's brother, it was well after midnight. Now a new game of hide-and-seek began. While the park rangers communicated his whereabouts with their car radios, we went looking for the little fellow with flashlights. Finally I got a rear-end view of him moving through the trees. I judged he weighed about sixty pounds. Taking a long shot, I fired the dart and managed to hit him. Heading after him on foot, we located him—down but crawling and far from immobilized. I pounced on the back of his neck and managed to hold him while Maurice ran to get our panel wagon containing the cub cage. As we struggled to put him in the cage, the cub emitted a low growl, a distress call meant to summon the mother grizzly that was now a captive. But had he acquired a foster mother? I thought and hoped not. His growl, I was sure, must have awakened the sleepers in a nearby trailer, but there was no sign that they had heard the commotion. Having finally jockeyed the cub into the trap and heaved it into the car, we took off for our headquarters, the laboratory at Canyon. Behind the car we pulled the trap containing the adult bear. We had done a good night's work—two problem bears immobilized with two shots.

When we peered in the culvert trap next morning to identify the large bear, we discovered that he was bear Number 1, the very first we ever trapped for our study. It had been over a year since we first tagged him, and we had not seen him since. So far as we knew, this was the first time he had visited a campground. At the time we marked him, he had weighed 200 pounds. Now he measured seven feet long from nose to tail and tipped the scales at 520—a gain of 320 pounds in about fourteen months, for an increase of 160 percent. Had this bear not been tagged we would have all agreed that he could not possibly be Number 1. Before putting him on the scale again, I had estimated his weight at 550. It was gratifying to have come within 30 pounds of the true figure. As our study went forward, our increasing ability to judge weights would be of great value in successfully immobilizing free-roaming bears that could not be weighed beforehand.

But we still had much to learn, as the fate of Number 1 now proved. Before we could release him, it was necessary to immobilize him again. Though we used a smaller dosage than the minimum one of the night before, it was still too much in this case; within minutes, to our dismay, the bear was dead. Apparently, the amount required for a captured bear was considerably less than that needed to subdue a free one. Perhaps, too, the factor of stress made a difference. We later found that it did. Such variables could be estimated or evaluated but not measured.

This was not the only casualty among the marked grizzlies that year. In early April, soon after coming out of his winter den, bear Number 19 had wandered into the small town of Gardiner, where he was quickly dispatched by an alarmed resident. Another bear, Number 49, was found buried along the shore of Shoshone Lake, where it had apparently been shot. The reason for this and the individual responsible were never determined. Number 4, whom we called Old Andy, was trapped for a third time in the same area and shot by a ranger. From the figures we had recorded, we estimated the known mortality for the years 1959–60 at 10 percent of the grizzly population we were dealing with and censusing—an estimated 170 bears of all ages.

We had known from the beginning that there were risks to the bears involved, particularly with respect to the drugging procedure. We had discussed the chance of losing a bear when we worked out our understanding with the Park Superintendent. Our research team recognized that variables such as age, sex, stress, and physical condition could affect the reaction of individual bears to being drugged and informed the Park Superintendent and his people that a few deaths were likely, but all agreed that this was a chance we would have to take. It was also agreed—based on our common knowledge that grizzlies and human beings do not always mix well, particularly in camp-grounds—that occasionally an aggressive bear foraging in a camp-ground might have to be killed to safeguard visitors to the park. Those bears that were trapped but repeatedly returned to camp-grounds after release were to be eliminated. Both parties also agreed, however, that no grizzlies would be killed without prior discussion except in an emergency. For our own part, we took all possible pre-cautions against mishap in immobilizing the animals. A marked bear became increasingly valuable to both us and to the Park Service as the study progressed and information accumulated year after year.

Ignatz was still alive as 1960 came to a close. With winter approaching, he took up his abode near Lake Lodge, where some construction and concession workers who were still in the park took pity on the lonely bear and put out food for him, thereby only reinforcing in him the ruinous association of food and human beings. As snow began accumulating, he moved to the high timbered country south-west of Lake Lodge, where he dug a cavelike shelter and went into hibernation. In spring he reappeared, his healthy condition living proof that a cub without a mother could survive the long, cold Yellowstone winter. But his ability to survive natural hazards could not protect him from his own bad habits. Early in the spring of 1961, Ignatz was shot by park rangers as a potential threat to human beings.

Another omega animal, Number 86, was orphaned as a cub in 1959. In 1961, we trapped and marked him as a two-year-old; at this point he weighed only 115 pounds, as compared to several hundred pounds for other animals of the same age. In the fall of 1962, we sorrowfully examined the body of the Orphan Runt after he had been hit by a car at night. This death by accident was unusual but the chances were slim that he would have lived much longer. Most omega animals are not destined to live a long life.

Hierarchical behavior was perhaps most readily observable when a number of grizzlies were present at or near a food source. Early on the morning of October 19, 1963, I followed a radio signal from the side of a hill in Hayden Valley, moving west on a bearing of 240 degrees until, in improved light, I observed one of the radio animals, Number 150, with her cubs. They were growling as they tugged at a stubborn piece of hide covering a tasty morsel. We knew that this bear, the Alum Creek Sow, was part of the hierarchy we were piecing together, but just where did she fit in? We had not observed her often enough with other animals to know. On this occasion Marian was nearby in the fringes of the timber, hesitant to approach the food. When she did move in, it was at an angle to the feeding bear, not directly toward her. Possibly Marian had already, in the darkness of early morning, had a brief encounter with the Alum Creek Sow and her cubs — perhaps she had just received a head-on stare telling her to wait. I settled down at the base of a tree to watch. How soon would Number 150 permit Marian to feed alongside her cubs? A considerably larger sow, having scented the food from some distance, now approached from the southwest and broke out of the woods at a run. This fast, direct approach suggested that this was a more dominant bear, and the behavioral signal was quickly translated. Number 150 and her cubs stopped feeding, watched the oncoming bear for a moment, and then turned and moved off. Marian retreated deeper into the shadows of the trees. In their hasty retreat, the Alum Creek Sow and her cubs ran directly toward me. Poor light and quiet air prevented them from detecting me until I was almost overrun. I grabbed a branch and swung up into a tree, one I had already selected for just such a contingency. The startled grizzlies veered slightly, rushing by almost directly beneath me. A slight breeze soon carried my scent to the new bear, whom I had by then recognized as the Grizzled Sow. She too raised her head and immediately took off at a run.

Timidly, Marian moved back in to feed. I could just barely see the red battery pack of her radio collar. Using her shoulder she pushed the carcass first one way, then the other in her attempts to get at the flesh within the rib cage. Again the wind shifted; fog moved in bearing human scent, and Marian took off at a run. It was now 7:30 A.M. In the course of three-quarters of an hour five different bears had approached, started to feed, and left the carcass. In that short time, I had learned that their hierarchical positions ranged from the Grizzled Sow down to Marian at the bottom.

My directional radio receiver told me that the Alum Creek Sow was now in the timber close by and Marian was off to the east not much farther away. By nine o'clock it was evident that the bears were slowly moving off to secluded daytime beds. It would be early evening before the bears left their beds and again came to feed. The ravens and magpies in the trees and the coyotes waiting in the timber nearby would have the carcass to themselves until then.

During the day magpies flew down to the unattended carcass and fed greedily. So intent were they on gorging themselves that a goshawk streaking out of the timber almost caught one. Coyotes tugging at the tough hide moved off; then one returned, edged close to the carcass, and ran in rapidly to drag off a piece of meat. His keen nose alerted him to what my radio signals told me: that the grizzlies were approaching and were close by. Minutes later Number 150 and her cubs moved in to feed while Marian circled to one side. When she had determined that the Alum Creek Sow would now tolerate her presence, all five bears proceeded to consume the still abundant supply of food.

This pattern of behavior took place at many carcasses. The first dominant bear to appear would temporarily hold off other bears, but before long, usually after feeding awhile, he or she appeared to acknowledge the submissive behavior of others, indicated by a slow, indirect approach to the food, and soon all would feed in comparative amiability broken only now and then by a short bluffing lunge or warning growls when the right to a choice morsel was being voiced. Here status had been established and accepted, and cooperative feeding resulted. At the carcass I was observing, more grizzlies joined the diners during the night. By daybreak only scattered bones and pieces of tough hide remained.

Marian and her companions were revealing to us the role of various individuals in the hierarchy and the meaning of the vocalizations, signs, and signals that compose bear language and communication. Four young bears that roamed over much of Marian's range gave us insight into a lower echelon of the social structure. Because these sibling bears from two families banded together as a group, we called them the Four Musketeers.

Ignatz and his brother had each faced the world of bears and the world of man alone; they were, as I have indicated, at the very bottom of the bear social system. In contrast, the Four Musketeers (one of whom was an orphan cub) chose to band together for greater security—at least this was the result of their cohesion. By the time they were yearlings, they rated considerably higher in the social hierarchy than did other yearlings that were weaned and on their own. To understand just how and why these four bears joined ranks we must backtrack a few months, to the summer of 1963.

The Owl-faced Sow, Number 148, and the Brown-headed Sow, Number 48, had frustratingly similar numbers considering that they were both having cub trouble. On July 1, we observed the Owl-faced Sow nursing two cubs, one with a white collar and the other with a partial collar or "necktie." Prior to this we had seen her with three cubs, the third sporting a very broad, unusually white collar. The Owl-faced Sow, as mentioned earlier, was also distinctively marked with dark circles around her eyes. On July 3 she was foraging in upper Alum Creek with again only two cubs, and sow Number 48 had three. All of the cubs of both sows had collars or neckties. Either the sows were switching cubs or the cubs were changing mothers. At any rate, one cub or more would follow one sow for awhile, then a few days later the other. They had us thoroughly confused. We were not sure which sow truly had three cubs and which had two, or which of the cubs was the true offspring of either. Both sows rated high in the social hierarchy and both were aggressive animals, quick to defend their cubs.

The Owl-faced Sow was the more antagonistic of the two, and her aggressiveness brought on her death. Several weeks after we tried to unravel the cub-switching mystery, a pickup truck driven at night along a dirt service road was suddenly struck a resounding thump that shook the entire vehicle and dented the fender. The driver had inadvertently driven between the sow and her cub, and Number 148 charged, hitting the front fender with all the force and rage that a mother grizzly can muster in the defense of her young. The attack broke her neck, killing her instantly. At this moment of orphaning, her cubs were doomed to slip far down the social ladder into a position of great insecurity. For a while, instrumented grizzly Number 150, the Alum Creek Sow, who had three cubs of her own, took care of one of the orphan cubs. But in early October we saw that this orphan was no longer with this foster mother. Had he been rejected by the sow, had he died, or was he on his own? We didn't know. Then, over a period of four or five days, nearly a dozen grizzlies moved to a carcass to feed, and among those attracted to the banquet was the Brown-headed Sow. She had her own three cubs and had adopted one of the orphan cubs of the Owl-faced Sow, the one that Number 150 had temporarily cared for. It was reassuring to us that the Brown-headed Sow had so well accepted the duties of motherhood that she had taken on the added responsibility of caring for one more cub, since during two previous years she had abandoned her cubs altogether. This complete turnabout was possibly traceable to a different combination or quantity of various hormones. When we last saw this family they were still together, and there was every indication that they would hibernate as a family.

The following spring all four yearlings reappeared, but the Brown-headed Sow did not. The fact that she was never seen again suggested that she had not weaned them but had died or was killed during winter or early spring. In the course of the summer of 1964, we captured and marked these orphans from two families, and Numbers 181, 192, 193, and 194 became the Four Musketeers. They remained close as orphan yearlings, often exhibiting unusual and interesting group behavior. The Musketeers were cautious but not timid, as were other single, weaned yearlings. They approached close to other feeding bears and closed ranks when facing a possible source of danger, whether it was a young but more powerful boar, or a human being tracking them by radio. They were always seen together whether they were mousing, digging up roots of tuberous plants, plundering red squirrel caches, resting, having confrontations with other bears, or extending their ranges by moving into outlying regions.

On October 16, 1964, we put a radio on Number 194 in order to learn more about the behavior of the group. We also hoped to locate their winter den and determine whether they hibernated singly or together. When first trapped at the end of August, Number 194 weighed 135 pounds, not a great deal for a yearling at this time of the season. When retrapped in October he had gained only 30 pounds, weighing 165. Orphaning had affected his growth, as it did most bears in these early age categories. In addition he was infected with round worms, but his rectal temperature of 102 degrees was about normal for an active bear at that time of year. We had misjudged the circumference of his neck so it was necessary to pad the radio collar with rubber foam to make it fit. Number 194 was an attractive grizzly with a narrow but almost complete white fur collar. One of his companions was nearly jet black with a wide white fur collar. He was the most handsome young male grizzly I have ever seen.

That autumn, we found the typical shallow daytime beds of the Four Musketeers grouped together in the snow, and we also located several deep burrowlike day beds with distinct claw marks in the earth at the rear where the bears had been digging. At first we thought these might be enlarged into winter dens, but although the instinct to dig a den for the winter apparently was already affecting the young bears, these beds did not actually become hibernation dens. While we were radio-tracking them we were also trying to monitor the radio signals and follow the movements of Bruno over on the eastern border of Yellowstone, Marian to the south of Hayden Valley, and Number 158, also far to the south traveling with his littermates and the large sow Number 39. The six to twelve inches of snow on the ground didn't make things easier. It was at about this time that the Four Musketeers suddenly took off and headed west. Like many young bears, they were abruptly leaving their summer foraging grounds and traveling rapidly to either a den site or a fall foraging area. It is quite likely that they returned to the site where they had denned the winter before. Unfortunately, we never found out where this was or whether they denned together. At this time of year the bears were fat, the researchers lean and weary. Fatigue forced a choice, and we decided to give up on Bruno, let the Four Musketeers wander as they would, and concentrate on following Marian and Number 158. Both were in the same general area, so it seemed reasonable that we might track both to their winter dens.

The following spring the Four Musketeers disbanded. As two-year-olds they had become more secure, better able to survive alone. Nevertheless, as lone young bears they took a drop in status, a step down in the hierarchy. This was evident when older, more dominant boars approached them. And because of this they would tend to wander over the next few years, some of this movement a result of evading more dominant bears, some to find new foraging areas, and some out of sheer curiosity.

It appeared that the grizzly bear hierarchy as revealed in this community resulted from the bears' innate tendency to form and maintain a social structure, and that the effectiveness of this social organization and its influence on the behavior of the bears was directly related to the number of bears assembling at any one time. The position of individuals was more readily observed where they came into contact with a concentration of bears. It was also under just such conditions that the hierarchy was most needed. A lone asocial animal only occasionally coming into contact with another bear of the community might not display much behavior related to the hierarchical structure. Nevertheless, he or she will still be subtly affected by hierarchical relationships, though perhaps expressing these effects only by avoiding or approaching the other bear.

We observed that the social hierarchy and related bear behavior served to minimize conflict between these powerful, potentially destructive animals when they got together during the mating season or when they concentrated at garbage dumps and along streams where trout or salmon spawn. Presumably the same was true in former times in places where the Indian killed his buffalo. The bears' recognition of status and the visual and auditory signals used to reveal dominance, and particularly subordination, decrease actual conflict and terminate combat before it results in death. The grizzly has evolved traits that prevent it from annihilating its own species even though it has the strength, ferociousness, and destructive power to do so. It would be reassuring to learn that its main enemy, man, had a comparable built-in deterrent to destroying his fellow creatures.

3

The Mating
Game

In June 1962, the boar we knew as Inge reappeared in Hayden Valley, but we did not recognize him until his ear tags revealed his identity. His once dark, shiny coat had become a dull, matted brown, and he walked like an old and feeble animal. The previous winter had evidently been a disastrous one for him, and it was not at all clear that he could retain his position as the alpha animal of the region. After Maurice saw him lose a fight to Scar Chest, a less aggressive male, we sadly wondered whether the coming winter would be his last. Apparently, a winter following a dominant male's loss of his ruling position can be fatal. But then we watched Inge fight off the challenge of a rival, a large boar we called Short Ear.

Inge had been making advances for the first time toward the young female we knew as Marian, when Short Ear approached in the company of another female. Immediately and with arrogant confidence, Inge moved to confront the challenger. The latter had tangled briefly with Inge once before, and this had apparently left him with no burning aspiration to become the top bear, for he retreated on the run. Inge followed in close pursuit, leaving the two sows without escorts. Short Ear finally turned and stood his ground, roaring and striking with his huge paws as Inge in one rhythmic motion lunged and seized him by the throat and then made a half turn, throwing his 750—pound adversary to the ground. Short Ear was soon back on his feet, and the two antagonists proceeded to lock jaws, cuffing each other with powerful blows.

As an aggressor who had bested his rival once before, Inge had the psychological advantage. Short Ear was fighting a defensive battle. When Short Ear finally turned and ran, Inge pursued him for a good half mile. Then, tired or bored, he gave up the chase and went back to resume his courtship. In the meantime, another boar—Number 88, whom we promptly dubbed Loverboy—had moved in and mated with the fickle young Marian. This mating produced no offspring; Marian did not give birth to cubs during her winter sleep of 1962–63. This and many similar observations led us to conclude that female grizzlies do not reach sexual maturity until they are at least four and a half years old.

The next spring, 1963, we came back to continue our study as the noonday sun, again higher in the southern sky, gradually warmed the high Yellowstone plateau. Tracks of red squirrels, martens, and snowshoe rabbits revealed active life in the timbered areas still buried in many feet of snow, but in early April there were as yet no signs or tracks of returning elk, mule deer, or moose. The windblown ridges and south-facing slopes absorbed more of the sun's heat; here the first green of new spring plants would soon appear.

The grizzly population was beginning to stir from its winter lethargy to begin another cycle of mating, foraging, weight increase, and winter sleep. Some adult bears and barren sows had already left their dens, and others were no longer sleeping soundly. By the time Inge, still the dominant bear in the Yellowstone social hierarchy, had traveled westward from the high country of the Absaroka Mountains that form the eastern border of Yellowstone National Park, Marian was moving north through lodgepole timber toward the open country of Hayden Valley. Her journey to this area, where many grizzlies congregate in spring, was comparatively short. Since she was relatively light, weighing not quite three hundred pounds, she had no trouble walking over the crusted snow. Inge, traveling westward, was now at a disadvantage due to his huge, hard-muscled bulk of nearly eight hundred pounds.

By piecing together the observations of various people at different locations and times, and by reading signs left in the snow, we got a realistic if incomplete account of Inge's spring journey from his winter den. The going was tough and exhausting, even for this powerful bear. Time after time he crashed through the thick crust and floundered in deep snow, but instinct and experience kept him on a steady course westward toward the spring meadows of Hayden Valley. He foraged as he went, rising on his hind legs to better sniff the air and making short side forays when his keen sense of smell located food. He stopped at times to feed on sedge shoots along stream banks, killed a moose, and was delayed for four days at the remains of a bison carcass.

The moose kill took place in upper Willow Creek. Inge had been following a ridge parallel to the creek where bare ground or the windpacked snow supported his weight, and moving generally into the face of the prevailing winds. Perhaps the scent of prey caused him to veer toward the stream. Perhaps he had found food here in previous years and was checking out the willow bottom. Ahead of him was a small grove of aspens and a few scattered spruce trees, surrounded by heavily browsed willow bushes whose tops rose above the deep snow. Inge passed between the trees, now breaking through the softer snow. Suddenly he faced a clearing, not much larger than a football field, where the snow was heavily tramped in places, packed solid in others. The clearing was bordered by numerous tracks leading spokelike into the deeper snow, and pelletlike droppings were both scattered and clustered.

As Inge raised his head to get a scent, a resting bull moose, now antlerless, turned his head and faced the bear. The hair had risen on the moose's back, his lips slapped defiantly and he started to rise to his feet. Inge took in the situation at a glance and charged. The moose had still not quite risen to his feet when Inge struck. The momentum of the bear's eight hundred pounds bowled his prey over, his right paw struck the upper back, and his long canines sank into the base of the moose's neck. There was a slight struggle, a quiver, and the moose was dead.

The moose was in poor condition, ribs showing beneath the skin and large patches of hair missing. His late winter yarding area had not been abundantly stocked with willow shoots. Nevertheless, he would have survived another year had not fate brought the big dark bear into this snowy corral at a time when he was weak and the snow was too deep for him to run. Malnourished moose, elk, and even bison fall prey to the hungry grizzlies in spring. Often the bear's killing instinct is aroused when the prey animal is incapacitated or struggling through deep snow. Such predation, however, is the exception rather than the rule. Far more often the grizzlies find and consume animals after they are dead. They act as scavengers rather than predators. The major predators on ungulate herds, the wolf and the cougar, and likewise primitive man, are no longer an effective control — they aren't even present. Starvation is now the slow killer of moose, deer, and elk when their numbers outstrip their winter food supplies. The grizzly's *coup de grâce* is often a mercy killing.

Inge remained in upper Willow Creek for nearly a week, gorging on the moose carcass. After taking full advantage of this early food supply, he moved on, eventually to join the grizzlies from distant parts of Yellowstone and beyond congregating for the summer in Hayden Valley, as they had done for at least the past eighty years. The attraction was an abundance of natural food supplemented by a Park Service dump, as well as the opportunity — as experienced in past years — of meeting members of the opposite sex. It was essential to the production of each new generation of bears that the males met, associated with, and mated with the females during the two- to three-week period when the sows were in heat — that is, psychologically and physiologically receptive to copulation with the males. The mating season, which in early June would alter their activities and behavior, had not yet noticeably started to affect the mature females in this grizzly population. When the sow's biological clocks ticked off the destined time the males, now ready but not yet stimulated, would respond instinctively.

Throughout the next month or so, we deliberately sought to be on hand when the grizzlies' annual mating activities took place. We kept a close watch on Inge and Marian in particular. Both grizzlies reached Hayden Valley at about the same time, but it was early May before they met. On this first occasion Inge, foraging head down along Alum Creek, appeared to ignore Marian's presence. The sow moved back into the timber, having recognized by both sight and scent the bear held in greatest respect by almost all other members of his community. Marian continued her spring foraging; along the Yellowstone River, in a patch of grass heavily grazed by bison, she flushed a sandhill crane as it fed on worms in the moist soil. She halted briefly to dig out and eat a few worms, too. Nearby, where the regular rumble of a sulphur spring could be heard, she encountered sow Number 39, with her cubs, pouncing on field mice exposed by the receding snowdrifts or digging the drier meadows for the bulbs of spring beauty *(Claytonia lanceolata),* some of which were already blooming in sun-warmed sites. The rounded bulbs, some an inch in diameter, were a storehouse of nearly pure starch; to us they tasted potatolike with a slightly peppery aftersting. However differently the bulbs may have tasted to the bears, they also found them good.

As the number of grizzlies per unit of area in Hayden Valley increased, some interesting social behavior could be observed. Each bear, from the most powerful, aggressive male on down to the most insecure orphaned cub, was finding its place in the somewhat reorganized social structure. By early June Inge was aggressive toward all bears and was fighting all challengers. Female hormones were at work and the sows, including Marian, who was now five and a half, were coming into estrus.

When Inge and Marian again met along the banks of upper Trout Creek a month after their earlier brief encounter, Inge was definitely interested, and though Marian displayed what might have been termed coyness in humans, she was not about to refuse him. The huge, galloping boar with the nearly coal-black coat dropped into a swale and emerged to rise erect like a man. He inclined his nose and turned his head as he sought to pick up scents from the windless air. His keen nose apparently detected Marian — or the scent of the Grizzled Sow, who had passed this way some fifteen or twenty minutes earlier. Moving down the sage-covered incline toward Marian, Inge walked stiff-legged, in a swaggering, slow but methodical gait. His head was lowered like that of a hound following a trail and his neck was bowed. Marian, though barely moving along, appeared to be completely ignoring Inge. As he closed the distance between them, he might have indeed appeared awesome to the timid young female. He was salivating profusely, and his course was direct and unerring. He slowed his approach only when his great bulk towered over her.

Marian stood motionless and subdued until, with his huge head, Inge nuzzled first her withers and then the side of her neck, whereupon she seemed to relax and assumed her normal stance. While she contentedly grazed, Inge repeated his overture, nuzzling her, smelling her new odor from all angles. He was gently rubbing his side against her when Pegleg, Number 76, suddenly appeared out of the sagebrush. With a few stiff-legged steps, Inge started toward Pegleg with his head down, Marian now completely forgotten. One quick glance at this awesome boar was enough for Pegleg, who turned and ran. He was still moving rapidly when he disappeared from my view. While Inge stood staring in the direction of the fleeing bear, Marian moved in close, turned her hindquarters toward him, and then backed playfully against his unyielding bulk. She was flirting, apparently aroused by Inge's aggressive attitude toward Pegleg. Twice more she nudged him with her rear quarters, clearly a hint. With no more challengers in sight, Inge's interest returned. At Marian's last nudge Inge forgot fighting and took up lovemaking. Without further preliminaries he mounted Marian. Twenty minutes later, side by side, they moved off together as though they had always been mates.

Marian, definitely in estrus, was Inge's choice, at least for the moment. Copulation had been relatively short as compared to previous matings we had observed between Inge and the Grizzled Sow. (Perhaps because of the Grizzled Sow's extremely large size the act was prolonged — in one instance we timed it at sixty minutes.) For much of the remainder of the day Inge seemed satisfied to stay close to Marian, nuzzling her now and then while she reciprocated.

With the setting of the sun, the members of the bear community began to rise from their daytime beds and to move about silently, placing their footpads so well that not a twig could be heard to crack. The light filtering through the lodgepole pines struck the rich brown coat of Loverboy, bear Number 88, and as my brother John watched, the bear moved off toward Inge and Marian. Unlike Pegleg when he stumbled upon them, Loverboy knew that Inge and Marian were directly ahead. His slow, stiff-legged walk was a deliberate challenge, and Inge's move to meet him was acknowledgement enough that the champion was accepting battle. As Loverboy slowed to a halt, Inge continued to move deliberately toward him. Loverboy seemed to hesitate, and then made a slight movement, perhaps to charge, but Inge lunged, sinking his canines deep into the rump of the contender. Loverboy stopped short in his retreat, if such it was, and Inge's momentum carried him onto and over his opponent, who was briefly flattened to the ground. Almost faster than the human eye could follow, Inge turned, seized his adversary's right thigh as Loverboy lay sprawled on his side, and shook this seven-hundred-pounder as a terrier shakes a rat. Loverboy broke away and his huge jaws clamped onto Inge's jowls. Inge roared, reared back and rose to his full height, and fought free. A great red gash marred the side of his face, perhaps presaging a disfigurement such as Cutlip's.

The two bears now stood on their hind legs eyeball to eyeball, each determined, neither afraid, and with their jaws wide apart they parried like monstrous boxers. Then they locked jaws, each levering to throw the other to the ground. Loverboy maneuvered to the left, trying to gain the advantage of some steeply sloping terrain. Inge headed his adversary off, gave him a lightning-fast karate swipe across the shoulder, and then lunged for his throat. The combined force of the blow and his own dodging move sent Loverboy staggering backward and to one side. Recovering, he rose to his full height as Inge came on. The two behemoths again stood face to face exchanging bites and blows, emitting growls and roars that could be heard half a mile away. Then both dropped to all fours, eyeing each other warily. Loverboy did not retreat, but by an almost imperceptible turn of his head may have indicated he'd had enough. At any rate, Inge deliberately turned his back, moving aside to claim his sow. His adversary did not take advantage of this opportunity, thus signifying that the contest was over. The objective was not to maim or kill but only to wrest an admission of defeat. Loverboy's "enough for now" was no clear-cut victory for Inge, but it was sufficient. Neither opponent appeared to be seriously injured, but both showed the marks of battle. There was no doubt that Loverboy would challenge Inge again. Marian, off to one side and seemingly forgotten during the fight, moved toward Inge as he turned toward her.

During most of June and the early weeks of July, Inge's main concern was to demonstrate and hold his dominance over the entire bear community. Aggressiveness at all times and under every circumstance was the key to his success. During his fights with other bears, his chases after them, and his occasional matings with other females such as the Grizzled Sow, Inge left Marian alone for long periods of time. One evening after they had been separated throughout the day, she sought Inge's protection, traveling nearly half a mile to get to him, apparently to avoid White Spot, another male who was pursuing her. The pursuer, finally realizing what her strategy was when she reached Inge, stopped only yards away from the pair. He stood there for a while before he finally turned and slowly wandered off. For Inge this concession to his own prowess was enough, and he chose not to fight.

By this time in early summer, Park Service employees were carrying the refuse left by a growing number of tourists out to the Trout Creek dump, and this source of food was beginning to attract the bears. Each evening they gathered there, following deeply worn trails made by generations of their predecessors. One warm evening, all through the long twilight, Inge slowly circled the area, perhaps trying unsuccessfully to pick up Marian's scent, for she was not in the vicinity. As darkness enveloped the landscape, he moved in to feed, scattering bears as he approached and with a turn of his head making them keep their distance. Was this to defend a food source, or was it merely a display of status? It was perhaps a little of both, but protecting food was not a major concern.

On some days Inge seemed young and agile, and on others he appeared old, with a slow, stiff walk that was almost a limp. One such occasion was the evening of July 3, when Inge was tired and not displaying his usual aggressive behavior. After grazing slowly along the banks of Trout Creek with other bears, both male and female, he wandered over the crest of a hill, lay down, and went to sleep. His numerous fights and sexual encounters over not quite a month appeared to have exhausted him completely. Before lying down he showed not the slightest interest in any of the sows, even though some were still in heat. For Inge the breeding season was obviously over. There could be little doubt that the day-to-day variation in Inge's behavior—one day acting like an old bear, a few days later like a vigorous adult—was due at least in part to his efforts to be everywhere at once.

A week after we saw Inge fall asleep in exhaustion, oblivious to the bears around him, I observed an encounter between him and Scar Neck, a large black male with scars on the top of his muzzle and on his right shoulder, both battle wounds. A bald spot near his hump, the result of rubbing his back against trees after emerging from hibernation, was also distinctive; by late summer it would be obscured by new hair. At about the time these two bears clashed, John, Maurice, and I had been following Marian in the hope of getting close enough to learn conclusively whether her estrus cycle was over. If so, it had lasted only about thirteen days, whereas the longest such cycle that our team had recorded had lasted twenty-seven days. We had also learned that most sows have a second estrus period, beginning after an interval ranging from four to eighteen days. When I saw Scar Neck he was following Number 112, a sow who was thus presumably still in estrus. Inge, who was lying down a short distance away, had lately exhibited little interest in the sows. The stage was set for a confrontation when another boar—Short Ear, a large, dark, chunkily built bear with a scar on his right cheek behind the eye—came toward Scar Neck. As the newcomer approached, Scar Neck walked stiffly to meet him, swinging his rear from side to side. He headed directly toward the dark boar, then quickened his pace and chased him away. Up until now, Short Ear had been this year's second-in-command at Trout Creek, but his aggressiveness was waning. Aroused by the scent of competition, Inge got up and chased Short Ear back toward Scar Neck. He took his time, and Short Ear angled away. Scar Neck likewise appeared unenthusiastic about confronting the oncoming Inge. He did not attempt to move toward Inge but took a few short strolls to one side as though looking for an out. Inge had to maintain his status, so he closed in on Scar Neck. Each acted as though the other were not present, yet each was very much aware of the other. When they were almost breathing in each other's face, Scar Neck turned and moved deliberately to one side, thus belatedly acknowledging Inge's superiority. The still dominant bear made no attempt to give chase or to test his dominant position further. It appeared that these bears respected each other, perhaps remembering fierce combats at other times and places.

Though it would take little to tip the scales in favor of Scar Neck, who slightly outweighed Inge, we now had no doubt that Inge would start the following mating season as the dominant bear. We were delighted to find that this aggressive bear, one we had come to like and admire, was still the top one. We respected his style; as they say in the fight game, he had "class." Our final observations of Inge just before he began his winter's sleep confirmed our impression that he had regained his strength and confidence. An abundance of summer and fall food, together with his natural recuperative powers, seemed to have reversed the downward physical trend.

By mid-July the mating season was unmistakably over; the mature males and females had all gone their respective ways, and sex was forgotten. We hoped and were later to confirm that Marian was pregnant, most likely by Inge. From now on throughout the next year and perhaps the one after that, Inge would be completely out of Marian's life, almost as though he were on another planet. Marian would be in sole charge of rearing the family. Occasionally in their wanderings their paths would cross, but she would give no more recognition to him than to any other bear; in fact, Marian appeared to prefer avoiding any close encounter with her former mate or any large boars. She certainly had no way of knowing, nor would she ever reveal by any recognizable behavior, that Inge was the father of her family. Neither did Inge convey any realization that he had sired Marian's first offspring. His promiscuous mating activities quite likely made him the father of more than one family.

As yet Marian's offspring were microscopic undeveloped cells. In bears, unlike most mammals, the embryos produced by the union of sperm and egg do not immediately become implanted, but remain free in the uterus. This state of embryonic arrest, or delayed implantation, continues for about five months, until after the female enters her den for her winter sleep. Soon after she curls up in late November, the microscopic blastocysts become implanted, and one to four infant grizzly bears begin to develop. The process occurs in a relatively short time; the actual gestation period for grizzlies is no more than from six to eight weeks, with birth occurring in late January or early February. The shortness of this period has survival value for an animal that must fast for six months while nourishing the fetuses and suckling her young. All energy for the process must come from food stored as fat.

Assuming that Marian was pregnant, we were already speculating on how large a litter she might bring back with her in the spring. We even had hopes of observing her and her tiny offspring in their winter den. First, however, we would have to follow her throughout her summer activities and track her to the final hibernation site.

During 1963, Marian became better acquainted with a group of bears we had designated family Number 2: sow Number 7 and her three offspring, Number 6, marked in 1959; Number 51, tagged a year later; and one unmarked bear. One of the favorite haunts of this family was the Sour Creek area east of the Yellowstone River, which is why Number 7 came to be known as the Sour Creek Sow. Number 6 had been the first cub we captured and marked, and we had been calling her simply the First Cub. In 1962 she bred as a three-year-old but produced no offspring the following year. In 1963 we instrumented the Sour Creek Sow, and we put a radio on the First Cub the following year and tracked her as well, sometimes accompanied by her mother. As a five-year-old the First Cub often scraped out her day beds close to those of Marian.

In early July 1963, I obtained a fix on the First Cub with bearings from our base station and from Big Game Overlook. Thinking that even at this late date she might exhibit some mating behavior, we decided to try to approach by following her signal, which emanated from a point close to where we had recently located Marian in a day bed. Just possibly, we thought, we might jump and observe both bears on the same trip. John with his son Johnny and I with my son Lance took off on foot to track the First Cub with our portable receiver.

We had previously determined that the First Cub was in a timbered area at Crater Hills. As we were closing in on her in rather dense timber, John and I decided to go ahead, leaving Lance and Johnny beside trees they could readily climb. Soon the signal indicated that the bear was only a few hundred yards away. Placing our feet slowly and with care on the matted pine needles, we moved to where the timber was even more dense. Thinking like a grizzly, I recognized a good spot for a day bed and stopped to look carefully before going ahead. It was then that I saw a huge sleeping boar directly in our path about a hundred feet ahead. I was astonished. My first thought was that he must be dead, and my next that we'd better get out of there — fast and quietly. We had been moving so noiselessly that we had not awakened the bear, and the faint "beep, beep" that had lured us directly toward this sleeping monster was turned so low that he had not heard it. Apprehensively, we backed off and retraced our steps to pick up our field glasses from Lance and to make sure that both he and

Johnny scrambled up into the trees. Then once again, following the contour of a wooded hillside, we approached the sleeping bear. This time we were above him and there were good climbing trees nearby. We had moved to a position where the wind took our scent to the bear, but fortunately an updraft or maybe mere exhaustion prevented him from detecting us. When he did not rouse, we each climbed a tree and shouted to discover what his reaction would be. From our respective positions in the trees, we saw another grizzly bolt out of a bed even closer to us. It was the Sour Creek Sow, whom we had radio-tracked the previous fall, but who was now without a radio.

Our shouts and the Sour Creek Sow's hasty retreat aroused the boar. Slowly, as though tired, he rose to his feet, then turned and moved away from us. His large size and light color identified him as White Face. Our signal was not coming from either of these bears. The First Cub, the instrumented grizzly we were tracking, was perhaps another one hundred yards farther ahead. The bed vacated by the Sour Creek Sow was about twenty-five feet from the boar's; both were in freshly dug earth at the base of fallen trees. The sow's bed did not have the usual flat saucer shape, but was burrowlike, approximately three feet high by four wide and nearly two feet deep. It had been constructed so that she could back into it, leaving her head and muzzle resting outside at ground level. This type of bed, we later learned, had the advantage of protecting the sow from unwanted attentions of the male. Not only had this sow and boar bedded close together during the mating season, but the First Cub was also apparently sharing the attentions of White Face. The Sour Creek Sow was evidently not concerned over her daughter's close presence. The fact that mother and daughter bedded so close together suggested a family association that had been maintained while the First Cub had reached maturity and might still continue for a number of years.

When we rendezvoused with Marian a little later in a jumble of fallen trees, we found that she was resting in a shallow day bed lined with several inches of dry grass. This interested us, for it was not a typical bed. Most were shallow excavations through a layer of duff to mineral soil, and very seldom did grizzly bears line day beds as Marian had clearly done. Was there an explanation for her departure from orthodoxy? Only one other sow, Number 187, had prepared such a bed, in the fall of the year when she was pregnant. If, as we assumed, Marian was also pregnant, perhaps the instinct which would later cause her to line her den with soft grass rather than boughs was already at work. If grass beds were consistently found to be made by pregnant bears this sign could be used as an indicator of pregnancy. A field ecologist is always alert for such possible clues.

In areas such as Sulphur Mountain, where we nearly stepped on the big sleeping boar, and within the extensive timbered areas above Alum Creek, we had to be continually vigilant while tracking instrumented animals. These timbered islands in a sea of sagebrush and grass were daytime retreats for the grizzly bears. Trackers following a radio signal to an instrumented animal in any of these locations were likely to come upon other bears, some sleeping, others active. In our encounter with White Face we had been fortunate. If we had moved on only a few feet closer, we would have jumped a sleeping bear at extremely close range—so close, in fact, that he would surely have attacked rather than run. We exercised added caution in the close-up tracking of any grizzly in dense cover, and this incident served to make us proceed with even greater care.

4

In Search of
Winter Dens

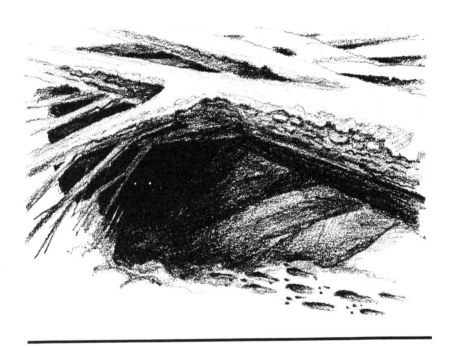

When we started our research, very little was known about the denning activity and prehibernation behavior of the Yellowstone grizzlies. We thought that perhaps they, like black bears and European brown bears, utilized natural shelters such as rock caves, hollow trees, and dense tangles of windfall. A few dens reported to us as being those of grizzlies turned out to be used by black bears. From fall and spring tracks in the snow and sightings of grizzlies, we knew that these animals spent about five months annually in winter sleep or hibernation.

Each fall from 1959 to 1963 the grizzlies had frustrated our attempts to follow them to their winter den sites. They lost us by traveling rapidly and far in falling snow, apparently to preselected winter sleeping quarters. It appeared to us that environmental conditions such as snowstorms triggered the urge to hibernate. But we had witnessed no prehibernation preparations — activity which might have alerted us that denning was imminent — prior to the final storms that put grizzlies in their dens. We had followed grizzly tracks through deep snow in heavy timber, only to lose them in open meadows where the blizzard's full force fused land and sky. The falling snow moved horizontally, not vertically, and tracks vanished in a matter of minutes. Where did the bears go? Did they make hasty last-minute preparations or were the dens already selected, dug, prepared, and waiting?

We were anxious to learn more about this lengthy and relatively inactive phase of the grizzlies' lives. To begin with, we had to observe the bears' behavior prior to winter sleep and again upon emerging from this period of lethargy. We also hoped to learn what kind of den sites grizzlies preferred, what sort of den they selected or prepared, and whether yearlings and two-year-olds denned with their mothers. If they did, would they have separate dens close to each other or a single den for all? Did mature males always den alone or were some winter quarters shared? What is the temperature inside a grizzly bear den in a frozen, snow-covered land where outside temperatures have been recorded as low as $-60°$ F? By the fall of 1962 we had instrumented three more grizzlies and hoped they would provide some answers to our questions.

The warm, orange light of an early October evening reflected off the tips of Marian's long guard hairs as I watched her through binoculars. I had noted her casual, unhurried gait when she left the lodgepole timber and moved into the open sagebrush and grass of Hayden Valley. Her brightly colored radio collar, along with the slight sway in her back, enabled me to identify her immediately. However, when I picked up the portable receiver and failed to get her characteristic pulsing signal, even with the volume turned high, I knew that her radio collar was no longer transmitting, that for some reason or other it was malfunctioning. Perhaps moisture had penetrated the battery pack following a swim or a bath in one of Yellowstone's mud pots. I was disappointed. We had instrumented three grizzlies — Marian, Number 96, and Number 37 — with the primary objective of tracking them to dens. We had already lost contact with Number 96, and now the same was happening with Marian. She was wearing the most powerful transmitter we had developed to date; it gave out 170-milliwatt pulses since Joel Varney had improved the equipment as a result of our experiences the year before. A few weeks after discovering that Marian was no longer transmitting, we lost track of Number 37 as he headed south, and though we monitored extensive areas of the park, we never again picked up his signal. He apparently left the park, crossing the southern border into Teton National Forest.

When we left Yellowstone that year, 1962, snow was on the ground, the bears were in their hidden dens, and a major objective of our radio-tracking efforts, to track grizzlies to their winter dens, was still a challenge unmet. Our radio-tracking equipment and techniques, the first to be developed and used on large free-roaming animals, had not been sufficiently perfected, and we had lost contact with our bears before the final "triggering" storm. However, we knew that we had a radio-tracking system capable of locating grizzly bears as they entered their dens, and we felt that it was now only a matter of time before we would achieve this goal.

The next year, in order to gather information on bear ranges and to increase our chances of following a grizzly to its winter den, we instrumented seven different animals. We actually tracked and obtained information on seventeen bears, because four of the females were members of family groups containing cubs and yearlings. However, some of the bears were instrumented too early in the season to be tracked in fall without reinstrumenting. This was the case with Numbers 75 and 96. We had not yet perfected our transmitter to the point, reached later, where they would operate continuously for approximately a year. Marian was sporting a radio collar for the third consecutive year. We had already acquired knowledge concerning her fall movements, so we had high hopes of tracking her to a den in 1963. But once again we were thwarted. On September 4, Marian's transmitter failed, and thus our best prospect was lost. It was unlikely that we would be able to retrap her, though we tried. Now the Alum Creek Sow and her cubs, who had for the last month foraged in a very restricted area, appeared to be our only hope of tracking a grizzly to its den. Number 96 had been reinstrumented but soon lost, probably due to battery failure. Pegleg, Number 76, had eventually evaded our electronic surveillance by traveling rapidly into the rugged mountains and canyons of the northeastern part of the park, where we lost him. The signal from the Sour Creek Sow faded as the battery power declined. Two different transmitters had performed their mission of informing us about her summer and fall movements, but we were unable to recapture and reinstrument her as planned.

John voiced my feelings when he said, "Dammit, let's try to instrument another grizzly." This would double our odds for success, as we now had only one bear — Number 150, the Alum Creek Sow — we could depend on. Accordingly, we made a determined effort to fit one more bear with a collar, even though capturing grizzlies had become increasingly difficult, since many had already dispersed to fall foraging areas and hibernation sites. On October 23, we trapped a sow at Rabbit Creek near Old Faithful. She entered the culvert trap in a snowstorm, and the next day we left her lying down, still a bit dopey from the anesthetic, but wearing a radio collar. Her two-year-olds approached and nudged her as though trying to help her get to her feet. They seemed to realize that something was amiss. The mother, even though partially drugged, warned them away when she raised her head and saw us move. Just before dark, Number 164 rose unsteadily to her feet and ambled off into the dark timber.

Our expectations of success skyrocketed, for we now had two instrumented grizzlies — Number 164 and the Alum Creek Sow — that could lead us to dens. The Alum Creek Sow would very likely hibernate with her three cubs. It was unlikely that 164's two-year-olds would hibernate with their mother, but this was something that we would like to verify. Continuous tracking of both bears would be difficult since they were located on opposite sides of the Continental Divide, one roaming the area of Old Faithful and the other foraging in the upper portions of Hayden Valley. We thus divided our activities between the two locations, trying to monitor both animals. Any day now a storm could put them in their dens for the winter sleep, and we wanted to be right behind them when this occurred.

Throughout most of the fall, the Alum Creek Sow and her cubs foraged over upper Hayden Valley, often along Alum Creek, where they dug out the starchy bulbs of onion grass *(Melica spectabilis)*, pounced on field mice, ferreted out pocket gophers, and raided the caches of red squirrels. From time to time we would make brief expeditions, following the mother bear's signal, to try for a sighting.

On one such occasion I had an encounter that clearly pointed up one of the chief hazards of tracking bears by radio, namely, the sudden and unexpected arousing not of the instrumented grizzly but of other bears whose proximity we had no way of knowing. I had hiked far out into the open sagebrush that bordered both sides of Alum Creek. I was well over a mile from timber and making a beeline for trees to the south when, at the head of a gently sloping ravine terminating at the creek, I saw another sow grizzly and her three large yearlings foraging along the stream and moving at right angles to me. I dropped to my knees, seeking concealment in the scanty sagebrush cover, and watched the family through binoculars. When they reached the draw, they turned and headed directly for me instead of continuing on downstream as I had anticipated. They seemed to be irresistibly drawn toward me, as though they were puppets I was unwillingly pulling on a string. What had made them change course? They had no inkling of my presence. Being afoot and far from timber, I had no alternative but to remain motionless, watching the grizzlies approach closer and closer. I thought surely they would turn before getting to me. The mother and her yearlings loomed bigger and bigger as they approached, and I became increasingly apprehensive, realizing that an encounter of some kind was unavoidable.

When the bears were about 150 feet from me and still coming, I knew that I had to act. If they approached any closer and crossed that invisible, unpredictable line where they felt threatened, they would surely charge at the sight of me. I rose slowly out of the sagebrush, knowing my .357 sidearm would be useless should all four bears attack. I would use it only if contact proved unavoidable. I had decided that after rising I would remain completely still, hoping that I was not violating the distance within which the sow felt compelled to attack. If the grizzly family came on, I would shout to distract them. After that I had no definite plans.

As I emerged out of the sagebrush, all four grizzlies, now less than 150 feet away, abruptly rose up on their hind legs and stared intently at me, definitely startled. For a few long seconds they seemed to tower above me attempting to pick up a scent, a clue to whether I was friend, foe, or food. Their behavior reflected first surprise, then curiosity, but not belligerence. That wonderful inquisitive look reassured me somewhat. Then, as quickly as they had risen, they dropped down on all fours, and I sensed the crucial moment had passed. While descending, the sow pivoted and took off at a run, the yearlings taking their cue from her. A tremendous sense of relief swept over me as I watched the rippling fur on their hindquarters become less distinct with distance. Once again our experience was confirmed: in a human—grizzly confrontation, the bears typically preferred to avoid us if possible. We could not eliminate the chance of surprising one or more grizzlies while tracking a radioed bear, since the very reason that one bear was in a particular locality was cause for others to be there too. We could only be alert to the potential danger and exercise the greatest possible caution. Surprising a grizzly is also a hazard, though not nearly so likely, to all who travel through grizzly country. It should be accepted as a matter of fact and a cause for healthy concern, but not for fear.

Throughout the fall of 1963, we continued to monitor the movements of Number 164 and the Alum Creek Sow. On October 30, at 7:30 P.M., Charlie Ridenour and I obtained a signal placing Number 164 near White Creek, a stream north of Old Faithful draining westward into the Firehole River. The signal was faint, indicating that the grizzly was quite some distance away—eight to ten miles, I judged. Perhaps Number 164 was heading for a den. We hoped that her signal would not grow still weaker.

On November 3, a fresh light blanket of snow gave a wintry aspect to the countryside. We routinely checked for a signal from Number 164 with our mobile unit but were unable to pick one up, so we decided to hike toward the last known source of the signal. Carrying a portable receiver, we started off through the timber, wended our way through a thermal area, and reentered the timber, climbing toward the headwaters of Nez Percé Creek. Hours later we still had not detected 164's signal, so we began climbing to a prominent point that would provide good reception for many miles. While scaling this high, rocky prominence where contrasting patches of snow formed an artistic mosaic on the cliff face, I glanced up and saw a tremendous bull elk standing on a rock slab, silhouetted against the wintry sky. The rutting season was about over, but I thought that the bull might bugle a challenge to other bulls. Slowly I reached into my backpack for my 200-millimeter lens, twisted it into place, and focused on the elk. I anticipated a picture such as photographers dream about but waited for the elk to turn his head so that light would reflect from his eye. But I never snapped the picture; the elk suddenly turned and instantly disappeared. Chagrined, I climbed on up to his overlook, checking for the grizzly's signal but thinking of the photograph I had lost. Not only had I missed the picture but there was still no sound of a signal. I realized that we had lost Grizzly Number 164—perhaps for the season, and if so, the opportunity to track her to a den. All we knew was that when last located she had been on an easterly course.

The day before, we had observed the Alum Creek Sow and her cubs foraging in the thinly snow-covered meadows of Alum Creek. We watched as the sow lay flat on her stomach motionless for twenty minutes, patiently scanning mouse runways. Then a paw flashed forward, pinning a mouse beneath it. The sow swallowed it at a gulp. The disappointed cubs, tired of waiting, began to wander, and eventually their mother followed. The cubs, now big and fat and sporting slick, heavy fur coats, alternately scampered ahead and trailed behind, adjusting their restless energy to their mother's methodical gait. We knew this grizzly well and had plotted her fall range. It embraced an overall area of twenty-seven square miles, but recently, though the bear was constantly roaming, foraging day and night and resting only for short intervals, she did not travel far and usually wound up a few airline miles (as the crow—or the plane—flies) from her starting point. Her three hungry, energetic cubs appeared to greatly influence her activities. They wouldn't have let her rest even if she had wanted to.

At 6:30 A.M. on the morning I lost Number 164, we obtained a clear signal from the other grizzly across the Divide—a pulse of 90 per minute indicating that the Alum Creek Sow was now in upper Alum Creek. She appeared to be working her way west and upstream, approaching the Trout Creek–Alum Creek divide. The Alum Creek Sow and Number 164, at least according to the latter's last signal, had been widely separated but generally moving toward one another. Surely, we thought, this change in activity from the Alum Creek Sow's confined travel routine of past weeks presaged a trip to her winter quarters.

Throughout the afternoon and night of November 3 and on into the early hours of November 4, we fought off sleep and continued to monitor the Alum Creek Sow's signal from our base station. With no indication of further movement and no signal from Number 164, the Alum Creek Sow seemed our best chance for following a grizzly to its den that year. We thought we knew roughly where her den might be, and so we again took to the field to investigate.

Late in the afternoon of November 4 we trudged through falling snow, following the signal from the Alum Creek Sow. This bearing and one obtained earlier from our base station provided an accurate fix — a pencilled "X" on our topographic map of the grizzly's known position. The Alum Creek Sow was in a heavily timbered area twelve miles from our base station and remained there throughout the night. But around 9:00 A.M. the next day the clear signal periodically faded. By 9:50 A.M. it became quite faint, and soon it was inaudible. We interpreted these signals to mean either that the bear was moving in and out of some kind of shelter such as windfall or cave that attenuated the signal, or that she was moving away and to the south. To determine which hypothesis was correct we had to move quickly.

Leaving our pickup parked along a service road, Maurice, Charlie Ridenour, and I shouldered our packs and headed into the storm to attempt to make visual contact. We followed a compass bearing and then picked up a faint signal on our portable receivers, whose receiving range was much more limited than our base station's antenna. Our destination was the radio fix on our map, in the middle of the Yellowstone wilderness. This was the last known position of our grizzly and, as the signal now revealed, she was evidently still there. In late morning the storm and haphazard piles of windfelled trees so slowed our progress that we despaired of ever sighting her. Fortunately, though we were unaware of it, she was not traveling. After a brief halt, the signal began to increase in strength and was soon coming in so loud that we had to turn down the receiver volume. Our excitement grew as we realized that we were fast closing in on our target. A bit later we began to look for footprints and signs in the snow that would warn us of the grizzly's presence, stopping often to listen and to peer ahead through the dense pines.

At one such stop I counted the signal pulses per minute, something we usually did automatically on first picking up any signal and at regular intervals thereafter. Amazement and disbelief engulfed me, and Maurice, seeing my look of consternation, asked, "What's the problem?"

"It can't be! Impossible!" I exclaimed. I had just realized that though the signal we had monitored over the last month from the Alum Creek Sow, and had counted and recorded recently, was ninety pulses per minute, the signal we were receiving now from the grizzly just ahead of us was thumping in at sixty-two a minute. Holding up and turning the receiver to emphasize the signal, I said, "It's not the Alum Creek Sow. The pulse rate's too slow."

"Hell, it's got to be," said Maurice. "Maybe the transmitter batteries are spent."

"No, the signal's strong. And even if it were weak, a change in pulse rate wouldn't be detectable." I counted again. "I'll be damned, its Number 164!" How could we all have gone so long without noticing the slow pulse of the signal?

We were closing in on an instrumented bear, but not the one we had expected. This was indeed Number 164, the sow we had instrumented on the west side of the Continental Divide, where all waters ran toward the Pacific. Here all runoff was to the east. Where then was the Alum Creek Sow and her family of cubs? She had been close by only a day or so ago, and if she were still in the area we should have been getting two signals. All day there had been only one—hers, we assumed. I shook my head but then realized it didn't really matter. This was not the time to solve the engima. The grizzly we had instrumented to increase our odds had moved during the storm from Old Faithful and Nez Percé Creek across the divide to Trout Creek. Now she was just ahead of us, and she as well as the Alum Creek Sow could lead us to a winter den.

We moved forward over unbroken snow, cognizant of the fact that we had traveled all day through country recently inhabited by grizzlies without seeing a single track. This indicated to us that the grizzlies had already moved to dens and were about to hibernate. Number 164 was probably at her den, and the Alum Creek Sow might already be inside hers—hence, no signal from the latter. We were now at the point on our map where the radio bearings had intersected, the area from which our signal had been coming.

We approached and examined every likely den site; yet we did not find a grizzly, nor was there any disturbance in the snow other than our own tracks. The woods were silent except for the signal. The deep wing beats of a great gray owl we flushed made no sound, nor did the flitting Canada jays utter their soft call. Even the usually noisy scolding of pine squirrels was oddly absent. We climbed up a slope and then to the top of some fallen timber, and from there I got a constant-strength signal; that is, a signal was coming in from every direction, and I could not detect a null to indicate the source, regardless of how I rotated the receiver antenna. A null or no signal occurs when the plane of the loop antenna bisects the bearing of the signal coming from the animal, and the lack of a null indicated that we were too close to the signal source to get one. Was the grizzly directly under me? The same thought struck Maurice, and he shifted his feet on the slippery logs so he could swing his gun freely. I switched the receiver to my left hand just in case I needed my sidearm. The grizzly could not be more than a few hundred feet away, but where? In the tangle of logs beneath us? Even the thought was alarming. A startled grizzly could rise up from underneath or to one side of us and be upon us in seconds — far too fast for us to climb trees or even run. Very, very slowly we moved another twenty feet, not knowing whether we were getting closer or moving away from the bear. I anxiously looked down at an opening between the fallen logs, but the snow was undisturbed.

"There it is," whispered Maurice, and I straightened up with a start, half expecting to see a grizzly. Maurice was pointing downhill to faint traces of dirt on packed snow fifty feet away. This bear-packed snow was the only sign in front of the dark den opening to suggest that a grizzly was inside, but our signal most certainly confirmed it. We retreated, circling to approach at an angle affording better visibility and greater freedom of action. At twenty feet I saw the den opening and snapped a photograph. The entrance led directly back into the hillside. A closer view through the binoculars revealed tracks but none that led away from the cave. The grizzly sow, rather than running, had retreated within her den as we approached. She undoubtedly knew we were present but chose to remain concealed rather than defend her den. With our film record we silently moved off to a more prudent distance.

"What about her two-year-olds? She doesn't seem to have them with her," said Maurice. There was no evidence of them at all.

"The few sharp tracks I notice all look the same, but we can't confirm that now. It would be too risky if we disturbed her."

We all agreed. We were looking at the big unclimbable lodgepoles towering upward without a branch for thirty feet.

We retreated silently and cautiously, thrilled by attaining our goal. I personally was elated. There are times in any venture when success depends on a lucky break. The right decisions are made, some intuitively, some by reasoning, some by pure chance. Finding the den of Number 164 was one of these occasions. We had worked hard, persevered, and made the right decisions, but luck had been instrumental in leading us to the den.

Radio-tracking Number 164 to her den provided us with the later opportunity to measure and observe the den interior and to gather information on bed construction and site selection—information we had been unable to obtain using conventional research methods. Along with the knowledge we had just acquired about environmental conditions that existed when a grizzly entered its winter den, this dramatically confirmed what we already suspected—that biotelemetry was a valuable and practical ecological research technique with tremendous potential for future studies. Perhaps it was symbolic of this technical breakthrough that a huge, uniquely three-forked lodgepole pine towered directly above the den opening, providing a landmark for our return either in spring or in midwinter, when ten feet of snow would greatly alter the character of the landscape. To ensure that we could find our way back, we followed a 60-degree bearing to the nearest recognizable meadow, making small blazes on the back sides of trees as we passed through the timber. These marks, indicating the reciprocal bearing of 240 degrees, would be visible on our return course.

As we backtracked the many miles to base, I reconstructed the happenings of the past few days. It was clear that at some time during the last forty-eight hours we had lost the signal from Number 150, the Alum Creek Sow, and had picked up Number 164's without detecting two simultaneous signals or realizing that a switch had occurred. The snowstorm had started Number 164 moving over the mountain to her den—a den already prepared. She traveled an airline distance of fifteen miles, but she covered many more on the ground, crossing the divide that had shielded her signal and arriving in the den area by November 3. She remained at or near the cave entrance during the afternoon of the fourth. At times she dozed on the snow-covered pile of tailing excavated from the den and periodically entered the den. The absence of tracks anywhere but at the den opening indicated that she had rested outside the entrance on the night of the fourth and during all of the following day, thus enabling us to pick up her signal while assuming it to be that of the Alum Creek Sow. Not until our approach on the afternoon of the fifth did she enter and remain inside the den. This, I thought, reinforced our theory that the grizzlies move directly to their hibernation dens during snowstorms, which eradicate all telltale tracks leading to their winter sleeping chambers.

Darkness and a storm enveloped us before we reached our vehicle. Snow fell all night and throughout the next day. The Yellowstone roads were closed to the south, east, and north. There were no more roaming grizzlies, no signals, and no bear tracks — only the deep ruts our vehicles left as we bucked the snow on our way out of the park.

It was a relatively unknown bear that led us to our first den. But we were still eager to follow Marian to her winter quarters, particularly as she would now have a family. We were certain that Marian was pregnant when she entered her den to spend the winter of 1963–64, but it was not until spring seven months later that we confirmed that judgment.

The tiny ten-pound balls of fur that bounced up and down in the gray sage were Marian's two cubs fighting their way through the shrublike forest that towered above them. Without their mother's leadership and care they would soon have been lost in the maze. But raising a family was new for this six-year-old bear, and she too was learning. In early summer she lost one of her cubs. Perhaps initially she was not strict enough in disciplining or in roughly demanding instant obedience to her instructions. In any case, her devotion and constant surveillance of her remaining offspring seemed to increase as summer gave way to fall. Marian's maternal instinct provided the basis for raising her family, but experience and acquired behavior would mold her into a better mother.

On September 4, 1964, when her burly youngster weighed over one hundred pounds and could well take care of himself for a few hours, we reinstrumented Marian with a radio that beeped at eighty pulses per minute. Wearing her red and yellow collar, she soon rejoined her cub while we monitored her signal. Once more we would try to track her to a den.

On September 8, the signal was intermittent — very loud and clear, then fading; returning loud, and again fading — the signal pattern that indicated she was moving in and out of a den. Could it be that she was already preparing winter quarters for herself and cub? Leaving our field station, I followed the signal through pine forests and over downed timber. During this tracking, I experienced more difficulty getting consistent bearings than with any previous bear. Adding to my difficulties, the signal increased and faded so often that I couldn't get a good null and thus a direction and course to follow. The anomaly, I eventually decided, was due to a combination of topography and heavy timber that caused signal bounce, usually not a problem with a 32 MHz signal. After three hours, my persistence in following the zigzag course indicated by the multiple signal reflections was rewarded. With the receiver volume first turned low and then off to prevent alerting the grizzlies, I moved slowly and quietly until I saw two dark, blurred forms vanishing into the more intense blackness of the forest. Marian had detected me before I spied her. I had interrupted her den-digging at the base of a large fir tree. She had been using her long front claws to dig an entranceway between two huge downward-projecting roots, but on examination the roots appeared too close together to allow for a sufficiently large entrance. Perhaps for this reason, along with my intrusion, she later abandoned the project and sought another site.

Two days later, signals revealed that Marian was den-digging again at a new location. We monitored this family daily as fall gave way to winter. On October 18, we followed her through a foot of snow. On October 31, we tracked her all day, her cub following in her footsteps. When we located a fresh warm bed on a timbered ridge we slowed down. Now we were using both the signal and fresh tracks in the snow to keep contact. Within a heavy stand of fir and lodgepole pine the tracks were so fresh that we knew the bears were very close, and the signal confirmed this. But just how far away were the grizzlies in terms of yards or feet? Could they be backtracking or perhaps even lying in wait for their tenacious pursuers? We decided to give them time to move on, so once again we stopped to wait before continuing. Marian seemed to have selected a course over the densest part of the jumbled windfall. Always she walked over the logs, never under them. Occasionally she sat down; once she nervously defecated. She led us past an old den that she may have dug in previous years, but throughout this day of trekking in deep wet snow she did not go near her den site. This was the final entry of my field notes at the close of that wearying day:

No indication today that Marian and other grizzlies are ready to enter winter dens. Although the snow is over a foot deep, the air temperature today was so warm that water from melting snow dripped off the trees. Wet globs of snow falling from trees soaked our down clothing. From past experience I do not believe the grizzlies will finally enter their winter dens while the temperature is above freezing and the snow wet though deep.

Among the grizzlies we had instrumented in the fall of 1964 was a yearling known only as Number 158, a dark-colored bear with a distinctive light tan collar. While trying to track the elusive Marian to her den, we were also keeping close tabs on this instrumented bear, from whom we gained considerable information on prehibernation behavior.

Grizzly Number 158, the offspring of sow Number 39, was born in the winter of 1962–63, probably not too far from Mud Volcano. We first observed him and his two littermates, later called Number 157 and Number 165, in the vicinity of this mud-spitting geyser, where their mother was catching field mice. We suspected that they had denned nearby on the slopes of Elephant Back Mountain. When Number 158 was trapped, marked, and given a number as a cub, he weighed 58 pounds; about a year later he weighed 117 pounds. And when retrapped in October 1964, almost four months later, he tipped the scales at 217 pounds, having gained exactly 100 pounds since June 22. As we had not yet instrumented a yearling, a member of this family seemed a good choice for tracking yearlings to a den. When we put a radio on Number 158, we found that his right front foot was cut and infected. We cleaned the wound and disinfected it with alcohol. The foot no doubt hindered his foraging, and this perhaps explained why he weighed considerably less than the 245 pounds of his littermate trapped the following day. From Number 158 we obtained the usual blood sample for later chemical analysis and took a rectal temperature of 102° F, about normal for active bears. We also photographed him as he wobbled to his feet and took off wearing a brightly colored radio collar. Turning to John I said, "Well, there he goes. If we can just follow him to a winter den we'll learn if yearlings will all hibernate together in the same den with their mother or in separate dens nearby."

We monitored Number 158 daily, and toward the end of October, with fresh snow on the ground, we followed his signal in the hope that we might now locate this family's denning site. We picked our way through sagebrush partially mantled in eight inches of snow. After we had entered the timber, the signal indicated that the bear was no more than a half-mile away. Bob Ruff, John, a visitor, Hersch Connally, and I moved up the steep-sided valley. At the top we came across the tracks of a large grizzly. We suspected they were made by the mother, Number 39. From this point we moved very slowly, carefully avoiding windfall and thickets whenever possible. Finally the signal beckoned us into a thicket of young lodgepoles growing among logs. I was in the lead with the receiver; John followed with the movie camera and Bob with a shotgun loaded with slugs, Hersch trailing behind. Our progress was very slow. We stopped repeatedly to look and listen. Our lives depended on our detecting the bears before they detected us, or at least determining their precise position before we got too close.

In the midst of a jumble of downed trees, just at the point where I felt we should go no further, I saw a slight movement at the base of a tree and recognized the ears of a grizzly rising to the alert position. With a brief pantomine I signalled to John that I'd seen a bear, and with a slow pointing movement he communicated that he'd seen another. We were dangerously close to the grizzlies, and the trees around us were mostly saplings, none suitable for a quick climb to safety. Very quietly and slowly we backtracked, only the soft snow making such a retreat possible. When we were about a hundred yards away, we talked loudly to one another in an attempt to oust the grizzlies so we could examine their beds. When the receiver gave no indication that this family of bears had moved, I shouted, but only after we positioned ourselves at the base of large climbable lodgepoles. While each of us stood close to his selected tree, the sow gave a terrifying roar. It was a sound undoubtedly designed to frighten and intimidate, and it had the same effect on me as the roar of a man-eating tiger I had once heard from a tree blind in the complete darkness of an Indian jungle.

Galvanized into action by the roar, John gave Hersch a boost to start him up a tree; then both John and Bob started climbing. I hesitated for a moment to put the receiver to my ear, trying to tell with volume turned low whether the bear was approaching. Within seconds I knew that though the sow had started our way, she was now retreating. In a few more seconds the signal had so faded that I had to increase the receiver sensitivity. Our radioed yearling, Number 158, and undoubtedly the entire family, was running away. Subsequently, fresh tracks in the snow showed that simultaneously with her roar the belligerent sow had charged toward us in the snow, and then turned and run off in the opposite direction. We knew it had been a close call, for had she been aroused when we were within a hundred feet of her there is little doubt that she would have charged with the intent of attacking. We already knew sow Number 39 to be a bad-tempered animal. In early spring she had charged John in a bluffing attack near Mud Volcano, so this latest roar and near attack were warnings that we did not take lightly. What would be her reaction when we finally tracked her to a den? Would an aggressive grizzly mother actively defend a den site? We didn't know, but we were sure that sooner or later we were going to find out.

On November 2, signals received at our base station informed us that radioed grizzlies Number 158 and Marian were on the move, traveling in a snowstorm to their den sites. Soon afterward, Marian's signal revealed that she was moving in and out of a den, perhaps excavating it a bit more at the last minute. This was what we had been waiting for.

Bob and I took off in pursuit of the bears, prepared to spend two or three days on their trail. Our backpacks were loaded with sleeping bags, dried foods, a cooking pail, tracking equipment, extra clothing, and camera gear. We were hiking, since the snow was not yet deep enough to cover brush and downed trees and snowshoes and skis were useless. The signal bearings that we had obtained from our base and field stations, using the sensitive five- and three-element yagi antennas, placed the grizzlies far to the south. The signals received at our base were weak, and now that we were hiking the signal source was too far away to be picked up at all by our less sensitive portable loop antennas. Thus during most of the first day we trudged in silence through snow twelve to eighteen inches deep, heading for a spot in uniformly timbered country marked on our map.

By nightfall of the second day Marian's signal, pulsing at eighty beeps a minute, was coming in loud and clear. We made camp in deep snow among fallen trees and under fir timber at a spot from which we could monitor the signal throughout the night. Air temperatures dropped to 13° F, but our down sleeping bags kept us warm. Nevertheless, it was not what one would call a comfortable night. The receiver functioned best if kept warm, and there was no option but to put it in the sleeping bag. Each time I rolled over during the night I came into contact with its sharp edges, but at least this helped me in the task I had set for myself—to periodically awaken, turn on the receiver, and listen for the signal of the nearby grizzly. All went well until 3:00 A.M., when the signal boomed in much louder than earlier in the night. The directional receiver indicated that the grizzly had moved. I wondered if she could have smelled the food we cooked for supper and was now approaching our camp. Such thoughts can be more than usually unsettling when one is half awake. I knew that I probably ought to monitor the signal, but I was drowsy, and the need for sleep dulled my apprehensions. It was daylight when I next awoke to check Marian's signal.

By midday we were approaching the den, moving slowly and cautiously. A growl from the cub revealed that we were very close. We followed the contour of a slope where the snow was deep, turning west to keep the tree-filtered sunlight out of our eyes. Directly in front of us a patch of fresh earth tailing darkened the snow — evidence of final "housecleaning" activities in den construction. Success! Here at the base of a huge fir was the entrance to Marian's den, but neither she nor the cub was inside. A flash of black had been the cub tardily following his mother. We didn't see Marian, only her tracks, but the signal informed us that she was only a short distance away. Mother and cub were apparently patiently waiting for us to leave. We moved on without approaching closer to the den. When we found a sunny spot we removed our packs, leaned against some accommodating trees, and ate lunch, basking in the sun and in the satisfaction of having finally located one of Marian's dens. The noon temperature in the shade was 40° F and much warmer in the sun, and the melting snow dropping from the trees moistened our rations of mixed nuts, raisins, crackers, and cheese.

It was not a suitable time for Marian and her cub to enter their den for the long sleep of winter. The triggering snowstorm of October 30 that had moved grizzlies to their den sites had been followed by clear weather and rising temperatures. Such conditions would keep the bears close to their dens but not inside where earth walls could effectively shield their radio signals. Thus the situation remained favorable for locating another den. "Why not try," I thought, as we rested. We had last radio-located grizzly Number 158 in this same general region, but so far on our trek we had not detected his signal. "If we hike to the southeast," I mused, "we should intersect the last radio bearing we have obtained from this bear." This signal had been recorded three days previously at our field station, but it was our only lead to Number 158's present location. Quite likely this last location was close to his den. If so, we were within striking distance.

"Bob," I said, "let's give Number 158 a try." I rose and threw on my pack, but Bob said nothing. The steak dinner and warm room he had imagined had been postponed indefinitely.

Our course took us to within a half-mile of the den we had located the previous fall, so we made a side excursion and determined that Lucky, Number 164, had not reused her former den, although she had raked out her old bough bed before departing in the spring. This information was worth the trip, since we would be gathering more statistics on this subject. However, when approaching darkness again brought us to a halt, we were tired and wet from fighting deep snow, and we still had not received the new signal we sought. The obvious reason, unless the bear was in his den, was that we were still too far away to detect the signal with our portable receiver—by at least three or more miles. But just how great was the distance between us, and in what direction should we go? Not knowing, we made camp.

The next morning we dined on the same fare we had had for supper—potato soup, dried beef, crackers, and tea. Then we continued our wide sweep to bisect the 165–degree bearing we had obtained at our field station. Our fervent hope was that when we finally picked up the signal from Number 158, it would reveal that we were farther back in the wilderness than was the bear and thus that our final direction of travel would be toward base and home rather than away. At 11:30 A.M. we routinely stopped to check for a signal as we had done many times already, but still there was nothing that even a lively imagination could interpret as a faint beep. We trudged a few yards up a slope and tried again. Perhaps the slight altitude made a difference, for here the rotating antenna picked up a weak signal. The sense antenna indicated that the bear was to the south on a bearing of 195 degrees—deeper in the wilderness country, not north in the direction of home.

We were simultaneously delighted and discouraged. A quick decision was mandatory; our companions had expected us back that morning, and we were already overdue. Hiking through snow with heavy packs had tired us, and we did not relish adding still more miles to the trek. We could have gone back to our base, but there was really never a question as to the decision. We would never be in a better position, nor would there be a more suitable time for locating the den of this family of bears. We turned and followed the signal, resigned to camping out with little food for another night. For the rest of the day the signal lured us on, pulsing weakly, often intermittently, and finally strongly at fifty-two pulses a minute. Several times it confused us by dying out completely for long periods when the grizzly remained in his den. At such times we brushed the snow off a log, sat down, and waited. We looked at our maps, but there were no recognizable landmarks in this expansive coniferous forest.

At 5 P.M. we were moving slowly and very carefully with the signal coming in loud and clear. We were apprehensive and alert as we entered a thicket of "doghair" lodgepole growing beneath towering pines. Here visibility was almost zero, and a sudden rapid increase in signal strength indicated that the instrumented grizzly, probably the entire family, was moving quickly toward us. The receiver sensitivity and volume were turned clear down. The distance now separating us could be no more than a few hundred yards. Simultaneously, Bob and I picked trees and started to climb. Twenty feet above the ground was a single limb where I could rest. From this perch, I saw Bob continuing to shinny upward. The signal was still loud though possibly diminishing. If so, it would mean that the grizzlies had turned and were moving away, but I wasn't sure. I remembered sow Number 39's record as a belligerent bear, and I also remembered that only Bob, of all the members of our team, had neglected to climb ropes daily in preparation for just such an emergency. He was tiring, and it appeared doubtful that he would reach the limbs above.

"Bob!" I shouted, "Get going! They're still coming." By now I knew they weren't, but within seconds Bob was straddling a limb. There are some things, I thought, that students must learn, even the hard way. While he gasped to catch his breath, I slid to the ground. The sow had elected not to defend her den.

A quick survey with binoculars of the nearby den revealed it to be large enough to have been prepared for the use of four, and since no other dens were visible, we were reasonably sure that Number 39's yearlings would indeed den with her, as we had speculated. Not wishing to further disturb the bears, we turned and headed north, intending to take a shortcut home. It proved a poor gamble. Much later in near darkness we were climbing, stumbling, and falling over natural log fences and barriers—piles of dense windfall covered with slick snow. A better fabrication for breaking bones could hardly have been devised. Time and again we scrambled up on slippery logs, momentarily balancing our heavy packs, then jumped down, climbed up again, tottered, jumped, and continued on. Since leaving the den we had been racing against time, traveling much faster than our tired muscles dictated, and after dark we would no longer be able to make our way through the windfall. The going would have been treacherous enough even in bright daylight; a twisted ankle or broken leg meant complications we didn't care to consider. So it was with real relief that we broke out into the narrow open valley of upper Trout Creek just as complete darkness settled over the landscape.

We could travel the open country after dark and still had many miles to go, but we stopped to brew some hot tea sweetened with our remaining sugar. Lunch had been scanty and was consumed many strenuous hours before. It felt good to take off my pack, and the brown needles and stalks of rye grass under the spreading fir branches provided a dry seat. While the fire flickered on Bob's face across from me and the snow in our kettle slowly turned to water, I leaned back, closed my eyes, and relaxed, weary but completely contented. I was glad simply to be in this solitary spot with the golden-brown grass, the dark green of fir needles overhead, the smell of evergreens, and the circle of snow rapidly fading into blackness. On down the bank under a layer of snow and another of ice flowed the waters of Trout Creek. Such moments invite musings, and mine turned to the question I had been asked many times: Why am I here? Is studying the grizzly bear worthwhile, important? But I knew the answer. If the grizzly should disappear from the Yellowstone ecosystem or from planet Earth it would be a tragedy but not a catastrophe. Life forms and processes would soon adapt to its absence. However, what is at stake is not just the grizzly, but the steady, often unnoticed attrition of the countless life forms, both plant and animal, that compose our complex biosphere and keep it functioning. The loss of the grizzly, the wolf, the great whales, the peregrine falcon, tropical orchids, would each by itself be more symbolic than crucial, but the combined loss of many species, whose intermeshing functions sustain life, is another matter. Somewhere we must assess the situation and draw the line if life, and particularly intelligent life, is to survive on earth. Our research on the grizzly would be a contribution to that larger assessment.

I had almost dozed off but felt the cold creeping in and rose. The bottoms of my feet were sore, and Bob and I felt like spending the night around our small cooking fire, but we knew that we had to move on. Our companions would be concerned over our continued absence, familiar as they were with the aggressive behavior of sow Number 39 in the past. Indeed, one reason we were studying her was to find out what caused her to be so belligerent. We had no wish to cause needless worry, so we set out on the last lap of our four-day trek, mechanically lifting one foot out of the snow and placing it ahead of the other.

Exhausted, but exuberant from success, we arrived at our parked vehicle at 9:20 P.M. As I hoisted my pack into the truck bed the brilliant flash of a meteor illuminated the pickup and reflected off the cab. I was thrilled and awed by this rare phenomenon; it seemed a fitting close to a season in which our efforts finally rewarded us by throwing light on the winter denning behavior of grizzlies. We now had evidence that some yearlings as well as cubs hibernate with their mother. We also knew, based on our observations so far, that all the grizzlies had dug and prepared dens well in advance of entering them for the winter. And we could at least speculate that it was instinctive for the grizzly to dig a den rather than appropriate a cave or natural shelter as does the black bear. Would our subsequent work in locating dens substantiate this conclusion? Would the offspring of the bears we had just tracked to their dens dig their own nearby next fall? Would they line them with boughs as Number 164 had done, and presumably Marian and Number 39? We would seek verification the following spring when we returned to the dens after the young bears had left them. Perhaps Number 158 and Marian's cub would help provide specific answers; we were sure they would raise more questions as well.

5

Holing Up: Preparation, Prehibernation, and Denning

In early spring of 1965, the crusted snow was slick and icy under our skis as we glided along through the monotonously similar coniferous forest, looking for a knife slash on a tree—the first blaze that would lead us to the next, then another, and another. John, Charlie, and I were returning to Marian's winter den. Miles back we had left our snowmobile and were now ski touring, our packs loaded with gear and enough food for three or four days. The sky was a bright blue from zenith to horizon, and the sun was beginning to warm the crisp morning air. By noon, the crusted snow on southern exposures would give way to our skis. On hillsides facing most directly southward, last year's brown flower stalks already jutted above the gray sage and splotches of bare earth showed, but when we entered the timber to pick our way through the thick lodgepole forest, we were skiing on snow six to eight feet above the ground.

When we spotted the last blaze we were within sight of the huge spruce tree under which the den was excavated. We now carefully side-stepped upward, sensitive to any sound or movement that might reveal the presence of the grizzlies. We were not sure what to expect, so we carefully reconnoitered the area. We found bough and bark beds laid on the snow near the den entrance but no fresh tracks. Judging from the signs, I decided that Marian and her cub — now a yearling — had emerged from their den in late March but had not left the den area until toward the first of April, perhaps a week before our arrival.

Marian and her yearling had spent the winter in their den sleeping on a bough bed, now compacted and well worn. There were also numerous bough beds outside the den, laid on snow at different levels indicating that they had been constructed at different times. Nearby, stripped trees revealed that mother and offspring had torn off spruce and fir boughs to build new beds. It was clear that on several occasions the bears had slept or reverted to a lethargic condition in these beds and had been covered by falling snow. When they awoke they had risen and destroyed these temporary snow caves with the exception of the section covering their heads. The story could be read from the partially melted snow caves, which had ventlike air tubes to the surface formed by the bears' warm breath rising through the snow.

After speculating about the formation and use of the snow beds high above the ground, we climbed down through the narrow den entrance into the bed chamber. Crouching on the evergreen boughs now tattered and flattened from a winter of use, we carefully and systematically searched the bed chamber. Using a flashlight, we looked for signs of excrement, urine — even a radio collar — but we found none of these. In one way or another the bears' hibernation physiology had taken care of the toxins that in most animals would

John and Frank Craighead remove a young drugged grizzly from a culvert trap. Photograph by Lance Craighead. (All photos, unless otherwise indicated, by Frank and John Craighead.)

Top: *Marian leaving culvert trap after being immobilized and instrumented with a radio.* **Bottom:** *John Craighead and Maurice Hornocker immobilize a free-roaming grizzly with a drug-filled dart.*

Top left: *Weighing grizzly Number 76, Pegleg.* **Top right:** *Maurice Hornocker and Frank Craighead instrument Beep, grizzly Number 37, with his first radio. In the foreground is a device used by the researchers to check the strength of a radio signal in the field.* **Bottom:** *Grizzly Number 158 wearing a radio collar.*

Top left: *The Grizzled Sow, Number 65, with her well disciplined cubs.* **Top right:** *Ignatz, the ill-fated "omega" cub.* **Bottom:** *Handsome, one of the group of cubs known as the Four Musketeers, was distinctively marked with a broad white collar.*

Top: *Two grizzly sows (right) aggressively warn a large boar away from the vicinity of their cubs.* **Bottom left:** *Immature male grizzly rocking in a seated pose.* **Bottom right:** *Bob Ruff and Charlie Ridenour monitor the signal of the Alum Creek Sow, attempting to track her to her den in late fall of 1963.*

Top: *John Craighead investigating a bough bed in the snow used by Marian shortly after emerging from her den.* **Bottom:** *Frank Craighead in the cramped entrance to Marian's den.*

Taking a milk sample for analysis from a lactating female grizzly.

Top: *Frank Craighead in the deep, denlike day bed dug in late fall by one of the Four Musketeers.* **Bottom:** *Marian and her yearling, Number 188, feeding on the carcass of a drowned bison along the shore of the Yellowstone River, soon after emerging from hibernation in the spring of 1965.*

have accumulated as a result of the slowed but continuous metabolic processes. The grizzlies had not eaten but lived off their ample fat supply throughout the winter. We knew that upon emerging Marian and her cub would have lost about 25 percent of their total body weight, according to results obtained by us and other researchers, using captive animals. Even so, they would still be carrying sufficient fat to provide energy during the lean spring months ahead.

At the time of our visit, the noon temperature inside the den and just above the bed was 32° F, but in the shade outside it was 40°, and in the sun a comfortable 50°. The warm outside temperatures probably encouraged the bears to emerge and sleep on the snow surface. While checking the den, I carefully measured the interior. The length of the bed chamber was four feet, the height also four feet, and the width three and a half feet. This would have been a snug sleeping chamber, just barely large enough for the mother and her yearling. The entranceway to the den was about three feet long and slightly less in width and height. Marian's den was a little smaller than the size we later averaged from ten dens, but Marian was not a large grizzly. Still, the average den was small — about five feet long by four and a half feet wide and three feet high. This particular den, like Number 164's, was dug at the base of a large tree and into a north-facing slope. It was situated so that the entranceway was covered with deep snow, forming a sealed chamber with little transfer of air. This small dead-air cell was marvelously suited for its purpose as a bed chamber; it was far more comfortable temperaturewise than the outside air. Just what the bed chamber temperatures might register we did not know but planned to find out. This year we intended to place within a den a device capable of transmitting, and allowing us to periodically record, inside air temperatures.

When Marian and her yearling left this isolated den, they traveled on deep snow through evergreen timber, making their way on the annual spring pilgrimage toward the open country of Hayden Valley. Here our direct observation and reading of signs helped to piece together their spring activities. In the valley, wind-packed snow still covered most of the sagebrush, but a light yellow-green was evident where the warm waters of Alum Creek had encouraged the early growth of sedges. Mother and yearling made their first meal on the tender shoots of these triangular-stemmed plants. Moving on down toward the Yellowstone River, they scoured the barren land, unable to find an adequate supply of food, both living off the fat reserves they still retained from winter.

At the same time, Inge, the Grizzled Sow, Ivan, Number 41 (who was missing teeth in his lower jaw), Fidel, Number 190 (one of the 34 new bears marked in 1964), and many other grizzlies were also busy foraging. Once active, all the bears would gradually lose weight until late spring and summer food supplies enabled them to recoup the loss. This decline in weight would be arrested if they found a carcass of an animal — perhaps an elk, bison, or moose — that had died either from the difficulties of winter or from advanced age. Many creatures in severe stages of malnourishment would not make it through the spring even though green forage was now available. The grizzlies' keen sense of smell would lead them to the ripening carcasses.

Marian located the carcass of a bison that had drowned while attempting to cross the Yellowstone River. The carcass, now beached along the river shore, formed a nutritious food supply for Marian and her yearling, and was also available to and shared by other bears. Here Marian once again encountered Inge, still the dominant bear in the Yellowstone hierarchy. Inge apparently was still attracted by this young grizzly, with whom he had bred in 1963. At this meeting, Marian paid no attention to Inge, but was very solicitous of her youngster. She watched over him with almost as much care and affection as she had done during the fall of 1964, seeming not at all anxious for a large boar to approach close to her progeny.

By mid-May still more sedge had added touches of green to the white landscape. Last year's grass was brown with no sign of new shoots, and corn snow stretched all around except for a few patches of bare ground. Bison, moving slowly with heads down, munched the sedge stems and dry grass. Muskrats, Canada geese, scaup ducks, baldpates, goldeneye ducks, and white pelicans rippled and dotted the Yellowstone River, but none of these was a likely source of grizzly food. Although this was a difficult time for grizzlies to obtain sufficient food to balance the energy expended in obtaining it, both Marian and her yearling looked to be in good condition and were apparently supplementing their stored energy with mice and green vegetation. Marmots, now out from hibernation, were a favorite meal when they could be caught. Some flowers were beginning to appear, including the snowbank, or sagebrush buttercup *(Ranunculus glaberrimus)* — a sign of spring and better days ahead.

Marian and her yearling followed another set of grizzly tracks up a hillside to grass and bare ground, where they began digging for field mice and pocket gophers. Open runways, tunnels, earth mounds, and girdled shrubs were signs of a high population of both these rodent species. A kestrel and a redtailed hawk were also hunting here; the redtailed hawk from a tree perch, the sparrow hawk hovering in the breeze. On another bared hilltop I saw a coyote pounce. An ermine, still almost completely white, was strikingly visible as it crossed the dark earth from snow to snow, and then vanished. When Marian, busily digging, located a mouse nest or excavated one, her yearling came running and she permitted him to catch and eat the mouse. A raven hopping close by was judging the distance, ready to rush in first and catch the prey. On several occasions the yearling chased his avian competitor, but the wily raven knew exactly how close he could approach the bear and still escape.

With a lightning-fast sweep of her remarkably prehensile paw, Marian picked up and consumed a mouse. Here, where the population of rodents was high, a collection of predators — the bear, coyote, weasel, badger, and their avian counterparts, the hawks and ravens — were reducing their numbers by day, aided by short-eared, great horned, and great gray owls at night. This varied assortment of hunters congregating where their prey was numerous and vulnerable would, over the next month, substantially reduce the breeding population of mice and gophers, functioning as natural regulators of prey populations. The grizzlies, the redtailed hawks, or any one or two species alone would have had little measurable effect, but the combined predator pressure from all of these bird and mammal species, operating day and night, would effectively prevent rodent population increase. Marian and her yearling were doing their part in maintaining an equilibrium between the rodents and their environment. Marian again unearthed a field mouse and affectionately, so it seemed, watched her greedy offspring catch and consume it.

By early June 1965, Marian's temperament began to alter as a consequence of hormonal changes. She completely ceased to lactate and weaned her yearling by chasing him away. (The duration of lactation varies widely among grizzly sows and according to circumstances, but one and a half to two years following the whelping of cubs is not uncommon.) Again and again he approached too close to her while she was busy feeding. Interpreted in terms of human behavior, her actions seemed to indicate anger. She charged her yearling in a very determined manner, chasing him for distances of several hundred yards. These frequent attacks on her offspring gave the impression that she resented his presence more than that of any other bear. It was a complete reversal of her former attitude. At first her yearling seemed troubled and confused as he continued to seek the companionship of his hostile mother, but eventually he got the message and stayed away. Several weeks later we observed Marian breeding, most often with Inge but at times with Bruno and even Loverboy. We felt sure that she was once again pregnant. The length of the breeding cycle varies with individual females, and in Marian's case we would compute it from this pregnancy to the next. This was the start of her second cycle.

On July 28, the breeding season over, we again trapped Marian. We removed her radio collar with its expended batteries and replaced it with a new collar containing a temperature-sensitive transmitter in anticipation of once again tracking her to her den. This device pulsed at varying rates depending on the temperature: the warmer the temperature, the faster the signal beep. By counting the number of beeps per minute and consulting a chart of pulse rates versus temperatures, we could readily determine the temperature changes occurring in Marian's immediate environment. This experiment would lead to developing and using transmitters for telemetering den temperatures and body temperatures of hibernating bears. With the new device we could tell when Marian was bedded down in the cool timber or was moving about in warm sunlight, from as far as ten miles away. We were now tracking Marian for the fifth consecutive year.

We also radio-tagged five other grizzlies including Marian's yearling, who, when trapped and marked, became Number 188. His yearling companion, offspring of the Grizzled Sow, was numbered 202. Our objective in instrumenting these weaned yearling males was to learn about their behavior following early separation from their mothers. How well would they forage on their own? Where, when, and under what conditions would they prepare dens now that they no longer had maternal care and instruction? During mid-August, our signal regularly placed Marian in the vicinity of her last year's den. Would she, I wondered, reuse this den? When I investigated I found that the roof had partially collapsed and the floor was filled with mud. There was plainly no chance for reuse. Weak signals on September 3 placed Marian in the timber to the south of upper Alum Creek, where we later located her new den. At this time she was selecting a new den site and even starting some excavation.

Summer gave way to fall, and on the clear, mild morning of October 15, Marian's signal told us that she was moving. The barometric pressure was falling. Could a storm be on the way? There were no visible signs of one. Small patches of snow showed through the yellow grass, still and unmoving in the quiet air of noon. However, the barometric pressure continued to fall, indicating that a storm was approaching. We had already learned that grizzly bears tended to move to their dens during a snowstorm. Back in the timber at higher altitudes, more snow was underfoot, and Marian was leaving tracks that we would be able to follow if we could cross her trail. She was moving fast and on a definite course, not a rambling, foraging trek. As the afternoon waned, the bright sunny sky turned gray; a storm was indeed imminent. Lazy, drifting snowflakes began to fall at 4 P.M., and by late afternoon a severe snowstorm was in progress. From afar we monitored Marian's travels and gradually closed in on her as we followed her signal. By dark we had radio-tracked her to a new den, and already her tracks were being obliterated by the snow. Within a few hours only an unmarred expanse of snow would surround her den.

Marian had started moving denward at least four or five hours before the storm was evident. Was there some way unknown to us that she had detected the oncoming storm? This and similar behavior of other grizzlies, starting the trek to their dens hours before storms appeared, suggests that they may be able to detect variations in barometric pressure or that they may be sensitive to infrasonic waves, very low frequencies that are initiated by storms and travel far ahead of them. Some such advance stimuli appeared to trigger grizzly movement toward dens before storm signs became visible. This and the bears' apparent instinct to travel to dens when their tracks were wiped out by falling snow were intriguing new areas of research that we hoped to investigate at a future date with radio and other equipment.

In the past when an early snowstorm was followed by sunny, warm days, grizzlies left their den sites and traveled long distances to forage, but this fall Marian remained close to her den. There were other changes in her behavior — she was less active and more lethargic than in previous years. We speculated that her pregnancy may have been the cause; we had had no opportunity to observe her pre-denning behavior while she was pregnant the preceding year. Due to the process of delayed implantation described earlier, the embryos had not yet started to develop and grow, but would do so now that she was about to enter her den for her winter sleep. (Although a delay in implantation had been proven for the black and European brown bears in the early 1960s, it was not until 1967 that John and co-workers conclusively proved this for the grizzly, by recovering unimplanted blastocysts from sow Number 180. This bear mated in 1967 at the age of fourteen years and was killed the first week in August as a troublesome and potentially dangerous animal.) We were anxious to learn more about the birth and development of young bears in the den, but we had already decided against a return winter visit as being an obvious danger to both men and bears. Above all we wanted Marian to successfully bring forth a litter in spring.

We now turned our attention to the two instrumented yearlings, Numbers 188 and 202. By tracking these two we hoped to learn whether former den selection by adults influenced den site choice of their offspring. We also hoped to determine whether the yearlings would den within the home ranges of their mothers or go their independent ways. What kind of a den did the male yearling prepare and use, and how might it differ from the dens of sows we had located in the past? Would it be dug in advance of winter? Would a first den be a crude affair, or would it be instinctively and skillfully constructed? And might young males den near each other or even together? Marian's yearling and the Grizzled Sow's offspring were apparently compatible, and their ranges were shared where they overlapped; we quite often jumped and observed both bears while tracking.

On October 12, before Marian had moved to her den site, signals from the Sulphur Mountain area told us that 202 and 188 were bedded down close together. Both signals, one pulsed at 80 and the other at 105 beeps per minute, were equally strong and produced almost identical bearings. I decided to move in through the thick timber to observe these bears, accompanied on this trip by Bob Ruff and two visiting scientists—a Dr. Thatcher, an M.D. with a consuming interest in natural history, and his friend. As we walked through the timber, moving ever nearer to the grizzlies, our visitors became tense and apprehensive—not surprisingly, since this was a new experience for them. I assured them that all was well and that I knew the approximate position of the grizzlies from the signal characteristics. We wouldn't suddenly surprise the bears.

Suddenly we heard a tremendous thrashing in the nearby thick timber and windfall. A huge animal was bearing down upon us. We couldn't yet see it, but our senses and minds were programmed for grizzlies, and our visiting friends assumed that a grizzly was charging. The blood drained from Thatcher's face as we got a glimpse of a huge brown monster moving through the underbrush. The animal crashed past us like a tank, and I recognized the blurred form of a large bison. The animal, sleeping in the dense timber, had been abruptly alerted by our scent and made a run for the open country, which for a bison meant safety. But it had approached and passed from view so quickly that none of my companions realized that it was not a rampaging grizzly. They were scared, and the incident left them shaken. When quiet again prevailed, we continued on and soon found Number 202 bedded down and reluctant to move. A little further on I saw Number 188 foraging as he moved slowly along the edge of the timber. I planned to follow him, but somehow the buffalo incident had dulled the enthusiasm of our companions for tracking grizzlies, so we turned and retraced our steps.

Two days later, in this same jumbled area of dense timber and windfall, John and I again closed in on 188. Instead of running when he detected us, he moved away slowly and soon stopped to sit down. We followed his example and remained hidden and motionless, watching through binoculars. Within a few minutes his head began to sway and he slumped forward, muzzle turned inward under his neck, nose resting on the ground. Although aware of our presence, he was indifferent and appeared unable to remain awake and alert. He made a number of attempts to lift his head and to rise from his sitting posture, only to slump forward with his muzzle again tucked between his front legs. Over the next half-hour we stalked to within a hundred feet of him before he rose and lumbered off. Following the other signal to 202, we observed a similar type of behavior. These grizzlies were already lethargic, apparently ready for their winter sleep. I wondered why they were exhibiting these signs so soon and whether they would remain in this condition. Or was it a temporary state that would quickly pass? These questions made me more anxious than ever to keep these bears under close surveillance.

Keeping watch proved not so simple, however, as the storm that moved Marian to her den also started 188 and 202 traveling. They left their regular summer haunts, and 202 moved to upper Elkhorn Creek where the snow lay deeper. A few days later he reversed directions and headed north, crossing the Yellowstone River on October 25 and then moving northeastward throughout the next day. By the evening of the twenty-sixth he had reached the south rim of Yellowstone Canyon. For the next three days his intermittent signal indicated that he was digging a den. To verify this we moved in on him, following his radio signal. We jumped him from a day bed but found no evidence of the den we thought he had been digging. We suspected that it was nearby, but we experienced difficulty with further tracking. Number 202's radio signal led us down along the rim of the canyon, where it plainly said in electronic language, "Your bear is directly ahead." But by going forward and then retreating we invariably reached a point where the signal, bouncing back from the vertical rock walls across the canyon, came in strong and refuted itself by indicating that our bear was now across the river. Was he? We doubted it. By hiking back from the rim to get a bearing and then continuing to move along the canyon edge we obtained and plotted a three-bearing fix, and when we hiked to this point the signal appeared to originate directly below our position on the edge of the canyon. Grizzly 202 should have been almost underneath us, perhaps far down on the narrow canyon bottom almost completely filled by a blue ribbon of fast-moving water.

Bob and I worked our way down the steep upper slope but were stopped by the perpendicular drop of a sheer cliff. We could go no further following his route, so we scanned the canyon below and its steep walls and talus slopes with field glasses. We saw neither bear nor probable den site, but as we started to leave, we accidentally loosened a large rock that crashed into the trees below. Simultaneously with the crash we heard a startled roar, followed by the "huff, huff" of a grizzly's alarm call. Eagerly we again scanned the rugged terrain below, focusing on the area of rock and trees. Finally I spotted

202's straw-colored form in a small opening almost directly below us, beside a pile of fresh earth that pinpointed the den site. The sudden noise had brought him to his feet and out from concealment. I could also see a pile of boughs and what appeared to be the den entrance.

For the next half-hour we watched 202, and during this whole period of time he remained motionless except for an occasional slow movement of his head when he raised his nose in order to test for a scent. He gave no indication of having detected us as we peered down from above. He seemed to be in an advanced state of lethargy, several times almost falling asleep, letting his head sink and resting his nose on the ground. This was similar to the lethargic behavior we had observed earlier, but now the bear was much drowsier and less active, clearly loath to move. His den was in a steep, narrow strip of trees bordered on one side by a gravel talus slope that looked like a snow avalanche run. There was a definable avalanche path on the other side. Here loosened, rolling, careening boulders had snapped the tops off trees eighteen inches in diameter and had gouged deep cuts and scars in still larger ones. The den and its close surroundings impressed us with their inaccessibility and complete isolation. Under the best of conditions it would be difficult to approach the den undetected, and it would probably be impossible to reach it in winter without considerable risk.

We scrambled back up over the rocks as darkness approached to begin the six-mile return hike. As I walked, I wondered what would make a young, inexperienced bear select such a den spot. One factor might be that this was the general area where he was born. It was well within the home range of his mother, the Grizzled Sow. Perhaps the family den, or dens, had been close by or in a similar site and early imprinting influenced his choice. We had some evidence that 202's mother might have hibernated somewhere within this rugged canyon, but as far as we knew, except in his spring trek from the maternal den and his travels with his mother to and from the den where he wintered as a fall cub, this bear had spent all of his life in the immediate vicinity of Hayden Valley. His first lengthy and independent move with an apparent purpose was when he crossed the Yellowstone River and headed straight for the site of his winter den. He had never been there so had not prepared his den in advance, as had Marian, but instead dug it within a few days of selecting the site. Another factor affecting his choice of location may have been the instinct of a single bear not part of a family unit to be alone and isolated during the potentially vulnerable period of hibernation.

After 202 had completed the preparation of his winter quarters, he remained nearby, sleeping in front of the entrance. His radio kept us informed. When we visited his den the following spring we found that he had not dug much of a cave in the steep rocky talus slope but had built a bough bed, very deep on the downslope side, that provided him with a level, cup-shaped sleeping platform. It measured thirty-one inches across and about eighteen inches deep. Curled up in this bed, his head could have fitted comfortably into the small opening he had dug. Here, partially protected and insulated by a deep blanket of snow, he had slept through the long winter.

When we tracked Number 202 the next fall, his signal again placed him on the snow-covered slopes of Yellowstone Canyon. In two consecutive years he dug dens only three hundred feet apart. The second year's den was a decided improvement over the first. He removed an estimated ton of rock in preparing it, and he amply lined the bed chamber with boughs. We found it interesting that Number 202 arduously dug his den, even though natural caves that appeared suitable for winter quarters were nearby. And though his drive to dig a den seemed instinctive, a learning process was certainly involved. At least in this case, den construction had improved with experience.

In contrast to the stay-at-home behavior of 202, Number 188 had moved off so fast to such a faraway hibernation site that we lost his signal and were unable to locate his den. He, like many other young grizzlies, wandered far into new territory to hibernate. We also temporarily lost radio contact with Marian when we approached closely and she retreated into her den, but by late October she was sufficiently lethargic that our occasional close presence did not disturb her. She was still scraping small quantities of dirt out of her bed chamber, and we noticed that instead of using boughs, this pregnant female was lining her den with soft mosses and grass. To avoid as much as possible disturbing them, we continued to monitor signals from Marian and 202 from afar as they napped at the entrance to their dens. This continued until November 11, when both bears entered their dens during a snowstorm and remained inside, as indicated by complete and continued radio silence.

The degree of lethargy exhibited by the grizzlies during the fall of 1965 was comparable to the condition they normally display later, after entering their winter dens. This early onset of lethargy appeared to be the exception rather than the rule, so we sought an explanation. Possibly weather conditions that year affected prehibernation behavior and movements to den sites. An early snowfall followed by unusual cold occurred from the fifteenth to twenty-eighth of September. At this time the minimum temperature dropped to 7° F. It was the earliest period of snow and low temperatures experienced in the course of our studies. Air temperatures in early fall were lower than at hibernation time in November, when still more snow covered the ground. The unseasonable cold spell was followed by warm, mild fall weather not conducive for grizzlies to enter their dens. Though the early snow and low temperatures did not stimulate the grizzlies to enter their dens, it did disperse some from summer ranges to fall foraging and denning areas, and it might have triggered the hibernation processes that caused the bears to become lethargic and physiologically ready to enter their dens and sleep by late October — before the usual environmental stimuli of low temperatures and a final snowstorm.

At the time she entered her den in 1965, Marian gave no sign of the momentous changes taking place within her. Though ovulation had occurred in mid-June, and conception shortly thereafter, the delayed implantation phenomenon meant that the tiny embryos would not start to develop until after she had denned.

After a short gestation period of about six to eight weeks, Marian's cubs would be born sometime in late January or early February. At birth they would be sightless, hairless, and helpless, and would weigh a little over a pound, perhaps even less. During this time and until she left her den, Marian would not eat or drink, but would nurse her cubs and produce enough milk for their growth as well as sufficient calories to maintain her own activities. The delayed development and small size of the cubs at birth are ideally suited for the confined conditions of their early lives. Larger, more advanced cubs could not be fed and handled by a fasting, lethargic mother.

As we had done with many nursing females, we later immobilized Marian in order to squeeze out a sample of milk, which was then packed in ice and sent to Dr. Robert Jenness at the University of Minnesota for analysis. Bear's milk differs from that of many other mammals in its low lactose content. Marian's milk was also typically high in protein, minerals, and fat—far higher in the last than cow's milk. In fact, half or more of the solids that the cubs drank in their mother's milk consisted of fat.

In spring 1966, Marian's two cubs, now weighing five or six pounds each, followed her from the den. For days they frolicked and slept near the den until the time was right for a journey to more abundant food sources. It was well into the summer before the cubs had their full complement of teeth and could chew and swallow food other than their mother's milk. With their pointed canines, four in all, they could rip away at meat, and their molars and premolars were adapted for both chewing meat and grinding vegetation. Their full set of teeth consisted of twenty in the upper jaw and twenty-two in the lower, a total of forty-two. The dentition of the bear has been modified over eons of time from that of the purely carnivorous eater to fit the diet of an omnivore.

We had many opportunities to observe Marian's maternal side during that summer. One warm day late in the season, as I tracked her through the pines, the increase in signal strength informed me that Marian had stopped walking and was just ahead, and I was closing the gap! Moving very quietly I slowly stepped from tree to tree, using each as a shield while approaching the grassy meadow ahead. About this time I heard a loud murmuring sound, like the buzzing of a disturbed swarm of huge bees yet soothing in tone. Its direction was difficult to determine. The first time I had heard it, I had been completely baffled, but by now I knew its origin and moved ahead even more cautiously. I crawled to the edge of the timber and then slowly rose to my feet beside a large-boled tree (checking for low limbs that would make it reasonably easy to climb).

Out in the meadow Marian was half sitting, half lying on her back, in much the same attitude as a rocking chair that a slight push would topple backwards. It was the mother bear's nursing position, and the two large cubs were sucking vigorously and roughly. The buzzing sound, which came from the nursing cubs, seemed to be one of contentment, and Marian's doting look reinforced my human assessment of this scene of domestic tranquility. Marian's mammary glands were, I knew, scratched, bitten, and raw from rough usage, but if she felt pain she gave no indication. When she tired of nursing, she cuffed her youngsters aside, rose to her feet, then rolled over first one then the other with a gentle sweep of her powerful front paw. This was all the energetic, ebullient cubs needed to start a wrestling melee, rolling, running, cuffing, growling, sometimes both pitted against their mother, sometimes wrestling each other. Occasionally all three were entwined in a confused jumble out of which a cub would dart, then turn and scamper back for more buffeting. As usual, the mother tired first and started moving off, only to be attacked by her tireless cubs. A sharp cuff that knocked both over terminated the play and reminded the cubs that obedience was essential and demanded by all mother bears. Disobedience when danger threatened could well mean death.

During the summer of 1966, Marian and her two cubs established a close relationship with sow Number 101 and her cub. Whenever we moved in to observe Marian we found these two families bedded down together or foraging for food. This mutually sought association extended throughout the summer and continued into the cold and snowy days of early November, and we thought that the bonds linking Marian and 101 might give us two chances to track grizzlies to their dens. By tracking Marian, who was instrumented, we might with luck discover the den of Number 101. There was not the slightest indication that the two bears were about to separate for the winter.

The strong mutual attraction of these sows was quite evident on November 4, 1966, when Henry McCutchen, Henry Tomingas, and I followed Marian's signal through the snow and over the slope to the west of Trout Creek. This signal, at 106 beeps per minute, led us to within sight of the day beds of Marian, 101, and their three cubs. This daytime retreat was about a mile and a half from a carcass on which the bears had been feeding. Around the day beds we found dark, watery feces similar to those we had recently seen at the carcass. This type of bowel movement was typical of bears just prior to hibernation. It is a scouring process that apparently permits them to continue to feed right up to the last storm and still rapidly purge their digestive system prior to winter sleep.

Although there was little left on this well-picked-over carcass, it appeared as though the bears were going to remain in the vicinity. Their next move might be to winter dens, so we established a base camp nearby from which we could monitor Marian during the night and keep track of her during the day. I strung a dipole antenna in the tree above our tent and ran a coax cable to the receiver inside my sleeping bag. When Marian's night travels took her beyond reach of the small loop antenna, I could plug in the more sensitive antenna and still monitor her signal. This antenna did not indicate direction, but it told me she was still in the general vicinity, not moving far. With this assurance I slept better. We were anxious to pick up the typical interrupted signal informing us that Marian was moving in and out of a den. Throughout the windy and snowy November night, the temperature falling from 24 to 13° F, I periodically monitored Marian's signal. When it increased in strength I suspected that she had moved to the carcass; when it decreased I assumed she had taken off to the west. My interpretations were verified next morning by the tracks of these two families in the snow.

We followed both tracks and signals, trudging through deep snow-drifts. When Marian and her two cubs scurried from their beds ahead of us, we failed to see them as they ran off. However, we followed their fresh tracks, and within a quarter-mile signs in the snow revealed that 101 and her cub had joined Marian. Before continuing on, we backtracked along 101's trail and soon saw the revealing earth diggings around the entrance to her den, at the base of a huge white-bark pine on a north-facing slope. I stopped and from a distance snapped a few pictures, then quickly left. We had located 101's den, just as we had hoped. After we had disturbed Marian, she had run directly to the den of 101 but only close enough to warn her with a "huff, huff!" Then both bears took off with their families. Number 101 had defecated soon after leaving her den and urinated on the run. She was obviously nervous and must have transmitted some of her fright to Marian, for she did likewise. We followed the grizzlies for another hour and then decided it would be best not to disturb them further.

The night was clear and the stars twinkling in the cold atmosphere when I crawled into my sleeping bag at base camp, a temporary bivouac area. The temperature was zero and falling; when I checked it again just before succumbing to sleep it was down a few more degrees. When I awoke to listen for Marian's signal, the thermometer read twelve below zero. Surely, I thought, with temperatures like these and snow on the ground, Marian will enter her den during the next storm. While we ate breakfast the next morning, the sky rapidly clouded over and the temperature rose to zero. I warmed the receiver at the nearby fire and connected it to the large collapsible quad antenna, which consisted simply of a large one-wavelength wire square, shaped and held in place by four fiberglass rods. A decided advantage was that it could be dismantled and was easy to backpack. The faint, interrupted signal thoroughly excited me; it meant that Marian was at her den.

Once again, with John joining us, we were off to see where our signal would lead. With the sky heavily overcast, we found it difficult to keep our sense of direction unless we continually referred to a compass. After following the erratic signal for hours, we picked up the fresh tracks of Marian and her cubs. Soon we located dark feces and scattered urine in the snow. Marian was not at her den as we had thought, but just ahead of us on the trail and nervous. Perhaps due to the cold, her transmitter was beeping erratically. The effect of cold and moisture on the transmitter, receivers, and on the batteries created problems that we identified in the field and Joel later remedied in his Philco Corporation laboratory at Palo Alto, California. We had at first assumed that the interrupted signal meant Marian was going in and out of her den. Now we were not so sure. On her trail we found a spot in the snow where she had sat down facing her pursuers. Judging from the melted depression, she had awaited our approach until we got quite close. We also came across places where her cubs had playfully scrambled over snow-covered logs, and again where they had slid on their rear ends down a steep hill. More loose feces and scattered urine indicated that Marian was still uneasy. I decided not to press her further, so we built a fire, melted snow for tea water, and munched on some crackers and cheese. When Marian later reversed her direction of travel, I felt sure that she and her cubs would not lead us to their den this day. There were other days, but I was worried. Would the interrupted signal, possibly due either to cold or to a loose connection, suddenly conk out altogether, thereby ruining our chance to track Marian to her den?

The next day, November 11, John, Hank, Harry, and I tried again, following Marian throughout the day. The chase led us over much of the same country we had traversed on the tenth, and evening found us at the identical spot where we had quit the day before. The interrupted signal of the previous day had corrected itself, and the radio was now pulsing steadily, making it much easier to follow the progress of the mother and cubs. As we moved wearily up the hill, a dark splash of earth at the base of a tree told us that we had come to the end of our search. For the third year we had located Marian's winter den. We immediately turned and headed back toward camp, invigorated by our success. With the dens of Marian and 101 located, we could now turn our attention to other things.

Almost any day now, I thought, the bears will enter their dens for the winter. The next storm should do it. In the short time left we might be able to observe Marian and even photograph her at her den. We had not yet attempted this. It would be interesting, too, if we could observe both families at a single den. Marian and 101 had dug their separate dens only a mile and a half apart. The former denning areas of these females had been approximately sixteen miles apart. Only a very strong bond could have caused them to seek new den sites, a sort of compromise location. Instead of returning to her former hibernation site in upper Alum Creek, Marian dug her den in the Trout Creek drainage. Now, rather than remaining close to their respective dens, the two families visited back and forth and appeared reluctant to terminate their summer relationship. This prehibernation behavior was contrary to what we had observed in all other grizzlies; as a rule the bears had sought solitude rather than companionship for themselves and families. Perhaps the close ties between Marian and 101 provided greater security for the young of both families.

When we again visited Marian's den and were about a hundred yards from the site, I saw the dark, indistinct forms of Marian and 101 moving between the lodgepole trunks. Although we stalked slowly, taking advantage of air drift and cover, the bears got our scent and took off. In their absence we hurriedly took several flash pictures of the den interior with its bough bed and then retreated to make bough seats concealed under the low branches of a small fir tree. Here we set up our movie camera and waited patiently until the barely audible radio signal increased in strength, telling us that Marian was returning. The bears — all five of them — approached within less than a hundred yards of us, cautiously sniffing our tracks as they neared the den. Upon reaching the den entrance they grew restless; they wandered off and then returned, making a partial circle as they investigated the area. The grizzlies were alert and checking out the human intruders, now no novelty to them. It was our turn to get restless. I shifted my position a few feet to obtain a picture of Marian, but she saw the movement. John, ready to start filming, froze at the camera, and a tense moment ensued, at least for us. We were relieved to see the sow and her cubs move away, for our sheltering fir was small, and none of the nearby lodgepole pines could have been readily climbed. This incident was of particular significance, because it was an instance of two adult bears visiting the same den without exhibiting aggressive or defensive behavior. It supported our observations that these female grizzlies were loath to separate for the winter and thus break up their close relationship.

When we visited 101's den and found no new tracks to the entrance, we concluded that our approach to her den had caused her to abandon it and dig another. Between November 19 and 21, Marian entered her den for the winter. Number 101 was not with her and we did not have the time or the radio aid to locate her new den.

In the spring of 1967, Marian and 101 met near Marian's den and in bear fashion worked out an arrangement agreeable to both. Number 101 took on the responsibility of caring for Marian's yearlings as well as her own. Her maternal instincts were still dominant. Marian stopped lactating, left her companion and family, and came into estrus and sought a mate. It is difficult to say whether she chased Inge or he came seeking her, but the eventual result of her mating activities was two more cubs. Inge could have been their father, but there were other possibilities. By not having to care for and nurse her yearlings, Marian's breeding cycle was shortened by at least a year. She was thus able to produce more offspring over a given period of time and still have her progeny well cared for. This phenomenon provided for increased reproduction by the individual and thus the population at large. Any such increase in the reproductive rate of the Yellowstone bear population might some day make the difference between extinction and survival.

In early November 1967, we tracked Number 101 to a new den. She had already finished her digging and was lining the bed chamber with a layer of boughs well over a foot thick. Outside the den was a huge pile of conifer limbs yet to be taken inside. But Number 101 never completed this bed. For a number of days we consistently got signals from a spot several miles from her den, and a radio fix positioned her at a new den site. Once again 101 had abandoned her completed den on being disturbed. On November 11, with Harry Reynolds, Jr., we revisited the old den and took time to observe numerous young trees that had been completely chewed down and boughs that had been stripped off nearby trees. Some apparently had been gathered as long as a month previously.

Leaving the abandoned den, we continued to follow the signal from Hedges Peak toward Dunraven Pass and Carnelian Creek, bucking two feet of snow on our radio course through heavy timber. We skirted the windfall to our north and then observed signs of a den site directly in front of us. We were awed and sobered by the sight of a tree six inches in diameter that had recently been felled by chewing. After a brief, hushed consultation we decided to turn back. The compacted, dirty snow in front of us, barely visible through the downed timber, was 101's new den site. Mission accomplished, we retreated to the unmistakable "huff, huff," accompanied by a muffled growl. We had inadvertently approached to within thirty feet of the den entrance, so we were fortunate that 101 merely growled and did not charge. It was possible that she, like Marian, was learning that though we were pests we were harmless. We marked our return route with colored plastic tape, and from a landmark to which we could easily return we recorded the bearing and distance to the den site. Perhaps realizing that we were not going to harm her, or because it was too late to move and dig still another den, 101 entered this one for her winter sleep.

Our success in tracking grizzlies to their dens was made possible by radio-tracking; of that we had no doubt. The bears purposefully or inadvertently concealed the locations of their dens, and without the aid of telemetry I feel sure we could have hunted for weeks, perhaps even months, and not found one, even if we had been able to narrow our search area to within one square mile. As it was, we were repeatedly able to select the time and place at which we wished to confront a grizzly or move in slowly to observe its activities. To have duplicated this for a specific bear without the use of a radio would have been impossible.

By following six different grizzlies over the years, we located eleven active dens, the last being one more of Marian's in the fall of 1968. Some grizzlies, such as Numbers 101 and 202, were tracked to dens in successive years. In all we found four of Marian's dens, three in consecutive seasons. Some dens were those of males, others females, and both adults and young bears were represented. By the time we had located a number of dens by radio-tracking, a general pattern of den-site preference emerged. Using this pattern as a guide we sought and found dens used in previous years, some still intact but unused and others in varying stages of disintegration. We revisited all active dens following the winter of use and recorded data on den construction and size. From the accumulation and eventual analysis of these data, we were able to draw some conclusions on the construction and characteristics of dens and on the prehibernation behavior of grizzly bears.

In general, dens were located at elevations above those where the grizzlies foraged in fall. They ranged in altitude from 7800 to 9200 feet. All dens were located in areas isolated from man, all were dug in timbered areas, and all but one were on north-facing slopes with the den entrance facing north. The dens were thus situated where the entranceways would fill with snow, forming a sealed chamber with little transfer of air. A north-facing den entrance is advantageous to the Yellowstone grizzly, because northern exposures accumulate snow dropped by the prevailing southwest winds. This snow serves admirably to insulate the den chamber from the extremely cold outside air temperatures. Snow on the northern slopes is also less likely to melt during winter thaws, which would cause water to trickle into the den with subsequent disturbance.

All the dens that we located were dug by grizzly bears; no natural shelters were used, or modified and then used. All the dens but one were dug at the bases of trees or stumps. By tunnelling under a tree between downward sloping roots, the grizzly could achieve certain advantages, but the selection was probably instinctive rather than premeditated. The roots limited the size of the den opening, and some openings were so narrow as to tax the credulity of the observer. How did the bear manage to squeeze through into the chamber? These tight entrances would have made it difficult for primitive man, the bear's principal enemy, to kill a bear inside its den. The tree bole and root complex above the den formed a ceiling that provided greater security from den collapse.

Within all of the dens the bears constructed beds, usually from conifer boughs but once in our experience from moss and grass. Occasionally a bed was elevated above the den entranceway as with a bed platform in a snow house; in other words, the bear would crawl up to the bed after entering. The bear's body heat warmed the surrounding air or microclimate; the rising warm air was trapped in the den and could not escape. Either the grizzly constructs such a heat trap accidentally or as a result of its instinctive knowledge of when soil and digging conditions are favorable for doing so. At any rate, the porous insulated bed, the small bed chamber and den opening, the deep snow covering, and trapped body heat all work together to provide a winter environment considerably modified from outside conditions.

No dens that we revisited were reused, though the sites were. Bedding and debris were scraped out of some dens before the bear left in spring, suggesting possible reuse of the den. Around the active den of one grizzly we found old boughs raked out the previous year, indicating that the den had probably been used the year before. This is both likely and possible but appears to be the exception rather than rule with Yellowstone grizzlies. Our sample, though admittedly small, is the first of its kind. As additional den data from our studies and others increase the sample size, our conclusions will undoubtedly be modified.

The prehibernation movements and behavior of grizzlies was as intriguing as their den selection and construction. Our studies of marked, unmarked, and radio-tagged grizzlies revealed that bears living under similar environmental conditions of elevation, vegetative type, and weather tended to enter their dens at the same time and during a storm, whether they were close to their dens or foraging some distance away. At this time of year snow was always on the ground, and both minimum and maximum air temperatures in the shaded den sites were below freezing. The grizzlies' habit of entering dens during falling snow served to conceal tracks that might reveal the den locations, to primitive hunters, for instance, and over the ages this could have been a factor favoring grizzly survival.

Over a period of nine years, the time at which grizzlies entered dens varied by as much a month, the earliest date being October 21 in 1961 and the latest November 21 in 1966. A combination of low temperatures and snowstorms appeared to condition bears and influence the time at which they entered their dens. The most wintry fall period coincided with the earliest hibernation date. The amount of illumination did not seem to affect the onset of bear hibernation as it appears to do with other hibernators such as ground squirrels. In general, the initiation of hibernation for grizzlies seems to be influenced more by environmental than by physiological factors. A convenient food supply, little snow, and relatively high air temperatures tend to delay hibernation. However, ample and available food will not deter bears from entering their dens if snow has accumulated and is falling and temperatures are low. All the bears we tracked to dens survived the winter, but I suspect that old bears that did not reappear in spring and were not seen again may never have emerged from their dens. No grizzlies that we observed defended a den or den area against other grizzlies or even man.

We were piecing together a sequence of events leading to hibernation, and we had already learned much about the activities outside the den. But still to come was an equally fascinating aspect of this work—finding out more about what happens within.

6

Hibernation and the Inner Bear

In January of 1963, my brother John and Maurice Hornocker webbed through deep powdery snow that had sifted down through the lodgepoles until it covered the forest floor to a depth of eight to ten feet. They entered the timber where a small blaze high on a tree told them they should start their course, following a bearing of 240 degrees. This would lead them back to the three-forked lodgepole that towered over the den where grizzly Number 164 was sleeping, the wintry scene of our first success in tracking a grizzly to its den. They had returned in the hope of determining whether she had her two-year-olds with her and to evaluate the site for later study of the sleeping bear and her winter den environment. They sank deeply into the fluffy snow, as did a marten who had passed that way earlier. This arboreal predator's tracks occasionally crossed small openings and then vanished as he took to the trees in search of red squirrels.

The north-facing entrance to the den of the female grizzly was covered with snow except for a tiny opening through which some warm air escaped. The den would have gone undetected had they not known just where to look. After compacting the powdery snow outside the entrance, they removed their snowshoes and used them as shovels. Before long they heard a sleepy growl that could have been interpreted as a groan, followed later by another with ominous overtones of a warning. They desisted, thought the situation over, and decided to leave Number 164 alone. They were not what might be called mobile, and had the aroused grizzly charged out of her den they would have been quite helpless. Unable to run, their only alternative would have been to shoot in self-defense, since an immobilizing dart could not take effect quickly enough.

Not wishing to put their own or the sow's life in jeopardy, John and Maurice reluctantly buckled on their snowshoes, shouldered their packs, and retraced their steps. Perhaps in another year, I thought on hearing the account, we would find a den more amenable for studying—one where the snow would be more compacted, the entranceway not so long and narrow, and the slope less steep. It would be helpful, too, to be able to see the bear from without and to find one in a more dormant condition. We required a set of circumstances in which we could safely immobilize the grizzly at least once and instrument the den and bear for temperature recordings. Number 164's den quite obviously was not ideal for our purposes, and I was not at all sure after later visiting the den myself that we would eventually find one that would meet our requirements. Indeed, several years later when we returned to one of Marian's snow-covered dens, we were still unable to immobilize her without excessive risk of having to defend ourselves, and Marian was not aggressive as grizzlies go.

In the meantime, we could perhaps study the winter sleep or hibernation of the black bear, *Ursus americanus*. This member of the bear family is in no way so aggressive as the grizzly, nor is it so powerful. Above all, its instinct when cornered is to flee rather than attack. It does not have the grizzly's complete lack of fear of *Homo sapiens*. Most importantly, many things that we could learn about black bear dens would apply to the grizzly. Why not, we thought, start our den studies with the black bear until we could safely work with a grizzly?

The black bear has evolved curved claws that enable it to nimbly climb almost any tree, whereas the grizzly is not adapted for climbing. Instead, its long front claws are ideally suited for digging. It may be that the ability of the black bear to climb and thus escape many dangers has made it less aggressive than the grizzly, which must face a challenge or turn and run. As might be expected, the black bear is more at home in the timber and prefers this habitat, while the grizzly is fond of open country — meadows, burns, sagebrush habitat, tundra, and open expanses above timberline. Because of its facility at digging, the Yellowstone grizzly excavates, shapes, and completely constructs its winter den. The black bear usually seeks out a natural cave or shelter that it can modify or use as is.

At close range it is quite easy to tell black bears and grizzlies apart. The black bear has two distinctive color phases — black and cinnamon — but the term black applies to individuals of both colors. Many black bears sport a white V-shaped collar. Many young grizzlies also have collars, but they are not V-shaped in front and tend to disappear as the bear ages. Grizzlies have a distinctive shoulder hump; black bears do not. The grizzly's face tends to be concave or saucerlike while the black bear's is the opposite, being convex. In general, grizzlies are much larger than blacks. The average Yellowstone male grizzly weighs 500 to 575 pounds (the lower figure in the spring and the higher in the fall), and the average female weighs 300 to 380 pounds. A large female will go as high as 500 pounds and a large male 1000 to 1200 pounds. The largest grizzly we weighed was 1120 pounds. The average male black bear weighs about 200 pounds and the female a quarter less. A few of the largest black bears on record have weighed over 600 pounds, but this is exceptional. Like that of grizzlies, the weight of black bears varies from spring to fall, reaching a maximum just prior to hibernation. They also tend to weigh more in areas of abundant food.

In the high Yellowstone plateau country, most black bears are in their winter dens well before the grizzly. Some enter dens at least a month before grizzlies do. One would go in and would not reappear, then another, until even the tardiest sleeper had retired. The Yellowstone grizzlies tend to enter winter dens pretty much at the same time when living under similar conditions, and, as discussed earlier, this unanimous urge to retire seems to be triggered at least in part by a snowstorm or blizzard coinciding with low temperatures and snow on the ground. Quite regularly black bear tracks led us to their winter dens. Never did we locate a grizzly den in this way.

When nuisance black bears or incorrigible grizzlies dangerous to visitors were killed, we performed autopsies on them. This work was done in collaboration with a lifelong friend, Dr. Morgan Berthrong, chief pathologist of Penrose Hospital in Colorado Springs. It was he who, during autopsies and from microscopic examination of tissue samples, first noticed the complete lack of arteriosclerosis in the bear's vascular system, including the coronary arteries. These findings led us to conduct blood chemistry studies to see if we could determine why the bear, unlike man, is not afflicted with arteriosclerosis. Perhaps such research would provide us with a better understanding of this disease in man. In pursuit of this work, we routinely collected blood samples from most of the grizzly and black bears that we captured. We had obtained and Morgan had analyzed numerous blood samples taken in spring, summer, and fall, but so far none had been taken in winter from hibernating bears. We needed such samples to continue our studies.

Our first good opportunity to make direct contact with a hibernating black bear occurred in 1963. Late in the fall of that year, when snow was on the ground and geyser steam in the air, we followed black bear tracks to a cave opening near thermal pools in the vicinity of Old Faithful. The bear slumbered while the snow deepened. Elk and buffalo moved less freely and centered their activities around relatively snow-free thermal areas. Whereas animals west of the Continental Divide congregated in small resident herds where limited winter food was available, the summer elk herds of Hayden Valley had long since migrated to the lower Lamar Valley, having left the abundant forage to a few sturdy bison capable of digging down through layers of snow to feed on it.

Winter was well advanced, and a coldness and uniform whiteness — sometimes in deadly calm, at other times swept by chilling horizontal winds—descended on the land. Over this frozen whiteness a raven flapped, undisturbed by countless snow particles hitting his eyes. While almost all other life quietly waited out the storms, the raven often seemed to revel in them, rolling, diving, banking in the winds as though it were just another balmy spring day. The approaching raven dipped low, apparently curious about the single human form motionless beneath him. Instinctively the raven knew that a creature alive one day might be food for him the next.

Below the raven stood Charlie Ridenour on snowshoes. The deep snow, unmarred except for a few human tracks, stretched beyond him to a dark green barrier of conifers. Charlie's attention was directed neither to the immobilizing gun beside him nor to the projectile syringes carefully arranged on a knapsack. Even the camera lay idle. Oblivious to his winter surroundings, he was listening intently, picking up the muffled sounds that seemed to emanate from the earth directly beneath him: voices, weak but distinct.

"Let's roll her over."

"Do you think there's room?"

"We can try."

"Good, now feel along the inside of her leg. Can you detect a pulse?"

"No, I can't feel a thing."

"John, how's she breathing?"

"A little rapid but steady. Now I feel a faint pulse. Hand me the vacuum bottle with needle. Shine the light over here; I think I've got a vein. There comes the blood. I didn't get the femoral artery but we'll get enough."

"The vial is almost full. Let's get out of here."

"If the drug effects wear off, we'll have to scramble."

Three of us—John, Maurice, and I—were packed in this small stifling den with a large black bear, and all the humans were sweating profusely.

"It's no wonder she hasn't built a bough bed," I thought. "The heat from this thermal area keeps the den warm throughout the winter."

John and Maurice began wriggling their way through the narrow entranceway toward the den opening, and just in time. The bear growled and raised her head as the flashlight disappeared. The effects of the drug were weakening and the bear's jaw control returning. Propelling my way with my elbows and knees, I followed John and caught a blast of light as he emerged; the glare reflected from the wintry Yellowstone landscape was blinding. As we appeared, Charlie Ridenour, who had been hunched over with his back to the wind, commented, "I'd give a fortune to have had a tape recorder. You should have heard that conversation."

Charlie might not forget that conversation; the three of us would never forget the experience. An hour before we successfully obtained a blood sample from the hibernating black bear, our movements and tramping around at the den entrance had aroused her. Her body temperature, already high because of the warm environment, kept her relatively alert and active. It rose a few degrees, and perhaps from curiosity she looked out the den opening. At the moment she appeared we hit her with a drug-filled dart. She growled and returned to the blackness of her cave. Half an hour later we thought the bear should be immobilized and helpless; the problem was, we didn't know for sure. Nevertheless, John, Maurice, and I, guided only by a flashlight, crawled into the narrow entrance and squirmed through the dark and confining tunnel. The tunnel seemed to extend on and on. It turned out to be nearly fifteen feet long, terminating in a chamber only slightly wider than the passage itself. While I was still inching forward with a wormlike movement, I heard John say that he'd reached the bear and she was anesthetized. Then I too was in the chamber, which was low-roofed with reddish walls and the air heavy and moist from the nearby thermal spring. The inside of the den, with the dark, formless shape of the drugged female bear occupying most of the space, is still vividly etched in my mind.

We had successfully immobilized a black bear in its den and obtained a blood sample, thus making our first intimate acquaintance with a hibernating bear. This sample, taken at a time when thyroid levels should have been low, might be revealing. Using a small centrifuge, we would soon separate the blood serum from the red blood cells and later ship it in ice to Morgan for chemical analysis.

Under similar circumstances we could never have dared to push our way into a grizzly's sleeping chamber. We had tried it with Number 164, the grizzly called Lucky, with Marian, Number 101, and later with Number 187, a female that mated at four and a half years whom we suspected to be pregnant and tracked to a den near Ice Lake. The response had always been growls and activity within the den, an aroused alertness. This reaction, combined with deep snow that hampered fast movement and the aggressive nature of the grizzly, put a damper on our enthusiasm to immobilize a grizzly and then crawl into its den to instrument it. Now, and at least for awhile, we were compromising by working with the black bears. In the meantime, we were developing transmitters and techniques that would enable us to implant a temperature-sensitive transmitter in a grizzly captured in fall, thereby obtaining at least one kind of information we sought without risking the hazards to both bear and men of an attempted immobilization in a winter den.

Our previous research had paved the way for the next phase of the work, which came in the winter of 1967. Joel Varney had modified the telemetry system we used to track grizzlies so as to make it capable of transmitting temperature data from tiny temperature probes (thermistors) inserted under the skin and in the muscle tissue. We had tested this system on free-roaming elk, monitoring their body-temperature fluctuations in both summer and winter. Now we were ready to employ the same technique on a black bear that we had tracked to a winter den in November. We planned to monitor temperature conditions in the den of the hibernating bear, and at the same time to obtain twenty-four-hour, or *nycthemeral,* body-temperature patterns from the sleeping animal in an effort to learn more about his temperature-regulating processes. Those twenty-four-hour temperature rhythms, similar to those of human beings, would give us insight into the winter physiology of the bear and inform us of the times when he was most lethargic or most active and alert. Would it be during daylight hours or late at night? Most though not all people are day-oriented, but bears at times appear to be both. Would the unbroken darkness of the cave tend to change the bear's pattern? How low would the bear's temperature drop from the 101° F normal during summer activity?

In January, at the cliff den above the Gibbon River, we immobilized the black bear by jabbing him with a drug-filled syringe at the end of a long stick that we poked into the entrance of the den. This was work at close quarters, and we were not sure how the bear would react. Would he ignore the needle injection and retreat farther into his den or would he charge? And how would we react if the bear rushed out of the den? The problem was definitely on our minds, but we had not determined a course of action. Four of us—John, Hank McCutchen (a wildlife biologist and former student), Klaus Nielsen (a Danish electronic engineer), and I — were crowded on a tiny ledge leading to the den entrance. Each of us would have to make his own decision.

After we injected the bear with the drug, sernylan, we heard a rustling movement, and then all was quiet. Lying on my stomach, I flashed a light into the interior of the den to observe the bear's reaction to the drug. The beam first caused him to press against the rock wall in the far recesses of the cave and then move restlessly about before making a fast break for the entrance. Our attempt to block the den opening with snowshoes failed. He moved too quickly. Suddenly he had joined us on the narrow snowy ledge above the river.

John's warning shout of "Watch out!" rang in our ears, but what to do? Our situation was precarious. Freedom of movement was drastically limited by the deep snow and our strong aversion to leaping off into space. Within the instant our crew individually but in unison moved in one direction, and the bear, fortunately and perhaps deliberately, in the other. He turned and began climbing a nearly perpendicular snow wall, pawing his way through snow five to six feet in depth. Carefully and with difficulty we followed on snowshoes. When we finally overtook him he was lying immobile in the snow.

Pulling him as if he were a toboggan, we dragged him back to the den entrance, where we brushed off the snow and proceeded to instrument him with a collar-transmitter. While he was under sedation, we slipped the radio over his head and inserted a thermistor probe into the muscle tissue through a small incision in the skin, which was then treated with an antiseptic and sutured. This completed, I crawled into the den pulling the bear head first after me, while outside John, Klaus, and Hank pushed against his fat-layered buttocks. Through our combined exertions we replaced the bear in his bed, but there was barely room for him and me inside the rocky den.

Nevertheless, I took time to marvel at this bear's beautifully constructed bed and also recorded a few measurements. The insulated bed was eighteen inches deep by thirty inches in diameter, cuplike in shape with nearly perpendicular walls against which the bear's body fit quite snugly. Within the confines of the thick accumulation of bed material consisting of a porous mixture of dry pine needles and finely shredded twigs, the bear had been hibernating as though enveloped in a down sleeping bag. This particular bear, I thought, must be a master in the art of making beds. To exit I slid over the bear's body, careful not to disturb the bed, and wriggled head first out the narrow den opening.

With the black bear again reposing in his pine-scented bed, we descended the steep hillside to our open tarp tent along the river. From this vantage point, with a fire and rock reflector for warmth, we monitored by radio the gradual rise in the bear's body temperature as well as the temperature changes of the den and the outside air. We determined the temperatures counting the pulses or beeps per minute from our radio receiver, using a stopwatch. The greater the number of pulses, the higher the temperature. These totals were immediately converted to degrees Fahrenheit by means of our previously prepared pulse rate/temperature chart. The bear's temperature was at first low due to the drug's effect. It then rose and gradually dropped again, indicating that he was reverting to his previous lethargic condition of winter sleep.

After the bear had returned to normal, we obtained body-temperature patterns. Over one twenty-four-hour period the den temperature remained relatively constant at 26 to 28° F, while outside air temperatures varied from 15 to 30° F. During the same period the bear's body temperature dropped to a minimum of 94° F at night and reached a high of about 96° F in the afternoon, suggesting a typical high day–low night rhythm, even though the cave was relatively dark. In still darker dens a diurnal rise in the bear's body temperature did not occur. The most significant changes in body temperature occurred in response to disturbance, and the greater the disturbance, the more the temperature changed. The disturbances expressed as frustration and anger, that is, emotional changes, altered body temperatures in both bear and elk. When no disturbance occurred, the bear's body temperature dropped as the den temperature declined. At a later date, during an unusual cold spell, the temperature of one of our captive bears reached a low of 89° F, after which it rose to over 90° F, even though the temperature of the artificial den continued to drop. It appears that 89° F is about the lowest temperature the bear can safely tolerate. Below that a spontaneous arousal takes place, and metabolic processes automatically increase, thus warming the bear.

While monitoring the bear in the cliff den, we remained awake to periodically count the radio pulses per minute, convert them to temperature, and record the data in a notebook. In order to obtain a twenty-four-hour temperature pattern, break camp, and return to

West Yellowstone, we went without sleep for forty hours except for an occasional nap. This grueling marathon was quite an incentive to develop equipment that would automatically record the changing temperatures. On the other hand we relished the close contact with the winter wilderness experienced during the long watch: the sound of our boots crunching in the cold snow, the brush of snowflakes on our faces, the flickering fire, the warmth of a down sleeping bag, the friendly visits of Canada jays, and even the infiltration of our camp by an audacious marten that stealthily cut the leather straps on my backpack and stole the frozen steaks we were saving for our last meal.

While we were monitoring the body temperature of the Gibbon River black bear, Marian was giving birth to a litter of three cubs. In the fall of 1967 we had been certain that Marian was pregnant, and we looked forward to visiting her winter den after parturition in the hope of seeing her tiny, helpless young. In late September, however, her radio transmitter had failed, and once again we lost the chance to track her to a natal den. We did locate her den the next fall, 1968, where she slept with her three large cubs, but immobilizing four grizzlies simultaneously seemed only remotely possible, and we had no intention of placing ourselves in a position where we might have to gun Marian down in self-defense. In the end, although we were never able to actually monitor a grizzly in hibernation, our studies of the hibernating black bears gave us some idea of winter conditions in the grizzly dens.

In 1970 we took a big step forward, electronically speaking, and radio-monitored a black bear and his den using the Nimbus satellite, a rapidly moving manmade star in the sky. We were embarked on a rather fantastic project, the culmination of numerous winters of studying sleeping bears using bio-telemetry methods. In collaboration with NASA engineers, we were committed to an experiment to test the feasibility of satellite monitoring of temperatures and light conditions in the den of a hibernating black bear. At the same time, we planned to obtain continuous body-temperature patterns from the sleeping animal by more conventional methods.

Hibernation in the bear is a complex adaptation to adverse environmental conditions, and it might, at times, well serve man. The capability to sleep for long periods of time could be an asset, for example, on extended space flights. As suggested earlier, bear and man have much in common physiologically, and the chemical composition of their blood, as might be expected, is much the same. But the bear has attributes we lack, such as the ability to handle metabolic products whose accumulation in man would be toxic. It is not inconceivable that if scientists can learn how the bear hibernates, we might, with modern technology, duplicate the process ourselves.

Our plans to satellite-monitor a black bear and his den proceeded by several stages. During October and November of 1969 we had tracked black bear Number 6 for twenty-seven days, using the radio-tracking system developed for studying grizzlies. Jay Sumner and Jim Claar followed and observed him while he selected and prepared his winter den. Our next excursion, in February, would be to reconnoiter the site, verify that our bear was still in his den, and cache part of the necessary gear. On the final trip we would pack in the rest of the equipment, and attempt to immobilize and instrument the bear and den without alarming him into flight.

Through NASA we had obtained the loan of an IRLS (interrogation, recording, and location system) electronic platform used for collecting and transmitting information from ocean buoys and weather balloons to satellites. Sensors within the den would gather information, which was carried by wire cable to the platform and an antenna situated outside and above the den. From here it would then be transmitted to the Nimbus 3 satellite in a polar orbit seven hundred miles above us. Twice every twenty-four hours the satellite would pass by and interrogate the instrumented bear den. We would thus obtain data from light and temperature sensors at twelve-hour intervals. We would also continuously chart the bear's body temperature on a nearby recorder.

Prior to each orbit, a ground station at Fairbanks, Alaska, would transmit commands to the satellite indicating the precise time at which the den platform was to be interrogated. When the satellite was within radio view of the equipment at the den, there would be an exchange of signals, and the IRLS platform would transmit the sensor information on temperature and light conditions to the satellite, where it would be stored until later readout over Fairbanks. The satellite would also measure the time required for the signal to travel to the platform and return: information that could be used later to determine the location of a stationary platform or moving animal on the earth's surface. When the satellite completed its orbit by passing over the Fairbanks tracking station, the accumulated data would be transmitted to the ground station and new sets of commands radioed to the satellite for the following orbit. Next the collected data would be sent by telephone lines and microwave to the Nimbus data processing center at NASA's Goddard Space Flight Center near Washington, D.C. In the course of processing, the data would be printed out by computer and then mailed to us.

In our efforts to test the feasibility of using satellites for wildlife research by remote recording of data from a hibernating bear and his den, we were taking a space-age leap from our earlier campfire monitoring. But if we had visions of satellites completely eliminating the backbreaking work of monitoring bear dens while we sat back and waited complacently for the data to pour in, we were quickly disillusioned.

The members of our February expedition ended a three-mile trek on snowshoes at the base of a steep slope that defied further travel except on all fours. Struggling upward, we had climbed slightly further than we slipped back and had gained the halfway mark, on a level with the bear den. Here we stopped to catch our breath and zip open our parkas. Before climbing higher, John and I looked for a rocky outcrop where we might position the antenna that would transmit to and receive signals from the orbiting Nimbus satellite. Farther up the hill was a site with a relatively unobstructed view of the sky. With the aid of ropes, Harry hauled up the cable spool, Joel and I each backpacked a battery, John and Derek carried the antenna tripod and transmitting equipment, and Vince Yanonne carried the antenna.

I peered through the snow-choked den entrance to verify that our bear was still sleeping. Although not in the torpor of a true hibernation, he was in a dormant condition — lethargic, with a reduced heart rate and somewhat depressed body temperature. By cautiously peeking into the dim cave I detected no movement, but as we had learned, the black bear could quickly awaken from his winter sleep, and if disturbed would even rush out of his den. We rarely looked into a bear den without having the animal open his eyes or growl, indicating that he sensed our presence.

By the time we assembled the gear it was noon and the satellite was passing by unseen high above us. It would complete another orbit of the earth about every hour and three quarters and pass over us again at midnight. On some orbits it would be overhead, on others close to the horizon. When it was low and to the west, the hill might interfere with data transfer.

On our next (and last) ascent, we hauled up a wire loop antenna to place under the bear's bed for the on-site recording equipment, more batteries, temperature and light probes, cameras, camping gear, and equipment for instrumenting and immobilizing the bear. We had assembled our field equipment and electronic gear in the little town of West Yellowstone, and then took off on snowmobiles pulling fully loaded sleds. Between West Yellowstone and Madison Junction, we left our snowmobiles and trekked cross-country carrying part of our gear in backpacks. Harnessed like dogs, we pulled and pushed the heavily laden sleds, threading our way through very dense stands of young lodgepole pine. Vince, with the bulky plate-shaped antenna strapped to his back, often had to step sideways in order to pass between closely spaced trees. Joel paused to take off his heavy parka and tied it on his sled. As he stepped into the harness again I heard him mutter, "And I thought this was going to be the easy way to monitor a bear den."

Two miles later we dropped some of our gear beside a huge rock where we would camp, then continued until our progress was interrupted by the steep, snow-covered ascent leading to the bear den. Again stashing the now useless snowshoes and skis, we struggled and crawled up the steep slope with our heavy burdens, grasping every protruding bush or tree to keep from slipping backwards. On the uphill side of a large spruce trunk I dropped my pack and traversed across to the den entrance. Accumulating snows had closed it since our former visit until only a slit remained. Peering inside, after my eyes adjusted I could detect the dark form of the bear, motionless and curled in repose. My silent approach through powder snow had not aroused him. But would the struggles and deep breathing of the others still bringing gear up the steep slope do so? I had no doubt that the bear would soon awaken.

When the whole crew finally reached the den we went quickly to work. It was a procedure we had performed at other dens, and we knew just what steps to take and when. While John, Vince, and Jay measured out a dose of sernylan and attached a hypodermic syringe to a long jab stick, Joel and I unpacked the electronic equipment. John's son Derek set up the movie camera at a vantage point, and his daughter, Karen, got ready to take still pictures. Pat Reynolds, a wildlife student, moved behind a big tree, and her husband Harry started unwinding cable that would lead from sensors placed in the den to the ledge above, where we had placed the IRLS platform and antenna. Though we had made our preparations as quietly as possible, our presence had alerted the bear. A black nose and one ear soon protruded from the narrow, snowy opening. The bear raised his nose and sniffed, turned his head from side to side, and then backed into the den. Seconds later he poked his head out again, nervously sniffing the still air.

Derek was taking movies, Karen was taking stills, and I was snapping pictures of Karen taking pictures. We were all apprehensive lest the bear should suddenly lunge out of the den before we could immobilize him, leaving us with only tracks in the deep snow. As he retreated into the den, John quickly peered inside, poised the jab stick, and struck the bear in the shoulder. With the momentum of withdrawing the syringe he backed off fast. Momentarily surprised, the bear retreated, but seconds later he burst out of the entrance and plunged down the snowy slope, stopping in a patch of brush. We waited for the drug to take effect before cautiously closing in on the motionless bear. We wrapped him in a tarp, and with the entire crew either pulling on ropes or pushing, we hauled him back up to the den entrance. Here we swaddled him in a blanket so that his body temperature, affected both by the drug and the cold, would not drop too low. The first bear that we had immobilized in his den had had a body temperature of 96° F soon after we anesthetized him. By the time we had replaced him in his den, his temperature had dropped to 83.5° F. We hoped to prevent such hypothermia this time.

While other members of the team were inserting a tiny body-temperature transmitter rectally into the bear and positioning the chart recording equipment, I crawled head first into the cramped quarters of the rocky den. Vince managed to squeeze partway in to help me place the tiny light and temperature probes and numerous wires, each terminating in either a photodiode or a thermistor sensor. He fed these to me through a small opening in the side of the den, and I fastened them in place with spikes pushed into cracks in the rocks. I distributed the temperature sensors so as to measure temperature at the front, rear, and sides of the den. I placed sensor number 2 under the shallow fir-bough bed along with the large wire loop antenna, which would pick up the emissions from the transmitter in the bear, thus enabling us to continuously and automatically record the bear's body temperature on the nearby chart recorder.

The body-temperature system that Joel had devised consisted of a temperature-sensitive transmitter inserted rectally in the bear and a wire loop antenna located under the animal. This particular transmitter was patterned after a model designed by Dr. Stuart McKay, professor of biology at Boston University. It was supposed to be swallowed, but in this case we reversed the procedure. The function of the antenna was to pick up the signals from the transmitter inside the bear and transmit them to a receiver outside the den. Changes in the body temperature of the bear would be reflected by changes in the rate of pulses broadcast by the transmitter. The receiving equipment was a broadcast band radio receiver with a pulse-rate converter wired to a chart recorder. The demodulated pulses would be counted automatically and converted to a direct-current voltage by the pulse-rate converter, thus making it possible to continually record the temperatures on a chart.

As I backed out of the den quarters, I placed the light sensor on the den wall and pointed it at the entrance so it would monitor the amount of light entering the den. It could thus be used to tell us when the den entrance was closed by snow or opened by the bear moving out. I diagrammed the position of each numbered sensor, and then Joel and I placed similar sensors on stakes and on trees outside the den—some high, some at snow level, some pointing skyward, others toward the snow cover. Because the satellite would only be able to monitor the sensors twice every twenty-four hours, we placed small clockwork-driven chart recorders inside and outside the den where they would continuously record the air temperatures. With the exterior and interior den sensors finally in place, the rectal transmitter lodged within the anesthetized bear, and a chart recorder operating to obtain continuous body temperature, we pushed the bear back into his den, closed the opening with snow, and climbed on up the slope to secure the transmitting antenna and connect the cable from the den sensors to the IRLS platform.

For the next seventeen days our visions of working in heated rooms at other tasks while the data poured in actually transpired. We even did some downhill skiing instead of cross-country touring and winter camping. Our chart recorder, powered by nickel–cadmium batteries, was accumulating on-site body-temperature information, and the capsulelike Ryan temperature recorders were providing a continuous record of the den and outside temperatures for comparison with the satellite-monitoring results. However, much of the work burden had been shifted to Chuck Cote and his engineers at NASA's Goddard Space Flight Center, where the Nimbus satellite data were processed, printed out by computer, and mailed to us for analysis and interpretation.

Sensor number 2, under the bear's bed, informed us via satellite that the bed temperature rose from 33° F to a high of 85° F over a ten-day period. Warmth from the bear's body maintained an average bed temperature of 70° F for the same ten-day period. The temperature in the rear of the den averaged 29° F compared with 26° F near the entrance and 20° F outside the den. The bear was acting as a heater to modify his winter environment. The warming effect of his body on den temperature was confirmed when he later left the den, and temperatures from all inside sensors dropped to coincide with outside air temperatures. In the earlier Gibbon River den experiment, the bed temperature had risen much higher than that recorded by satellite. In the microclimate—the thin layer of air between a very well-constructed and insulated dry, pine-needle bed and the bear— we recorded a maximum temperature of 97° F, just slightly lower than the body temperature of the active and aroused bear. It was clearly evident from the accumulated bed temperatures that hibernating black bears considerably altered both the localized environment and the microclimate by their presence. The average temperature in the bed of our satellite bear was 50° F above outside air temperatures. However, peripheral den temperatures were not greatly altered, suggesting that little heat is radiated from the bear's body and that the heat lost by conduction is minimized when a well-insulated bed has been prepared.

Voltage readings from the light sensors placed outside the den varied from about five volts during the day to zero at night. For about a month we obtained zero readings from the light sensor inside the den pointed toward the entrance, an entrance which was sealed with snow. On March 14, the reading indicated that the entrance was probably open. As this coincided with a sharp drop in bed temperature, we suspected and then verified that the bear had left the den. The relay of data from den to satellite to us had almost immediately informed us of this movement of a bear isolated in a wilderness area of Yellowstone. It was just one example of how a satellite system could provide an unusual capability for studying animals and their environment in remote locations.

While den and bed temperatures were being monitored twice every twenty-four hours by Nimbus 3, the bear's body temperature was continuously displayed on the chart recorder in an insulated box near the den site. The bear's body temperature leveled off at around 95° F, comparable to that of the Gibbon River bear, whose temperature ranged between 94° F and 96° F. This body temperature recorded during winter sleep is only five to six degrees lower than the temperature of an active bear in summer. This small differential was expected; the bear's body temperature during winter sleep does not drop so low as to approach ambient temperatures, as is the case with small mammalian hibernators such as dormice or ground squirrels. Unless disturbed, a bear may sleep for as long as a month without changing position, but, as we repeatedly experienced, it can quickly be awakened to action.

Some researchers suggest that bears are not true hibernators, even though they go into a deep sleep and are inactive for considerable periods of time. Their reasoning is that bears do not become torpid and helpless as do most hibernators, and that the drop in their body temperature is not so extreme. Because various species of animals differ in the degree to which their body temperatures drop and their metabolic activities are depressed, and in how specific organs function in the hibernating state, a number of definitions have been advanced. One such definition, by Raymond J. Hock, is that hibernation is a periodic phenomenon in which body temperature falls to a low level, approximating ambient, and heart rate, metabolic rate, and other physiologic functions fall to correspondingly minimum levels. By these criteria the grizzly is not a true hibernator, so for the bear Hock proposed the term "carnivorean lethargy" to describe the bear's winter sleep. Another researcher, P. Morrison, suggests that because of the relatively slight drop in body temperature, bears might be considered "ecological" as opposed to "physiological" hibernators. Dr. Edgar Folk takes the opinion that there is no conspicuous reason not to use the term hibernation for bears as well as for the small mammalian hibernators. The condition, from lethargic to dormant, achieved by different animals appears to be a matter of degree and largely related to size. The bear is somewhat less of a true hibernator than, say, the ground squirrel, but for our purposes the term hibernation is appropriate enough, for the bear's ability to sleep through adverse winter conditions is truly remarkable.

Because of its large size, the bear enters its den with an immense supply of food. This potential energy reserve in animals is proportional to the animal's size and weight, but the metabolic rate is likewise weight dependent. An animal as large as the bear thus has a low metabolic rate and can fast for long periods without the drastic reduction in metabolic level necessary in smaller animals, which have a high metabolic rate when active. Our den temperature measurements also verified that, because of its small surface area relative to total mass, the bear has a low thermal conductance and cannot like smaller hibernators lose enough heat to reach and maintain a body temperature near the ambient air temperature. In other experiments we found that the bear's body temperature dropped as outside and den temperature declined, but only up to a point. Our data showed that upon reaching a low body thermal point of about 89° F, a spontaneous arousal mechanism went into operation in the bear. Folk has found that small mammalian deep hibernators cannot be quickly aroused and remain dormant with a body temperature of about 41° F. They awaken periodically and eat, urinate, and defecate, and at those times their body temperature rises. The bear, in contrast, hibernates at a considerably higher body temperature and can be quickly aroused by a disturbance. Apparently the bear cannot reduce its body temperature more than about 10° F below normal but does not need to.

While hibernating the grizzly does not eat, drink, defecate, or urinate for about five months. According to the physiologist Dr. Ralph A. Nelson, it produces metabolic water and energy through the combustion of fat stored up in thick yellow layers during late summer and early fall. Each gram of fat produces a little more than a gram of water, and this metabolic water satisfies the bear's requirements. The body does not dehydrate but remains normal, its blood volume unchanged. With protein metabolism discontinued, no catabolic end products that require excretion are produced. The bear thus frees itself from the need to urinate. Nitrogenous end products do not accumulate in the blood, nor are they excreted as urine or stored in feces. Nelson believes that either these substances are not formed, or, if they are, the nitrogen is removed or recycled in some undetermined manner. The bear's ability to regulate the production of urea so that no net increase occurs may be related to the unusual lobulation of its kidneys, and the exceptionally long renal papillae may function to concentrate urine. Whatever the mechanisms, this adaptation is a major factor in maintaining winter sleep.

Other investigations have shown that the bear's summer sleeping heart rate of forty to fifty beats per minute drops as low as ten beats during the winter sleep, and that oxygen consumption is reduced by 50 percent. Our additional studies of the bear's blood, some conducted during hibernation, showed that the bear is in some ways physiologically "smarter" than humans. Up to this time, our chemical analysis of the blood showed high levels, by human standards, of circulating fats, including cholesterol. Comparable levels would place a human in a very high-risk category for the development of arteriosclerosis and coronary heart disease; why did they not do so for the bear?

In humans who develop arteriosclerosis, blood lipids have been transported on different blood proteins. An unstable combination results, and the fats are deposited as arteriosclerotic plaques in the coronary arteries. We learned that the bear, in contrast, circulates the fats or lipids attached to a blood protein that provides stable transport, so the lipids are not deposited in the blood vessel walls. The bear can thus become quite obese in fall without suffering the consequences that would afflict man. We found, too, that the bear's protein-bound iodine is definitely low, particularly during hibernation. According to Dr. Berthrong, comparable levels in man would indicate hypothyroidism. Together with the small thyroids, this also suggests a metabolic difference from man, perhaps a lower level of cellular metabolism. The generally high levels of serum cholesterol may in turn reflect the lower level of thyroid activity. All in all, the bear is a highly efficient hibernator.

The use of an earth-orbiting satellite to monitor a bear den provided interesting data on hibernation and demonstrated the feasibility of applying this data-gathering system to the study of numerous animals in their immediate environments, particularly if these are located in remote and inaccessible areas of the globe. As we learned, even physiological functions and responses could be monitored. Also, this technique permits information to be gathered almost simultaneously from many instrumented animals distributed over an extensive area. In a wider sense, the development of an economical and efficient satellite-wildlife technology will demand an integration of effort that could promote communication and understanding among diverse cultures and widely separated peoples. But the full application of satellite information-gathering systems, or a combination of these and ground monitoring techniques, implies far more cooperation and coordination of effort by ecologists and engineers, by private and governmental agencies, by foreign and domestic scientists and our respective governments, than has existed in the past. Had there been adequate cooperation from Yellowstone Park officials after 1968, our "space-age" grizzly, Marian, might have been the first grizzly to be tracked and monitored by satellite. She had been groomed for a role she would never play.

Man has adapted to changing conditions and has freed himself, to some extent at least, from the vicissitudes of cold, drought, food shortages, population pressures, and a host of other disabling forces by his ability to alter his environment. The bear, more so than man, has itself adapted to changing environmental factors. It is a marvel of biological adaptation, of physiological and chemical perfection developed to cope with existing natural environments, and its ability to sleep through adverse winter weather is among the most remarkable of its adaptations. But if the ability to hibernate is of great advantage to this large species, it is also true that during the winter sleep the bear is highly vulnerable to its chief enemy, man. It is gradually losing out to the rapid changes man is now making in the environment, and it cannot cope with man's highly developed and sophisticated technology of killing.

Black bear Number 6, whose den was monitored by satellite, moved out to a Yellowstone highway in spring. According to a concerned ranger, he was given an overdose of nausea pills as an experiment. The purpose was to discourage bears from begging food from tourists. His radio collar was removed while he was unconscious from the drug, and he was hauled away. This black bear, who had made history, vanished like so many others in Yellowstone and was never seen again. The fate of the Yellowstone black bears is perhaps best summed up in a statement written by a ranger in the Yellowstone Park Lake Bear Logs, July 8, 1970, after seeing a black bear: "1408 — ranger reports a real live black bear at Sand Point — M.G." A few years earlier, it was not uncommon for a ranger or visitor to see forty to fifty bears in a single day.

7

Homebodies and Nomads: Ranges, Movement, Territoriality

Animals require definite but varying amounts of space in order to live and function. The size of the area each needs is related to the total requirements of the animal; some, such as bears, need far more than others. The area traversed by an individual bear in its normal activities of mating, food gathering, resting, denning, and raising a family is often referred to as its "home range." The home range provides all the bear's living requirements; its character and extent, therefore, are influenced by the size of the animal, by its mobility, its food habits, morphology and physiology, as well as by environmental constants and changes.

If an animal defends all or part of a home range against other members of the same species, the defended part is designated a territory. The territorial animal is aggressive toward others of its own kind, serving notice of ownership of a given area by readily observed behavior such as warning calls, bluffs, or other hostile actions. If these are ignored a fight may result (though physical combat is usually minimized, to the benefit of the species as a whole).

Although female grizzlies without families, and mature and immature grizzlies of both sexes, often live alone for extended periods of time, we have already seen that the grizzly is for the most part a social animal. In the Yellowstone ecosystem, the bears developed a linear hierarchy in which each animal recognized the position or status of others and acted or reacted accordingly. This hierarchical behavior among large carnivores with the ability to destroy or mangle one another serves much the same purpose as territorial defense among other species — that is, to reduce friction within the community and thereby increase the species' chances of survival.

Is the grizzly a territorial as well as a hierarchical animal? From our research to date, we did not think so. We had found, for example, no evidence that a grizzly would defend the entire extensive area over which it ranged. But would it defend a den site or a food source? This was among the questions about grizzly ranges that we hoped our radio-tracking might answer. Some of our marked grizzlies traveled extensive distances while others apparently did not. We knew that home ranges differed in size, but to what extent? In what other ways did individual ranges vary one from another? And how might they be related to sex, age, to movement and migration, to the abundance of food, to the availability of mates, and to the suitability of certain areas for winter denning? One of our key objectives in following radio-tagged grizzlies in their daily and nocturnal activities, and in their seasonal and annual movements, was to determine the size and characteristics of certain individual ranges in order to learn about grizzly bear ranges in general. While doing so we would very likely learn whether or not the grizzly had territorial tendencies.

The first step in this work was to determine the physical and biological parameters of ranges. From the day we first put a radio collar on Marian in 1961, we plotted radio fixes and recorded bearings, sometimes moving in on foot to observe her where our fixes indicated she should be. By plotting these radio locations on topographic maps and then connecting the peripheral fixes by lines, we outlined the range inhabited by this particular grizzly bear. Within the complexity of bear society, Marian's discrete home range gradually emerged. Within this area we could expect to find her day after day, season after season, and from one year to the next. While we radio-tracked Marian in her travels we also tracked other grizzlies, twenty-four in all; thus, in addition to learning about the ranges of single animals, we were obtaining insight into the relationship of one range to another.

Delineating ranges required many long hours of observation, but on some occasions we were fortunate enough to locate several grizzlies close together. From such situations we could derive a wide variety of information. One morning in the summer of 1963, my son Charlie and I awoke at 4 A.M. in upper Hayden Valley and shook the moisture off our sleeping bags. The light was quite poor but not gropingly black and there was promise in the east of more light to come, but a heavy grey mist hung over the valley. I flipped on the directional radio receiver but got no signal. We set off in the chilly air of this July morning and hiked along a ridge, keeping just within the timber so we could occasionally peer toward the open expanses of the Alum Creek drainage. I had slung my camera over my shoulder and was holding my binoculars. Soon we were cautiously approaching the carcass of an elk. There was no indication of a grizzly—no movement, no sound, though we had expected a confrontation with one or more. The light was still poor, however, and our sight impeded by the mist; a grizzly outside the limits of our senses could easily locate us with its keen nose.

We slid quietly into a sitting position at the base of a lodgepole pine to await a clearer view of the carcass, and had barely settled down in the pine needles when we saw the emerging shape of a small grizzly moving toward the carrion. It was now 4:45 A.M., which I jotted down in my notebook along with the information that the grizzly was a female, young, and not extremely large. She angled toward the food timidly and warily. She had appeared from the southwest, then circled to approach from the opposite direction and paused at the carcass briefly—just long enough for us to identify Marian's radio collar. Marian then hurried off upwind, coursing the sagebrush fields like a bird dog, her nose to the ground, occasionally stopping to sniff or to rise up and look about. She circled to the north, then roamed east of the carrion before again approaching, but this time from the northeast. She had almost completely circled the carcass in this reconnaissance operation.

Apparently satisfied that she was alone, she finally reached the carcass and began to tear ravenously at the meat of the rear quarters, tugging at the flesh and tendons with her powerful jaws. She coordinated the use of her teeth and long front claws to rip the hide or to push a stubborn leg first one way then another. Occasionally she grasped part of the carcass with her teeth and pulled backwards, moving the entire animal. At times she partially rolled, then pushed the elk, or grabbed a leg and tugged, to shift the position of the carcass, apparently trying to find an easy way to the tasty meat inside the tough outer hide. I was close enough that at times I could clearly hear her paws strike the legs and her jaws snap shut on bone. While Marian concentrated on filling her stomach, a single cow elk followed by a small band moved from the misty distance toward the feeding bear. The elk were barely visible in the fog that still hung low to the ground, but as heat from the rising sun gradually dissipated it, I took photographs of both bear and elk. The air was quiet, so still that apparently the elk could not scent either us or the bear.

Nor did Marian detect Charlie and me. She was still gustily eating when for no apparent reason, and exhibiting no signs of alarm, she left her meal and moved out of sight over a nearby hill. Her radio signal indicated that she had not gone much farther. Only after she disappeared did I spot another grizzly coming in from the southwest; evidently, Marian had detected this bear by scent before I spotted him. Was it also possible that she had detected us but was not concerned?

The newcomer was larger than Marian, dirty brown in color—not quite black, but close to it. While this bear approached, I saw yet another hurrying toward me from the east: a rangy, black grizzly that reached the elk first and started immediately to tear up the carcass. He ate as though he had not had a meal for several days. Shortly after his arrival the larger brown grizzly poked his head up over the hill just behind the feeding bear. As big brown came in, small blackie ran off a short distance, then immediately returned and was not threatened by the larger bear. Both fed amicably together. In about ten minutes the larger bear, though not alarmed, appeared nervous as if he had obtained a whiff of a scent which he could not decipher, though it did not signal danger. He ambled away. My first reaction was that the stirring air currents created by the rising sun had wafted our scents to him — but not so, for shortly after this the black grizzly that had been feeding for some time left the carcass and came directly toward us.

I whispered to Charlie, "Get ready to climb a tree," then cautioning "Not yet!" when he seemed ready to act immediately. The bear appeared to be starting a typical circular reconnaissance to determine who or what might be nearby or approaching; he might still veer away from us. The trees at the edge of the meadow sheltering Charlie and me had limbs but would not be easy to climb. The grizzly continued to approach. I quickly snapped a couple of pictures, telling Charlie to start moving back toward the lodgepole pines with lower limbs, then I too began moving. The grizzly had been only two hundred yards away when he started in our direction, and though walking — not running — was covering the ground rapidly. Lugging camera and tripod I followed Charlie, who was already climbing, and when within sight of a limby tree, I started to run. Only then did the grizzly detect me. He turned and took off in the opposite direction, and when I looked around from my perch in the tree there was not a bear in sight.

Assured that the coast was clear, we climbed down and moved off to a more distant site from which to watch the elk carcass. Within ten minutes Marian, who had been hanging around nearby but out of sight waiting for the black grizzly to leave, reappeared and moved in directly to the food. She fed to her satisfaction, then like the others left the carcass. I'd seen no coyotes, ravens, or magpies in the neighborhood prior to the arrival of the first grizzly, but soon after Marian left a coyote appeared, followed by wheeling ravens and finally magpies. These three scavengers had waited until the bears had opened up the carcass by tearing the tough hide, then fed after the bears left.

Eventually all three grizzlies returned and ate side by side. In the course of one day and night they consumed the bulk of the carcass. It was well within Marian's summer range but she neither defended the food source nor exhibited territorial defense of this area. Neither did the other grizzlies whose ranges coincided with Marian's. Each was willing to share the food with other grizzlies. In this instance, however, Marian was the least aggressive of the three animals. The bears' behavior was governed more by their positions in the bear social hierarchy than it was by any instinct to defend a food source or a territory; being relatively low in the social order, Marian was making sure that she was welcome at the feast before participating.

On October 10, 1963, subtle variations in the signal reaching our Canyon base station told us that, as usual for this time of year, the Alum Creek Sow, Number 150, was on the move. We decided it was again time to rendezvous with this grizzly. Only a few days earlier, with the onset of a snowstorm, she and her family had moved rapidly south into higher country and dense timber, thus extending her plotted range. We suspected that she had visited her den site. Now she was again feeding on mice — moving, moving, moving, her cubs seriously hunting one minute, running playfully ahead the next.

From our field station a strong signal indicated 275 degrees as the direction we must hike to intercept the Alum Creek Sow and her family. Mike Stephens and I hurriedly swallowed a sandwich and a handful of mixed nuts before starting toward the signal source. With the help of landmarks we followed our course, checking occasionally with the directional receiver. We knew our exact location on reaching the top of hill 8020 on our topographic map, so rotated the loop antenna to the null point where the signal became inaudible and took a bearing with our compass. We sketched our travel route on the map and continued on. By 1:15 P.M. we were splashing through the warm, algae-laden water of Alum Creek, losing the polish the grass and sagebrush had given to our boots. From the next ridge we spotted four grizzlies grazing in a thermal area, but none of these was the Alum Creek Sow. The signal had already told us that she was off to the right and much farther ahead. By 2:30 we were close to the grizzly, the signal coming from a peninsula of timber extending into a sea of sagebrush.

Turning off the course indicated by the directional receiver, we swung to the east so as to approach the grizzly with our faces into the wind. This is a dangerous approach because the grizzly would not be forewarned by our scent, but the only way to get close. Minutes later the signal was thumping in, even with the volume turned down. It seemed to shatter the silence of the forest. The grizzly was quite close, probably within 100 yards. I was in the lead carrying the receiver, followed by Mike with the shotgun. Simultaneously Mike and I spotted the bear outlined by back light shining through her guard hairs. Then the hairs on her hump rose and glistened in the sun. She still had not scented us, the slight air movement being toward us, but she knew of our presence. She had heard the signal from our receiver, which until now I dared not turn off as it was our only means of telling her precise location. She turned her head as Mike moved and she spotted him, but because of wind direction, she still did not scent us. She stared as though sizing up the situation, then turned, gave her alarm, "Huff, huff," to the cubs and ran. I got a fleeting look at her colored collar, brightly taped for just such identification. I feared that after rounding up her cubs, the sow might return, but she was intent only on getting them away, for the radio signal soon told us that she was departing. I paced off a distance of 140 feet between the bear and the spot where we first jumped her. Such measurements, when averaged, would give us some idea of the critical distance beyond which the grizzly would be more likely to retreat than attack.

Earlier in the season the Alum Creek Sow had adopted a cub belonging to the Owl-Faced Sow, Number 148, who had been killed by a truck. Was she still caring for this adopted cub? When we jumped her I learned she was not. The grizzlies were not bedded down as I had anticipated but when intercepted had been tearing apart an old log in which a red squirrel had stashed a supply of pine cones. The airline distance we had tracked them since our lunch break was three miles, although we had traveled nearly four in circling to approach upwind.

We continued to follow the family after they entered a rocky ravine, an area of thermal activity with small, constantly playing geysers, rising steam, hot springs, small mud pots, and boggy areas of doubtful footing. It was a natural greenhouse with ample food for bears, but to us it possessed an air of mystery and even gloom. The changing density of the moving mist generated by the cooling after-noon air caused objects to fade, then disappear, and the steam from hotter thermal waters contributed to the ghostly atmosphere. When Mike and I emerged into the timber from the gorge, we nearly ran into three grizzlies — a big sow with two yearlings, all grazing toward us. Though we were only a stone's throw away, a large log partially hid us from their view. I dropped to one knee behind the log and with my binoculars looked for ear tags (there were none), but not before having taken a quick glance to locate a tree. As the bears moved nearer I motioned Mike to start climbing, then slowly grasped the limbs above me and started up myself. Mike bypassed the nearest tree for one easier to climb, and as he did so the grizzlies saw him move. A protracted moment of suspense passed before the sow turned and ran with that incredible speed which, if she had charged, so eas-ily could have overwhelmed us. Again, we heard the anxious "huff, huff," this time not only an alarm call to her yearlings but also a warning to us.

This family had been grazing the autumn growth of white clover in soil warmed by thermal activity. Droppings left by elk and Canada geese told us that the grizzlies had no grazing monopoly in this hot-house garden. The cubs would acquire a taste for clover here and would learn where and when to seek it. In later years they would return alone to forage. Where food is concerned the grizzly does not forget, but returns year after year and always at the right time.

Another routine check with our receiver showed that the Alum Creek Sow and her cubs were circling toward us and might soon break through the timber into this lush pasture to feed, so we decided to depart from this hot water section of Alum Creek and turned east toward our lunchtime starting point. En route we came across five more grizzlies around an elk carcass — the remains of an old bull. We watched them awhile, unseen and undetected, and identified Number 48, the Brown-headed Sow, with her two cubs. I studied the very unusual brown head and face of this mother grizzly, who was also easily recognized by the aluminum tags in each ear and a colored rope marker in her left ear. (Her black and white cub, although not as yet marked or named, later became known as Handsome, one of the bears that we called the Four Musketeers.) I could not avoid the an-thropomorphic tendency to endow the mother bear with human feelings. She seemed to oversee her litter with affection and pride, now and then tempered with a pretense of indifference inspired by modesty. This, as it turned out, was to be my last long close-up view of this model mother. The next spring she did not appear, and we had to presume her dead.

During a five-hour expedition covering a distance of eight-and-one-half miles, we had tracked the Alum Creek Sow and her three cubs, seen nine other grizzlies, and obtained varied information that would be entered in our records. For example, we would tabulate the number of marked bears seen compared to unmarked ones. Over a period of time, these relative totals would help us to compute the grizzly population. All of the animals observed were within the seasonal range we had plotted for the Alum Creek Sow and most were within the known boundaries of Marian's range. Thus, one day's radio-tracking of a single animal informed us, directly or indirectly, of thirteen different animals and added more information on the sharing of ranges — and this was only one of many such days.

Darkness that day ended the tracking but not the monitoring of the Alum Creek Sow. We would check her signal periodically at night to make sure that if she strayed beyond her known range, we recorded the move. For a month now, we had tracked, observed, and studied this grizzly family. We knew that except for short foraging excursions, the Alum Creek Sow and her cubs had managed to obtain practically all the food they required in an area of about one square mile. Most of this was open meadow habitat supporting a high population of meadow mice and an abundant supply of onion grass bulbs under the frozen soil. This information alone gave us clues to the carrying capacity of this vegetative type for grizzlies. A family of four grizzlies had found ample food here for a period of one month at a time when they were feeding constantly to accumulate additional layers of fat. (Carrying capacity is the average number of grizzlies a given area can support year after year without deterioration or adverse changes in the environment.)

This square mile fall foraging area was the nucleus of the Alum Creek Sow's summer and fall range, a considerably larger area. Overlapping this range was the northern half of Marian's range. The two bears frequently met, but Marian's intensively used feeding and daytime bedding area was in a side drainage of upper Trout Creek, a much more heavily timbered region. There in the shade of lodgepoles, spruce, and a few whitebark pines, Marian and her cub dug their shallow daytime beds on a steep slope. The odor of damp earth and evergreen needles was more evident than the musky bear scent, except on those occasions when we disturbed Marian while she rested. She and her cub had torn up the hillside beneath a large tree seeking the nut cache of a squirrel, and the shells of pine nuts in her droppings showed she was also feeding on the green nuts of the limber pine before they ripened and fell from the drying cones.

This wooded area, some two square miles, was the nucleus of Marian's 1963 summer and fall range, the first of her seasonal ranges we were to delineate. The size of this range was determined from a group of 140 bearings and 32 radio fixes to be approximately eight square miles. The same year, 227 bearings and 35 fixes showed the Alum Creek Sow's seasonal range to measure twenty-seven square miles. Movement to dens and to new food sources would expand these seasonal ranges, and when a new radio fix or a sighting revealed such expansion we would plot it on our maps. If the lines linking our peripheral fixes encompassed a den site, they could be considered to define a home range. Thus with the location of a den in 1964 we learned that Marian's home range was fifteen square miles, and similarly that it expanded to twenty in 1965.

The accumulation of locations on our maps revealed centers of activity where bears were found much more frequently than elsewhere. This smaller area, where often both food and day bed sites were close together, was the nucleus of a given range. It is the area of most concentrated use and is sometimes, though not always, close to the geographical center of the range as well. In Marian's case in 1963, even the nucleus of her seasonal range was shared with other grizzlies.

The winter of 1964–65 had not been kind to the small bison herd that foraged along the Yellowstone River in the vicinity of Sulfur Mountain and the thermal areas of Hayden Valley. At least three had succumbed by spring, but their loss was the grizzlies' gain. An ancient lone bison had bedded down on the warmed, snow-free earth near Mud Volcano on a bitter winter night and had never risen again. Grizzlies had found and were feeding on his remains by mid-April. Another had survived a few more weeks until green sedge shoots and new grass blades were available, but for him these plants were useless. His stomach had shrunk from a dearth of food, and the bacterial flora were so altered that the pentose sugars and cellulose from these succulents could not be digested and absorbed. His condition deteriorated and he died in the midst of plenty.

The third, a young and vigorous buffalo, had died in mid-winter. Still in his prime, he did not face a winter food shortage; he could feed by pushing and shoveling snow with his huge head until he reached edible forage — dried grasses and forbs — far beneath the snow surface. But he made a mistake that winter, and one mistake in the bitter cold of a Yellowstone winter — whether for buffalo, elk, moose, or man — can result in death. The young bull had attempted to cross the ice spanning the Yellowstone River, perhaps to seek better grazing conditions, but had picked a spot where warm water gushed into the river beneath the surface. The warming had reduced the snow-covered ice to a thin, treacherous layer. The bison broke through, and although he floundered towards shore breaking the ice in front of him, he was never able to extricate himself from this deadly trap. His energy ebbed, hypothermia set in, and he drowned.

When we located the carcass of this unfortunate animal in early May, the bottom had gone out of the snow — a sure sign that spring had arrived. Uinta ground squirrels, just out of hibernation, scampered around on the surface of the snow, but our skis were ever dropping into the melted hollows surrounding the sagebrush. Even our ski poles sank down to the handles. We approached the drowned buffalo a little after noon of a warm day, the temperature 54° F, the sun bright. Coyotes had also just discovered the carcass, and grizzlies, including Marian. Succulent sedge shoots were available, but the buffalo carcass provided more nourishment.

We had not anticipated that Marian and her yearlings would be feeding in this area, which was beyond the home range we had plotted for her over a four-year period. Her lifetime home range had been evolving as we annually added the new radio fixes, gradually increasing in size as she matured. It expanded slightly in the summer of 1964 when Marian foraged with a cub and again that fall when she made a trek to the southwest to prepare her den site. Now in the spring of 1965 she was again extending her range, but this time to the northeast across the Yellowstone River, and her keen sense of smell had detected the ripening buffalo meat.

In the cover of some trees, Charlie Ridenour, John, and I settled down to observe Marian, who was sporting her radio collar and was followed by her energetic yearling Number 188. However, a large, brown-headed boar had preceded her. This unmarked boar, we learned, fed on the carcass in late afternoon or after dark, while Marian and her yearling patiently awaited his departure on a terrace across the river. They fed only toward morning or during daylight hours after the boar had satisfied his hunger. We did not see them feed together. On one occasion, the boar and the sow with her yearling approached the carcass simultaneously. The boar, upon detecting the sow, turned and slowly circled back in a maneuver to get between her and the wooded retreat to the east. This caused Marian to move off, keeping a respectful distance from the boar as he circled towards her. As the boar approached, the timid Marian moved back. Could we interpret this as an exhibition of territorial defense by the boar, that is, defense of an extensive area surrounding a temporary food source? It did not appear to be a mating advance. It is possible that territorial behavior is more pronounced in spring when food is scarce; aggressive action at this time does seem aimed at intimidating other bears and thereby gaining a brief monopoly of the food source.

While discussing this incident back at the lab, John, Maurice, and I agreed that aggressive behavior related to hierarchical position — such as we had observed with Marian and the boar—also suggests territorial defense. Hierarchy and territoriality here appear to merge and are difficult to distinguish precisely. A territory is a specific area from which an animal excludes all others of its species except mates and its own offspring (usually of that year), and within territorial boundaries an individual animal usually reigns supreme regardless of its relative rank, order, or position. Having studied Marian's position within the social hierarchy, we were inclined to believe that under these conditions, where Marian was expanding her established range and perhaps felt somewhat insecure, she and her yearling exhibited submissive behavior—manifested by an unwillingness to feed while the boar was present — and concluded that it was not typical territorial behavior.

While again watching for Marian to return to the buffalo carcass, we observed a considerable range of territorial behavior in many of the species of birds then nesting in the vicinity. A pair of Canada geese had selected a nest site on an island in the river and permitted no intruders near. We listened to the winnowing courtship flight of the common snipe high overhead and occasionally caught sight of a blurred shape in the sky where the snipe was performing for its mate. Their nesting site was in the marsh below. Ospreys flew by, scanning the river, whose low spring flow made fishing excellent. Numerous osprey congregated to fish in the common hunting territory where Alum Creek enters the Yellowstone, but flew off to nest in Yellowstone Canyon or on islands in Yellowstone Lake where each actively defended a nesting territory. White pelicans in groups flew up and down the river, then landed, herded fish together, and scooped them up in their large bills. Theirs was a shared feeding area and a cooperative fishing endeavor; only a small nesting plot on Pelican Island was defended. From the densest part of the lodgepole forest, we could hear the mating hoot of the great gray owl. It was a thrilling sound. Those rather rare birds were even now establishing a nesting territory, though it was unlikely that they would have to defend it from another pair of their species.

Snow still covered much of the valley, but as Marian and her yearling again approached the site of the buffalo carcass, they stopped on a bare slope and began digging. They had conveniently switched from a meat to a vegetable diet and were consuming the tasty bulbs and succulent leaves of the shooting star *(Dodecatheon)* and the nippy-tasting bulbs of the inconspicuous salt-and-pepper plant *(Oregonia)*. The poisonous death camas *(Zygadenus elegans)* with its linear lily leaves was not touched, nor had I ever found the grizzlies to eat any part of the plant, including the onion-like bulbs. Did they instinctively know that it should be avoided? Would it be toxic to them, as it is to man and many other animals? Or do they have digestive adaptations that would enable them to eat it safely? All we learned was that this plant was not eaten by the bears.

Not far from where the grizzlies were feeding, a moving black spot in the whiteness of the snow caught our attention. At closer range we could make out four ravens, one flapping helplessly in the snow while the others pecked at him viciously. He appeared unable to fly. The other three, I thought, were surely hammering him to death. With our approach they flew off, although reluctantly. When John webbed closer the injured raven waddled away over the snow, gaining air speed as he hopped. He finally managed to take off and flew clumsily to a low branch where he had difficulty in landing. He fell down through the limbs, managing to perch on one just above our heads. When he flew again he did better, and the next time was still an improvement. But he flew like a blinded bird — he tended to go straight up. His attackers had quite possibly blinded him in one or both eyes. (Ravens instinctively go for the eye of a victim.) When it was evident that we could not catch and examine the raven, we returned to the scene of the struggle. Here green-colored droppings made us suspect that the raven had been sick. Was this the cause of the strange behavior? Food at that time of year is still scarce; perhaps the raven in distress had stimulated the predator instinct in the other hungry ravens so they set out to kill him. It was also courtship time for the ravens and the period when they were claiming their nesting territories, but if he had invaded the territory of a pair of ravens, why were there three attacking him instead of two? We saw no nest nearby and we knew that ravens often permit other ravens to closely approach their nests without defensive action.

Whatever the cause, there seemed no doubt that had we not intervened the three ravens would most surely have killed their victim. This merciless behavior toward a disabled individual can, but usually does not, occur in grizzly bear society. In general, recognition of defeat and a signaling of such to an opponent serves to terminate grizzly bear fights; as suggested earlier, it is a built-in mechanism for preventing the murder of members or destruction of a species by its own kind. By the same token, as the establishment of nesting territories by birds tends to eliminate friction and minimize conflict, the social hierarchy within which each bear recognizes his or her position precludes the need for grizzlies to establish and defend territories.

In 1963, we got our first inkling of the size of an adult boar's summer range by tracking Pegleg, Number 76. We had difficulty instrumenting Pegleg, for when we hit him with the immobilizing dart he took off on the run. The drug took effect as he splashed into Trout Creek. After laboriously hauling him out of the water, we slipped a radio collar over his head, then released him. Subsequent tracking revealed that Pegleg had the largest summer range of any of the bears we had yet monitored — an area of 168 square miles. In the course of one of his foraging trips out of Hayden Valley, he made a circular

Simplified Field Map of Grizzly Bear Ranges and Nuclei Plotted by Radio *The circled area within each delineated range represents its nucleus or center of activity, the bear's most heavily used feeding and bedding area. The irregular arrowed line shows Pegleg's 50-mile, 7-day foraging trek in the summer of 1963.*

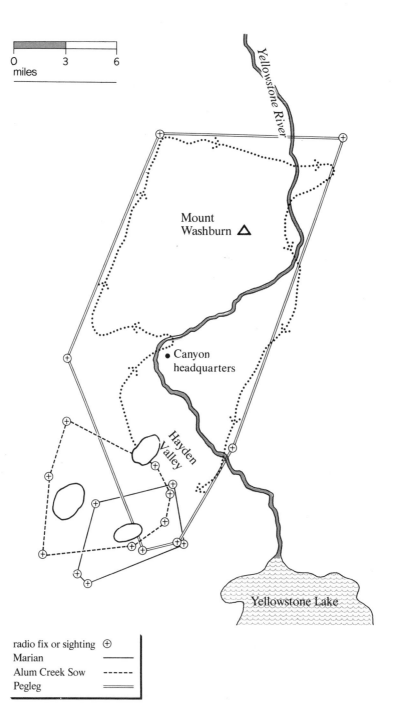

0 3 6
miles

Yellowstone River

Mount
Washburn △

● Canyon
headquarters

Hayden
Valley

Yellowstone Lake

radio fix or sighting ⊕
Marian ————
Alum Creek Sow - - - - -
Pegleg ═══════

fifty-airline-mile trek in seven days. He of course logged far more ground mileage than this as he plodded over hills and valleys, wandered back and forth in search of food, climbed high on the side of Mount Washburn, and then dropped nearly a thousand feet from the rim of colorful Yellowstone Canyon down to the rushing white water. He swam the Yellowstone, then climbed the steep south canyon slope following a line of scanty vegetation and timber, a course that took him over talus slopes and huge rocks but was free of cliffs. While we tracked him that summer, he made five known crossings of the Yellowstone River and was the first radio bear to show us that rushing water, deep pools, and steep-sided canyons were no barriers to travel when a grizzly got the wanderlust. In fall he left his summer range, which he shared with other large boars such as Inge, Bruno, and the Short-eared Boar, and many others in the Hayden Valley community of bears, and established a fall range in the northeast corner of the park.

Sow Number 34 was no slouch either. During the summer of 1964 she crossed the Yellowstone River eleven times in less than a month. On one occasion, when her signal told us that she was approaching the banks of the river at night, we stationed ourselves on the opposite side of the river and waited. Out of the darkness across the river came the low growl of a grizzly, joining the subdued beep, beep from our hand-held radio receiver. The sow and her family entered the water and swam almost directly toward us. One bear growled softly while swimming. I could barely make out their shapes through my binoculars as they emerged from the water, bounded up the steep bank, shook themselves, and took off at a run.

Toward the end of July we were able to trap and mark the yearlings of this sow. They became numbers 177 and 178, thus adding another completely marked family for us to study. With Joel Varney and Hoke Franciscus, I moved carefully as we closed in on the day bed where this mother bear was resting. We had weighed, measured, marked, and taken a blood sample from one of her yearlings the day before. He was with his mother when we jumped them; apparently they had been reunited during the night. The other yearling was at that moment in our trap. We would weigh and mark him in the afternoon. Close to the daytime bed of Number 34 we jumped another grizzly, then flushed out two cow elk that had been resting no more than seventy-five yards from the grizzlies in this same dense timber.

In early spring, grizzlies will attack and kill sick or weakened elk and even healthy ones temporarily incapacitated by floundering through deep snow. But in summer other food sources are abundant. These grizzlies and elk were living closely and amicably together, the elk sensing that the grizzlies were disinterested and would not attack. (Perhaps in the same way grouse or snowshoe rabbits can tell whether a goshawk is well fed or is hungry and hunting. Many prey species apparently have evolved this ability to ascertain the condition and consequently the intentions of predators by one or a combination of their senses.)

From grizzly bears Numbers 101, 150, 202, and others, we accumulated data on the size and character of home ranges, but with Marian we went a step further. By tracking her closely over several years we were able to establish that the lifetime home range of this animal was evolving and expanding. During 1961–63, when she was a barren sow, her range embraced approximately eight square miles but did not include her winter den, which we knew was not far from the southern border of her range. In 1964 we tracked Marian and her cub for sixty-seven days and located her den as they were about to enter it for the winter. The increased foraging activity required by the presence of her cub together with her movement to a higher elevation to dig her den increased the size of Marian's home range to fifteen square miles. In 1965 we tracked her even more intensively for a period of 106 days. It was in the spring of this year that she extended her range to the east by moving to feed on the buffalo carcass and by swimming the Yellowstone River with her yearling. Her 1965 range ultimately embraced twenty square miles. In 1968, when very little food was available at the Trout Creek dump, Marian again had cubs with her. She covered an area of twenty-two and one-half square miles, including some new territory where she had not previously foraged. This expansion was in part due to the partial closure of the dump and in part to fall movements in search of pine nuts.

Some years she moved into new areas and did not visit older haunts, so that in general the average annual size of her home range was about fifteen square miles, and the total area over which she roamed in her lifetime in search of food, mates, and den sites totalled thirty square miles by the fall of 1968 when she and her two cubs again entered a newly dug den for the Yellowstone winter. This was not a large area for a grizzly. Some ranges that we plotted through radio-tracking and spotting of marked animals were considerably larger. Marian was definitely a homebody.

Within the peripheries of the ranges that we delineated, the grizzly bears were constantly moving about in the course of their daily and nocturnal activities. The extent of this day-to-day movement was determined by radio-tracking and by measuring the airline distance between radio fixes made approximately twelve hours apart, and it could best be described as considerable roaming without going very far. Both the Sour Creek Sow and the Alum Creek Sow provided examples of such movement, each day foraging for many miles but winding up not far from their starting point. The Sour Creek Sow averaged 3.2 airline miles each day for twelve days and the Alum Creek Sow 2.3 miles for thirteen days. The maximum straight-line distances that these two grizzlies traveled in a single day's foraging were 5 miles for one bear and 6 for the other. Males under similar conditions traveled farther than females; Pegleg, for example, averaged 7.2 airline miles in eight twelve-hour periods. (This included one afternoon when he traveled 9 miles.) In contrast to this leisurely type of foraging, grizzlies would travel rapidly and directly when they detected carrion, and this often resulted in the expansion of ranges. One grizzly quickly covered a distance of 18 miles to feed on a carcass. Beep, Number 37, traveled an airline distance of 19 miles from one food source to carrion. Adverse conditions can impede this purposeful movement, however; it took the Alum Creek Sow sixty hours to locate a dead bison only one and three-quarter miles away when the wind was unfavorable.

Other factors in the evolution and expansion of home ranges are the annual fall dispersal to den sites and the dispersal of young bears into previously unvisited territory. Within a twelve-hour period in November of 1963, Lucky, sow Number 164, moved sixteen miles from a foraging area to a den site. Similarly, Pegleg left his already extensive summer range and rapidly traveled well over twenty airline miles to a fall foraging range, and sow Number 96 traveled almost double this distance to reach her winter den site. This fall dispersal—the coincident and seasonal movement of members of the grizzly population to distant areas, some even beyond the boundaries of Yellowstone—took on a pattern of migration. One of the longest migratory movements we traced was made by the Old Faithful Boar, who traveled from Rabbit Creek to Hawk's Rest, just outside the southeast corner of Yellowstone—an airline distance of fifty miles. Here our records of this bear were terminated. He was shot in the Teton Wilderness during the fall hunting season.

In the fall of 1961 male littermates Numbers 37 and 38, who had been inseparable companions as yearlings after an early weaning by their mother, sow Number 39, split up as two-year-olds to wander in different directions. Number 37 moved from Hayden Valley south to the West Thumb thermal area. Number 38 swam the Yellowstone River, foraged south along the east bank, and entered Pelican Creek campground near Fishing Bridge.

I pieced together an itinerary for Number 38 by means of occasional sightings and visible clues he left in his progress. From what we know of grizzlies' habits and of the terrain he crossed, it is possible to draw a composite picture of this bear's activities during his travels. He did not linger at the now almost deserted campground, but plodded his way northeasterly up Pelican Creek. In this open valley he dug tubers and caught mice in the scattered company of other grizzlies. Still restless, he climbed to the higher meadows of Mirror Plateau, where he had probably fed in spring on the leaves and seed pods of the glacier lily (*Erythronium grandiflorum* Pursh). Now he consumed the gnarled woody roots of the alpine bistort *(Bistorta vivipara),* too meager in starch to add to his layers of fat for the coming winter but nutritious enough to furnish energy for his travels. Elk and their large, frisky calves were abundant, but all had grown fat, sleek, and healthy in their summer home and were no source of food for the young grizzly.

As Number 38 moved across open meadows and through small stands of conifers, a few of his silver-tipped guard hairs were left on the barkless trunks of trees rubbed bare by the passing bison. (There were far too many of these to be mistaken for "bear trees," trees used by grizzlies for backscratchers. At one rocky outcrop a shrill whistle betrayed to him the presence of a marmot, and after an hour's toil rocks were strewn in all directions as though catapulted by an explosion. At their center Number 38 had dug a large crater in rock and soil, but one huge rock that even the bear could not budge still protected the marmot in its burrow beneath.

Number 38 moved on, his hunger undiminished. He overturned "buffalo chips" (bison droppings) and licked up the ants and other small insects he found underneath. He passed the magnificent petrified trunks of ancient trees on Specimen Ridge, where living forest stands on top of other forests that over successive eons have been inundated by volcanic ash. From these rock replicas of the giant sequoias of the past, over which thousands of generations of bears had moved in search of food and mates, Number 38 dropped down into thick lodgepole stands and out to the edge of the Lamar Valley. The bordering aspens were high-lined and their barks scarred by the teeth of hungry elk congregating here in winter. No young aspens were visible. Each shoot that managed to sprout in summer was consumed in winter, an indicator that the carrying capacity of this range for elk had been exceeded. Moving across the valley, where grass and sagebrush vegetation was scarce, the boar did not stop to forage but continued upstream, picking his way through large boulders, traversing ridgelike moraines, and splashing through shallow, marshy ponds—all signs of the glaciers that retreated and finally disappeared with the warming climate, in the process transporting rocks from granite outcrops in the high mountain headwaters of Soda Butte Creek.

Number 38 was now traveling northeast along Soda Butte Creek and paralleling the highway. Without knowing it, he was moving toward the northeast entrance to Yellowstone Park, beyond which lay Silver Gate and Cooke City with its garbage dump. For the time being he was content to browse the fall meadows for the drying stalks and extensive root of the elk thistle. (Humans, too, enjoy the stalks of this plant when it is young; raw or lightly cooked they make delicate tasting greens.) Goldenrod and fireweed dotted the meadows, giving color to the valley while denoting the passing of summer. Again and again the grizzly waded into the stream, and where it narrowed in its upper reaches he pushed his bulk through low willow thickets, trampling unconcernedly on the red leaves of geraniums and their seed pods shaped like a crane's beak. The willows, the major winter food of moose, did not interest him, but along their fringes he occasionally stopped to eat a few late-ripening strawberries, often licking up several beetles at the same time. Even an occasional butterfly or a moth immobilized by the cold was automatically consumed. Where the willows gave way to timber they were interspersed with a shrub whose leaves were brown and velvety on their lower surfaces and whose branches bore an abundance of luscious-looking red berries. These buffalo berries are consumed in large quantities by Alaskan grizzlies, and though they might have been a food bonanza for grizzly Number 38, he completely ignored them. Perhaps he had tried them before and found them as distasteful as they are to humans. Possibly he might acquire a taste for them when food grew scarce.

On the upper slopes of the valley, he passed through scattered whitebark pines that, unfortunately for the bear, were not loaded this fall with pine cones. These trees produce cones with large seeds only periodically, not annually. Had there been a pine nut crop he could have grown fat on the rich nutritious seeds found in this small patch alone, even though Clark's crows, blue grouse, and red squirrels would have competed with him for the ripening seeds falling from their pitchy containers.

Where a very large and gnarled pine grew close to a cliff, the bear walked between tree and rock, nearly touching both but not noticing the blackened interior of a shallow cave in the cliff. He was not interested that the soot covering these rocks came from a fire kindled by men long dead; that the cave served as shelter when they came here to gather pine nuts, perhaps in competition with this bear's ancestors. A flake of chipped obsidian pressed into the rocky soil by the bear's rear foot gave evidence that man was once an integral part of this vast ecosystem. His onetime presence throughout the Yellowstone region is apparent from flint arrowheads and obsidian knives found near thermal pools and along river banks. Even above timberline he left his stone implements: tiny scrapers, perhaps used to peel the *Lomatium*, or biscuit-roots, another food relished by both bear and man; a large spearhead that might have been carried as protection — for early man, like today's backpackers, must occasionally have come face to face with prowling grizzlies.

In the narrowing upper valley of Soda Butte Creek, the clear waters ran a little faster. Majestic mountain peaks loomed up and the colorful yellow strata of sedimentary cliffs towered overhead, truly spectacular scenery to humans but unappreciated by the bear: the distant peaks were beyond his range of sight, and the colorful cliffs, white clouds, and blue sky no more than a blur. But as he hurried on, apparently unmoved by all this grandeur, he was acutely aware of changes in his own environment. His nose told him of spruce trees ahead, the entrails of cleaned trout on the stream bank, elk on the wooded slope above, humans close by where the narrowing canyon forced him ever closer to the highway. We can imagine, too, how differently the elk with its keen sight must experience the same scene. Or the soaring golden eagle, whose eyes can at one moment take in an entire valley, then focus instantly on a scurrying mouse or pika.

On the slopes beneath Abiathar Peak, Number 38 raked away the thin layers of humus and duff covering the mineral soil and curled up in a shallow day bed. He lay with his nose into the wind, probing a slight updraft from the valley below. He was well hidden by the thick growth of trees, but the sounds of passing automobiles told him of the highway nearby. He slept until dark, and when the sound of moving cars ceased, he dropped down to the valley floor and plodded on, crossing the highway several times before passing through the outskirts of Silver Gate. He moved on eastward through the night and arrived at Cooke City before sunrise. Behind a restaurant he knocked over a garbage can, then walked down a deserted street past a log cabin and back into timber, his nose leading him to the town dump. There he found enough tasty morsels that he returned to feed for two more nights. Then he continued eastward into the Beartooth Plateau, where sheepmen grazed their flocks on Forest Service land. Here for the first time he encountered domestic animals. He was hungry and he killed. When he returned the next night to feed and perhaps kill again, a bullet from the waiting sheepherder ended this young bear's wanderings. He was two and one-half years old. His movements that autumn and his fate were not unlike those of many other young bears that never lived to reach maturity.

It became evident from our radio tracking and from observations of our marked animals that the Yellowstone grizzlies inhabited an area much vaster than Yellowstone National Park, and in their travels or migrations moved in and out of the park. The establishment and evolving of their individual ranges went on without regard for man's arbitrary boundaries; inevitably this led to circumstances where bears and civilization came into uncomfortably close proximity. During the first nine years of our study, when we often handled troublesome grizzly bears for the Park Service, we transported many of them to distant areas of the park, and in doing so learned a great deal about the grizzly's attachment to a home range. Most transported grizzlies either returned to the area of capture or to their established ranges. Instrumented grizzly Number 170 traveled thirty-four airline miles over rugged country in sixty-two hours to return to Gardiner, Montana, her point of capture. When we again trapped her and released her along the eastern border of Yellowstone, she returned a distance of fifty-three miles. Male grizzly Number 38, when released on Promontory Point on Yellowstone Lake, traveled thirty-one airline miles in four days to return to his established summer range. To do so he had to first go south around the lake, then swing north along the eastern shore. Many more such examples of this induced movement revealed to us the strong homing instincts of the grizzly bears and their desire to return to familiar country even when transported fifty or more airline miles away. This strong homing instinct helped maintain a certain cohesion in the bear population. Spring migratory movement to previously established summer ranges provided opportunities for grizzlies of both sexes to meet during the short breeding season. However, these same behavior traits of the grizzly were soon to prove disastrous to the population.

Like Number 38, the big subdominant boar we called Bruno was a nomad. Although in summer he shared Marian's home range, sometimes scraping out his daytime beds in the same dense patch of timber she used, he covered far more countryside in his daily travels and, like Pegleg, took off on foraging trips that greatly extended his summer range. At times he went south to a day bed high on the slopes of Elephant Back Mountain, within the daytime haunts of sow Number 75, and like her, he sometimes went up and over the crest of the mountain. He did just this on September 11, 1964. He ambled south, then moved rapidly up the slopes of Elephant Back Mountain, left his summer range, and moved eastward. The next day signals received at Lake Butte, on the shore of Yellowstone Lake, placed Bruno on Pelican Cone, a mountain at the north end of Pelican Valley. He was approximately fifteen airline miles from his Hayden Valley bedding area. We were tracking Bruno to learn about his fall movements and determine his fall range, and to find his den site if possible. We had instrumented him on the night of September 5 and found that he weighed 890 pounds, a gain of 370 pounds from the time we had first captured and marked him in July, 1959. Knowing that he would continue to put on weight until hibernation, we figured that this large boar could easily weigh 1,000 pounds by the time colder weather and deepening snow sent him into his winter sleep. (He thus gained another nickname: the Thousand-pound Boar.)

After Bruno's rapid trek to his fall range, we plotted his daily movements and found that his fall foraging range included the upper part of Pelican Valley and the country surrounding Pelican Cone. It extended eastward to the upper slopes of Mount Chittenden and the rugged eastern border of Yellowstone Park, and reached northward to upper Mist Creek Trail, including Raven Creek. Our base camp was along Pelican Creek where the stream emerges from timber to meander through the open grass–sagebrush valley. When a radio fix from here placed Bruno on about the 8,800-foot contour line northeast of and beneath Mount Chittenden, four of us (Bob Ruff, Charlie Ridenour, John, and I) followed the elusive signal all day but were unable to close in, as he was traveling faster than we. At 5:35 P.M. we reached the top of a small mountain, elevation 9,390 feet, with Bruno's signal coming from the rugged timber expanses ahead of us. It was too late in the day to go on. We would have to return to camp and start again prepared to spend a number of days and nights on Bruno's trail.

It was already dark when we emerged from the heavily timbered north face of the mountain and headed for base camp using the stars as a guide. For a while we followed Mist Creek Trail, then left it to head directly for camp — the north star now ninety degrees to our line of travel. In the blackness of the night we were unable to locate a shallow spot to ford Raven Creek even though we followed the stream bank a quarter-mile off course. So we stripped off our clothes and shoes and waded into waist-deep water on which ice was forming. I made two crossings to carry my boots, clothes, day pack, and tracking gear. By this time my feet were so numb that I had trouble putting on my boots, and I stumbled along through the sage for the next quarter-mile. Still cold and tired by the time we reached camp, we built a small but cheery fire and cooked supper hastily, then immediately slipped into our sleeping bags. The silence was broken by howling coyotes and the distant bugling of bull elk, but sleep came quickly. Several times in the night, I awoke to change position on the hard ground and heard the elk still bugling and the coyotes yipping — sometimes close, other times far away — normal comforting sounds that made me feel contented and secure as I rolled over to go back to sleep.

In the morning we set out, backpacks loaded with all our gear: sleeping bags, tarps, cooking utensils, receivers, quad antenna, cameras, film, binoculars, and skimpy rations of food—mostly de-hydrated but at least enough for several days. We hoped to supple-ment our provisions with trout from Raven Creek, but because Bruno led us into the mountains away from streams, we never did. For three days we followed Bruno on foot with packs on our backs and tracking receivers in our hands. Each night we slept where darkness overtook us, continuing to monitor Bruno's movements from our fixed camp locations. In airline distance Bruno moved only about twenty miles though he traveled many more, as did we in our attempts to close in and observe him. Bruno frequented the dark, very dense spruce–fir timber where the ground was littered with dead trees and windfall. Sometimes we climbed over logs as much as we walked on the ground. Visibility was often less than fifty feet. During this entire tracking period Bruno stayed in dense timber with the exception of two nights when he moved into the open country of Pelican Valley to forage on pocket gophers and meadow mice. By camping on moun-tain tops and ridges at altitudes of 9,000 feet or more, we were able to monitor his nightly movements in all directions. The greatest dis-tance that he moved away from us at night was four miles, and once he moved in very close to our camp. The increasing loudness of the signal alerted us and we prepared for his imminent appearance at the edge of our circle of firelight. It was scary, yet thrilling, to listen to this signal coming from the surrounding darkness. How close would Bruno come? Would he try to ransack our food, cached some distance from our beds? Might he come so close that we would have to take to the trees? But the signal diminished without an appearance of the boar, and we succumbed to fatigue and slept until daylight.

The next day we approached to within an estimated quarter-mile of the big boar, but we never sighted him. We found it difficult to keep up with him for he traveled day and night, only occasionally stopping to rest, while we were limited to diurnal movement by darkness, rough terrain, and dense timber. We were also slower and hampered by packs and gear. Huckleberry patches were numerous, particularly on north slopes, but the berry crop was waning. The green leaves of the whortleberry were turning yellow. The bear fed on both its berries and leaves, and we tracked him into a number of lush berry patches. Although Bruno was active both day and night, it became apparent that he was more active, traveled farther, and foraged more vigor-ously after dark. Though Bruno was just plodding along, here turning over a rock, there tearing a log open or digging for a pocket gopher, he led us a tiring chase. We climbed two mountains, one twice.

At 5:20 P.M. on September 27 I recorded in my field notebook:

We decided to make camp on the south side of the mountain. This meant a dry camp on this waterless slope, so we threw for the line to see who would hike down into the timbered valley for water and haul it back. Bob lost and went off with a pail. Charlie, John and I built a fire and cleared level spots for our beds. We rationed food for supper and breakfast; potato soup for both meals with dried beef on crackers for supper, and oatmeal, two pieces of bread and coffee with sugar for breakfast. From our camp at 5:20 P.M., we obtained a signal at 220 degrees. Our bear appeared to be moving westward. At 8:10 P.M., we had lost the signal as Bruno had moved west around the mountain which effectively shielded his signal. At 12 midnight, 1:30, 3:00 and 4:30 A.M., I turned on the receiver and checked for Bruno's signal, but with no luck. I found it difficult to awaken and force myself to action. This morning while eating breakfast, I placed the receiver near the fire to warm the batteries and checked again but still no signal. We broke camp and climbed to the top of the mountain to check for a signal from the far side. At the top of mountain #9177 we got a very strong signal at 360 degrees. We started off on this bearing and followed Bruno throughout the day. We again made a dry camp for the night.

At 12:45 P.M. on September 29, we were following Bruno's signal westward back towards our base camp and starting point. When we hit the open country south of Pelican Cone we obtained our first drink since the afternoon of the previous day. Although we had filled our plastic water bottles the day before, there was not enough to quench the thirst generated by hard exercise during the heat of the day. The clear, cool water of the mountain brook tasted better than any cocktail.

From these days of tracking Bruno, and others that were to follow, we determined that his fall range was located in wilderness country, far from roads and human activity. Although he had visited the Trout Creek dump in summer, he was not at all dependent on this human food source, and all the food that he consumed during the last two months before hibernating was foraged from nature (and was quite varied, including even frozen mushrooms). However, each year he would return to the dump as well as to other places where he had successfully found food in the past. Bruno led us almost to the eastern border of Yellowstone, and we suspected that we had been close to his winter den site, but as the snows of late fall grew deeper, we were unable to make the daily seven- or eight-mile trek necessary to get back into his range. We tried horses, but they were a handicap in the heavy windfall and downed timber. Finally we had to decide whether to keep after Bruno or follow Marian and some of the other grizzlies that were more accessible. With reluctance we gave up tracking Bruno to his winter den. We had plotted his fall range at about twelve square miles. Although he stayed within this area for approximately two months, we knew that his annual range was much larger and that his lifetime home range might well embrace a sizable part of Yellowstone National Park. The following spring Bruno was observed on the south side of Yellowstone Lake at Flat Mountain Arm, feeding on cutthroat trout that ran up the small streams to spawn. As the bear traveled, this was at least fifty miles from the point where we had last picked up his signal in the fall of 1964. From tracking and other sightings, it was evident that Bruno had a lifetime home range of a thousand square miles or more. Although he stayed for long periods of time in limited locales, he was a wanderer compared to many other bears.

During our study we delineated twenty different grizzly bear ranges. We worked out the home ranges of eight different bears and plotted the lifetime range of Marian. We found that the size of grizzly bears' seasonal and home ranges varied widely and was influenced by many factors, including the availability, amount, and distribution of food; availability of mates; den site locations; and the age, sex, and condition of the animal. Other factors were the variety and combination of habitat types, and long-established patterns of travel and feeding. The radio-measured home ranges varied in size from a maximum of 125 to the smallest of 20 square miles. In general the ranges of recently weaned or mature males were larger than those of females, but we measured the Sour Creek Sow's range at 106 square miles, and Marian's close companion, Number 101, had a home range of 41 square miles. Both of these were larger than the home ranges of yearling boars Number 188 and Number 202. Sow Number 96 had a split seasonal range much like Bruno's. In the course of a week, she and her cubs traveled thirty-one airline miles from her spring range and den area to her summer range in Hayden Valley. Her summer range was considerably larger than the twelve-square-mile range of Sow Number 34; it was about the size of that of Sow Number 75, which embraced thirty-six square miles.

Bear movement and the size of individual ranges are influenced by the availability of food sources such as carrion and berry and pine nut crops. However, the ranges of almost all the Yellowstone grizzlies were affected to some extent by the presence and abundance of food at the Trout Creek refuse area. Many bears fed there for varying periods of time. It was becoming apparent that the grizzlies congregating in summer in Hayden Valley and at the Trout Creek refuse area were not only bears from close by but included a number that moved in from points far beyond Yellowstone National Park. Our findings on the extent of the grizzlies' annual migrations seemed clearly to indicate that these grizzlies were all part of a single ecosystem population. (See map on page 159 for a simplified picture of this long-distance movement and concentration.)

Out of our work there emerged two types of grizzly bear home and seasonal ranges. One was a discrete, well-defined home range used throughout the year, and the other a larger area consisting of a summer foraging area connected by a migratory corridor to a late fall and early spring range that contained the winter den site. Marian's range was typical of the former; Bruno's exemplified the latter, an annual early and late summer range separated by considerable distance from the spring and fall range, wherein lay his den site. The yearling male

Movement of Grizzlies From and Toward the Center of Yellowstone National Park *Each of the straight lines represents the recorded movement of a single bear between two points of observation, capture, or radio fixes (the lines merely connect the points; the bears do not, of course, travel in a straight line). Much of this movement is seasonal migration, the bears congregating in the Hayden Valley area for summer foraging and dispersing in the fall. The quantity and extent of such movements supports the existence of a single ecosystem population rather than one group of bears in the central region and a separate "backcountry" population.*

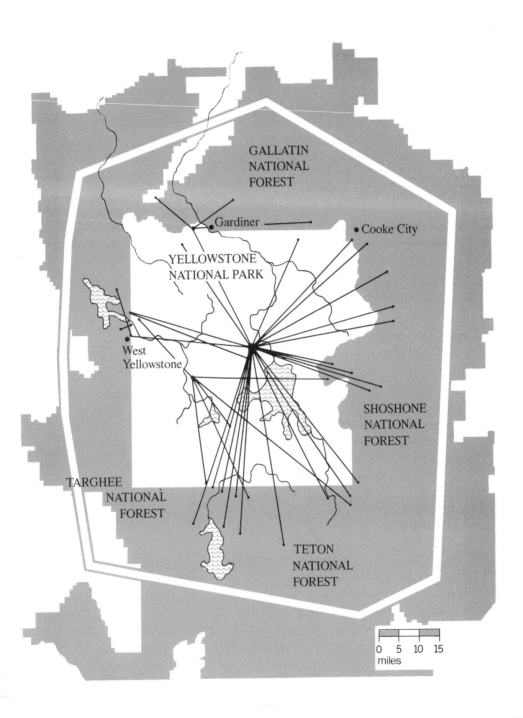

GALLATIN
NATIONAL
FOREST

Gardiner

Cooke City

YELLOWSTONE
NATIONAL PARK

West
Yellowstone

SHOSHONE
NATIONAL
FOREST

TARGHEE
NATIONAL
FOREST

TETON
NATIONAL
FOREST

0   5   10   15
miles

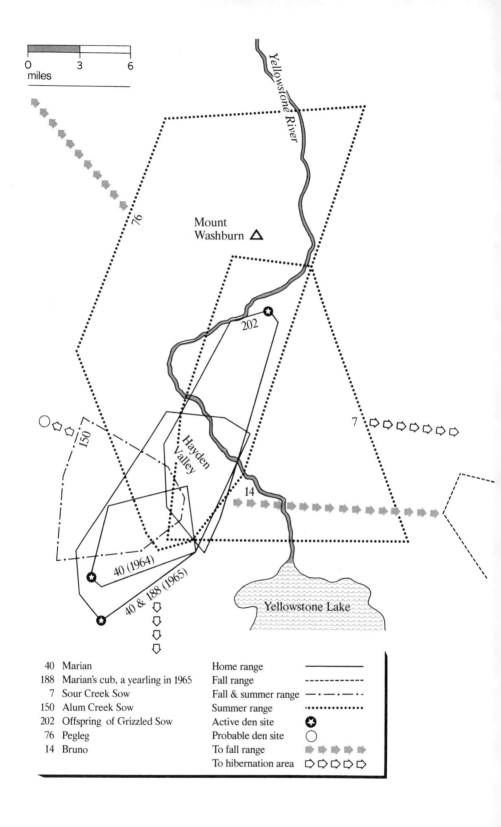

40	Marian	Home range
188	Marian's cub, a yearling in 1965	Fall range
7	Sour Creek Sow	Fall & summer range
150	Alum Creek Sow	Summer range
202	Offspring of Grizzled Sow	Active den site
76	Pegleg	Probable den site
14	Bruno	To fall range
		To hibernation area

Number 158 and Marian's cub, Number 188, had summer ranges of twenty-two and twenty square miles, respectively. These were identical in size to those of their mothers, from whom they had not strayed far. In late fall of 1965, as a yearling on his own, Number 188 traveled rapidly to a distant denning site, thus greatly expanding the size of his summer range and initiating a range pattern similar to that of Bruno. We found that Number 202, in contrast, developed a discrete range pattern similar to that of his mother, the Grizzled Sow, and to Marian's. His range expanded from 27 square miles in 1965 (when he was yearling) to 125 square miles in 1966. Our study of this bear's lifetime range ended when he was killed after re-entering Canyon Campground in August 1966.

Although grizzly bear ranges tended to conform to the two patterns just described, each was a discrete entity that existed from year to year with only minor modifications. Within any of these spatial entities numerous grizzlies carried out daily and seasonal activities without major conflict or territorial defense. In other words, ranges overlapped; they were the habitats picked out and utilized by individual bears but shared by many, and were not spatially separated, as is the case with territorial species. Marian and her companions congregated in the vicinity of food sources: refuse dumps, carrion, berry patches, pine nut stands, clover fields, and sedge seepages. Their daytime retreats or beds were made in nearby dense timber, and numerous grizzlies regularly used the same retreats at the same time. (In one small timbered bedding area, we jumped thirteen grizzlies within a matter of minutes. The forest seemed to erupt bears.) We did not observe territorial defense of a seasonal range or home range, and all behavior indicated that defense activities related to territory were largely nonexistent. The peripheries of ranges were definitely not defended, nor were den sites nor feeding areas. At refuse dumps or

Pattern and Overlap of Grizzly Bear Ranges *This map distinguishes several types of grizzly ranges according to season (see legend). Some bears, as indicated, travel considerable distances to a separate fall foraging range or to a hibernation site; others, such as Marian and the young boar Number 202, develop a discrete range pattern. The map also shows that sharing of large parts of ranges by many grizzlies is common, suggesting the absence of territoriality.*

around carcasses, a show of dominance that temporarily postponed communal feeding seemed to substitute when needed for any clear-cut defense of a definite territory, large or small.

As noted earlier, the grizzly social hierarchy and the territorial behavior of other creatures have a parallel function: to minimize conflict between members of the same species. It was quite noticeable that cooperation was fundamental to the activities of the bear community. Although aggressiveness was readily used and consistently observed, it was this underlying cooperation that enabled the bears to function in harmony with one another and with their Yellowstone environment, which included other wildlife and people as well. Any intrusion on this delicate balance would cause disturbances both to this well-adjusted bear community and to man.

8

The Yellowstone Population

Through our radio research we were learning many things about individual grizzly bears: where Number 202 dug his winter dens, the size and characteristics of the Alum Creek Sow's home range, Number 170's strong homing instincts, Number 101's sharing of Marian's family burdens, the Sour Creek Sow's fall feeding habits, the lack of territoriality exhibited by Marian and other instrumented grizzlies. We instrumented Number 101 at age ten and a half in order to learn more about early-season mating. Female Number 187 was observed mating at four and a half years of age and was later reinstrumented for a sixty-five day period in an attempt to determine the time interval between mating and implantation of blastocysts. Information we gathered on individual bears often applied not only to the individual but to the population as a whole; indeed, the ability to generalize was essential to our study.

The grizzly population wandered through the sagebrush country and across the alpine meadows, roamed the coniferous forests, swam the rivers, and climbed the multi-flowered mountain slopes within the Yellowstone ecosystem. At times it was widely dispersed throughout this extensive wilderness area, some bears living in family groups, others as lone males or young females. Seasonally, as we have seen, large segments of the population moved inward to concentrate at relatively small feeding areas. This distribution pattern characterized the population as a unit and could be observed in microcosm in a single bear as well. Many other life processes and cycles were exhibited throughout the population: it reproduced, grew, consumed various types of food, slept through the long winter, dug dens, fought, mated—and in time, like the individual, each generation died.

As we realized from the start of our study, in order to understand the grizzly bear and to formulate recommendations for its management, we needed to compile and analyze information that represented the entire bear community. A major goal was to arrive at as accurate a figure as possible for the total size of the population. It was also essential to know its composition in terms of age and sex and its growth trends; was the population static or were bear numbers increasing or declining?

These were the larger questions, but to fully understand the dynamics of the grizzly population we needed still more details. Only by observing individuals could we learn at what age the females first produced young, the number of cubs per litter, the number produced annually, causes of death, longevity, as well as the average life span of a grizzly. Particularly important was the reproductive life of females—at what age could sows still give birth to young? Such data, accumulated slowly, bit by bit, in the field, could be averaged over the years to give a representative picture and correlated with such factors as the bears' daily and seasonal movements, size of ranges, habitat preference, food supply, and other influences—the hows and whys of population characteristics and trends.

To gather this wide range of information required both trained personnel and a variety of research methods, chief among which was to develop and maintain a reliable grizzly bear census. The data we sought was similar to that acquired through making censuses of human populations: the type of information compiled in the actuarial tables of life insurance companies. Gathering such information about bears, however, presented some challenges. We couldn't put out questionnaires, interview our subjects, or otherwise communicate with the animals. Our task was further complicated by the vast, largely timbered area over which the grizzlies roamed, and by the fact that they tended to be nocturnal.

The most effective technique in censusing was to capture bears and mark them so that we could recognize individuals from a distance, year after year, and even keep track of entire families. Marking was essential to accurate counting, so we early gave it high priority, and we made special efforts to mark grizzlies of known ages. Harry Reynolds, Jay Sumner, Jeff Nelson, Mike Stevens, Jack Seidensticker, Jim Claar, my sons, Lance and Charlie, John's son Derek, and numerous others all participated in the trapping and marking procedures. They baited and set traps, helped measure out drug doses, recorded data, assisted in weighing and measuring the animals, and learned to place a good tattoo in the bear's armpit or lip. The number of marked animals increased year by year; 30 were marked by 1959, 77 by 1960, and 122 by 1961. We marked 19, 24, and 34 in the years 1962–1964, respectively, and still more bears in subsequent years. Through 1970 we had captured and marked 264 grizzlies. There were never this many marked bears at any one time, but by keeping track of deaths we could compute the number extant in any given year. Once a substantial number of animals were marked, we were able to observe and count marked bears as well as some individuals striking enough to be recognized on their own, thus greatly reducing the chances of duplication.

Although we studied the Yellowstone grizzlies throughout their habitat, it would have been impossible to obtain accurate counts when they were dispersed over thousands of square miles of rugged wilderness. But the grizzlies' pattern of migrating each summer to the Hayden Valley area and gathering at earth-filled dumps such as those near Old Faithful, Trout Creek, West Yellowstone, and Gardiner provided us with the opportunity to observe large numbers of bears in concentrations. At Trout Creek, for example, eighty-eight grizzlies were observed on a single night in 1966; in the 1965 season 132 individuals were spotted there. The dumps, then, became the logical places to conduct our periodic counts, and we systematically censused bears at six such locations. Because the bears' habit of visiting the dumps was well established throughout the population—sows passing it on to their offspring, and the grizzly's excellent memory and strong homing instinct perpetuating it—there was a dependable gathering of bears at the dumps each year. We could thus compare the counts and information acquired in one census to others, and the summarized data for one year to the tabulations for other years.

From 1959, the first year of the study, through 1967, we made 367 censuses, each lasting three and a half hours. John, with help from University of Montana graduate students, concentrated on this aspect of the work. Marked bears were identified, unmarked bears tallied, and the sex and age of each recorded. (With unmarked bears, estimating ages was more problematic.) The censuses we made during this period revealed that the portion of the bear population we counted—both marked and unmarked animals—ranged in size from 154 animals in 1959 to 179 in 1970, with a peak of 202 in 1966. The average size of the population we censused during this period was 177 grizzlies.

But what percent of the total population did this figure represent? To calculate this we used the ratio of marked to unmarked animals encountered in our daily observations and recorded in the death statistics, and as it turned out the distribution of marked and unmarked deceased animals suggested that we were censusing a large proportion of the entire ecosystem population.

Our information on ranges and movements, and the death statistics, showed that our 264 marked grizzlies represented animals from all parts of the ecosystem. We recorded 267 deaths from 1959 through 1970, 143 of which occurred outside Yellowstone National Park and 124 inside. Of the bears that died outside the park, thirty-one were marked, seventy-two unmarked, and the status of the remaining forty unknown. By hypothesizing that the kill of marked bears outside the park is random, this particular statistic became our "control" in estimating a total population.

We took the average percentages of marked and unmarked bears killed outside the park during the twelve-year period and compared these with the average percentages of marked and unmarked grizzlies recorded on the censuses for the same period. An average of 30 percent of all bears killed outside the park were marked ones (31 animals). For the same period an average of 39 percent of all bears censused were marked (a total of 69). Assuming the kill outside the park is random, the average percentage of marked bears killed over an extended period should equal the average percentage of marked grizzlies counted in the censuses, but this would apply only if all the bears in the ecosystem moved to the census sites and were counted. If the percentage of marked grizzlies killed outside the park (30 percent) had equalled that of marked grizzlies counted in censuses (39 percent), it would have indicated that our census had included virtually all the bears in the population. Since the percentages differed, we assumed that not all the bears had been counted. The approximate number of uncounted bears would have to be determined, and the variance in the above percentages was used in calculating this. Letting x represent the unmarked bears that never visited the dumps and were thus never censused, the total ecosystem population would be 177 (the average number of bears censused) plus x. With further computations we figured that x equalled 52 animals never counted in our annual censuses; thus the average population for the total ecosystem was 177 plus 52, or 229 grizzlies. Translating back into percentages, this meant that our yearly average of 177 bears censused at the dumps represented 77 percent of the total ecosystem population.

The estimated figure of 229 was the average number of grizzlies that inhabited this extensive ecosystem during the period of our intensive study. There were fewer in later years when, as we shall see, grizzly numbers declined. Some of the fifty-two grizzlies that we did not count probably lived in rather restricted locales, similar to Marian's home range, where all the necessities for their existence were supplied for a year or more. In the course of a long lifetime many of these grizzlies would probably be attracted to the dumps, but temporarily they lived singly and in family groups within the park and in the bear habitat surrounding the park.

Prior to using our population data to compute these uncounted bears, we encouraged the Wyoming Game and Fish Department and U.S. Forest Service to carry out a census of grizzlies in areas surrounding Yellowstone National Park at a time when the grizzly concentration at dumps reached a peak. This was to be a direct observational count of grizzlies. One purpose was to determine whether there was a separate population unit unaffected by seasonal movement to dumps.

The two-agency census was carried out in August 1969, and the technique was to place carcasses in strategic locations in the Clark's Fork and Wapiti Districts of the Shoshone National Forest bordering Yellowstone Park on the east. Thirteen bait stations or carcasses were placed in open areas near timber sites preferred by grizzlies and where black bears would not come if grizzlies were present. After the baits had ripened for four days, observers watched them from a distance. The conditions were such that the deteriorating carcasses should attract all or most of the grizzlies inhabiting the area in August. On the basis of our knowledge of the grizzlies' movements we did not expect that many bears would be observed, and this proved to be the case. Only three grizzlies were seen at bait stations, but twenty-two individual black bears were sighted. In addition, more grizzlies were observed throughout this extensive area in spring and fall even without the attraction of bait, prior to the bears' migration to the park and after their dispersal throughout the park and beyond its borders. These results confirmed that we were dealing with a single population most of whose members sooner or later visited a Park Service or municipal dump.

According to Forest Service biologist Larry Mullen, approximately twenty-five to thirty percent of the grizzlies seen during 1969 and 1970 in Shoshone National Forest were marked animals that we had tagged in Yellowstone. These observations and the census results tended to confirm our conclusions that in summer we were counting about three-fourths of the bears in the entire grizzly bear ecosystem.

We also needed to know the average age structure of the population, that is, what percentage of the total was accounted for by each age class: cubs, two- and three-year-olds, subadults, and adults. Each age class consisted of one or more cohorts. All bears born in a given year belonged to the same cohort or generation; thus at any given time all the cohorts, or all the living generations of bears, composed the population. The members of a cohort were all born in dens at about the same time—midwinter—but the time, place, and conditions of their deaths varied greatly. In general, the older the cohort the fewer the individuals composing it, as members were continually dying off. Marian, born the year before our study began, was a member of the 1958 cohort. We relegated bears to this cohort by aging yearlings and two- and three-year-old bears captured in 1959, 1960, and 1961 (we later modified this somewhat after perfecting more precise methods of aging younger bears as well as adults). In any event, we could definitely assign only a small number of bears to the 1958 cohort: by 1962 it consisted of five age-established bears, compared to seventeen for the 1959 cohort.

The techniques by which we were able to tell the age of a grizzly varied. The most obvious of these was observation of the individual as a cub or yearling. Another important method for young bears was to compare tooth development, emergence, and wear. It was neither possible nor desirable to collect a large and representative set of real jaws, as can be done with an abundant game species such as elk or deer, so to circumvent the need for this, we made a geltrate mold and subsequently a cast of the upper and lower jaws of each immature bear we captured. We aged the older animals by counting the rings or annuli in the cross-sections of the fourth premolar, just as is done with trees. A broad cementum ring is laid down during the summer period of activity and a very narrow one during hibernation.

From information on the birth and death of known-age individuals, we would eventually determine the mortality rate at specific ages and obtain longevity figures, average life span, and eventually the time it took for a population to completely turn over. This type of data would trickle in for years.

In the course of marking and processing more than six hundred grizzlies, we were bound to have a few thrilling, and occasionally traumatic experiences, though these were rare exceptions to the routine.

In one such episode the bear that we later named Ivan the Terrible (Number 41) recovered rapidly from the effects of the immobilizing drug while we were still working. Because we tended to underdose rather than over, thus erring in favor of the bear, an untimely return to consciousness was not unheard of. In this case, we already had Ivan's jaw impressions, from which we would later pour a cast, but had yet to mark one ear with a tag and make a plaster mold of his right front paw. By working up to the last possible moment, we found ourselves trying to hold down a struggling giant. With a tremendous effort he threw John aside, rolled to his feet and took a few menacing but wobbly steps forward while our entire crew raced for safety. For a few seconds Ivan's attention was diverted by our marking and tattooing equipment, which he batted around in all directions, then sank his large canines into the heavy metal box holding our immobilizing darts and drugs. On later examination, the holes looked like they had been made by rifle bullets. We managed to reach a station wagon and had barely slammed the doors when Ivan's charge propelled him against the front of the car and on up and across the hood. At that moment there seemed little reason to doubt that he would keep coming on through the windshield. That was his intention, but his coordination was still not up to par. He slid to the ground as we gunned the motor and started off through the sagebrush. Ivan regained his feet, chased us, and managed to rake the back end of the station wagon with his lethal front paws. There remained a clear shiny imprint of bear claws, a memento that we chose not to obliterate with a fresh coat of paint. Among the human population that coexisted with the bears, and especially within the small group labeled "bear researchers," the marks were a status symbol. Not everybody could own a car distinctively decorated by a grizzly.

When we captured cubs or yearlings, the sows usually temporarily deserted their offspring, seldom waiting around until we checked the traps. Typically there were exceptions, and one occurred in the case of the Sour Creek Sow, grizzly Number 7. We had captured her cub Lonesome (Number 6) and she was still lingering around when we approached the trap. We planned to quickly weigh, measure, mark, and release the cub, then get away as fast as possible. Keeping an eye on the sow in the distance, we removed the cub from the trap. While we were engrossed with marking her, the Sour Creek Sow came directly toward us—slowly at first, then on the run. We hurriedly lifted the immobilized cub into a pickup and started off to a new location where we could complete our work. Several miles away we stopped and had no sooner renewed our operations than we saw the cub's mother coursing back and forth through the sagebrush like a bird dog on a scent. She was trying to locate her youngster, and with each passing minute she was approaching closer. At that distance her eyesight was of no value but her nose would soon tell her where we were. We worked frantically with the now struggling cub and finally released her just as the sow got our scent and once again started directly toward us. Only the reunion of mother and cub a stone's throw away from us prevented another tangle between researchers and an enraged grizzly.

An incident with a still different twist occurred when we trapped the Sour Creek Sow but not her cubs. They hung around the trap, providing us with the unexpected opportunity to immobilize and capture the rest of them along with the mother. Marking an entire family was a bonanza for making future observations. We weighed the sow in a nylon net hoisted by winch from a metal tripod, and we took a blood sample for chemical analysis and some samples of her milk. When we were finished we released the still immobile sow and moved off. One of her cubs was already moving and he was hungry, his mother having been in the trap the previous night. He walked over to where she lay sleeping, trampled roughshod over her face and head searching for her nipples, and tried to nurse. Finding this unrewarding under the circumstances, he again walked over her body and face, nudged and smelled her, then left looking both perplexed and discouraged. When the Sour Creek Sow regained the use of her muscles she lumbered off and by evening had rounded up her cubs.

In early July of 1963, female grizzly Number 96, whom we had lost while trying to track her to a den the year before, appeared in Hayden Valley with her radio collar still intact. It was riding quite well with the battery pack tucked under her chin but almost invisible beneath the long guard hairs on her neck. She arrived with only one cub but had earlier been observed with two at Cache Creek, thirty-two airline miles away. The second cub might have been killed, died from natural causes, or been picked up and adopted by another mother bear. We never found out, but we could keep tabs on Number 96's remaining cub by reinstrumenting her. When the immobilizing dart struck her, she took off at a run toward Trout Creek, but her movements slowed as she approached the stream, and we hoped she would collapse before plunging into the water. Though her muscle coordination was now obviously affected, she nevertheless attempted to swim but collapsed in midstream. Her head was still above water when we ran to the creek, waded in waist-deep, and pulled her safely to shore. It had been a close call for one of our instrumented bears, and one for whom we had developed quite an affection.

Our census data gathered over the eight-year period from 1959 to 1967 revealed that the Yellowstone population varied in age from cubs to ancient citizens twenty-six years old or older. When we totalled all our counts and averaged the various totals, we found that the composition of the population by age was about 19 percent cubs, 13 percent yearlings, and 10 percent two-year-olds. Almost 15 percent were three- and four-year-olds, and close to 44 percent adults, that is five years or older.

At the end of this period Marian was an adult, ten years old and several times a mother. In 1958, when she was born, her sex had been in the minority, for in the younger age classes there were more males than females. As an adult, however, her sex represented the majority, for by then the sex ratio of adults was slightly in favor of females (54 percent). This change of the sex ratio in favor of mature females might have been due to the fact that although outside the park the grizzly was considered a trophy animal, sows with cubs could not be legally killed by hunters in either Wyoming or Montana. Thus the selective killing of males, especially large trophy specimens, caused a differential mortality which over a period of time resulted in a population with more mature females than males. Had the population not been hunted, the sex ratio would very likely have been one to one.

In our census we kept close track of females with cubs, since it was of particular significance to get accurate counts each year on the number of cubs and the size of litters. The average annual litter size varied from 1.80 in 1959 to 2.50 in both 1963 and 1967. The nine-year average was 2.2 cubs per litter. Using the data from annual counts of adult females with cubs and information about the females' reproductive cycles, John and his University of Montana collaborators were able to determine reproductive rates for both individuals and the total population, in other words, the number of cubs produced per adult female per year. This was calculated by dividing litter size by the length of the reproductive cycle.

A reproductive cycle is the time from one pregnancy to another, determined by observing various females year after year. Marian, for example, had three reproductive cycles over a seven-year period; thus her reproductive cycle averaged 2.3 years, relatively short for a grizzly. The average reproductive cycle for thirty Yellowstone grizzlies was 3.4 years and varied from 2 to 7 years. In terms of breeding cycles and production of litters, Marian was prolific. She had three reproductive cycles—two 2-year cycles and one 1-year cycle. Her reproductive period was seven years and she produced a total of seven cubs: thus her reproductive rate was 1.0.

Her close companion, Number 101, who had adopted Marian's yearlings in 1968, had three reproductive cycles in a reproductive period of eight years but produced a total of only four cubs, thus reducing her reproductive rate to 0.5, or just half that of Marian. At the other extreme was Number 65, the Grizzled Sow, with three 2-year reproductive cycles in a period of six years. She produced nine cubs, including a litter of four in 1965. Her reproductive rate was 1.5, the highest of any individual measured. The average rate for the thirty female grizzlies in our sample was 0.658, and 0.626 for all observed females. The highest annual reproductive rate for the population as a whole was 0.735 in 1963 and 1967. Between 1971 and 1973 the average reproductive rate declined to 0.56 and the average litter size dropped from 2.2 to 1.93.

We found that the females can first breed successfully at four and a half years, thereby producing young at age five, though many may not reproduce until they are eight or nine years old. Only about 45 percent of the adult females, or roughly fifteen animals in the censused population, produced cubs each year, because of the wide variation in reproductive cycles. Thus each year the grizzly population level was being maintained by relatively few productive females. It was obvious that an increase in the death rate of adult females and a consequent decrease in the number of cubs produced annually could cause a rapid and serious decline in this relatively small population.

After tens of thousands of years of adaptation the grizzly bear population, just like one of elk or mice or birds, lived in a particular environment normally suited to its needs. The bear population, of course, was not separate from this environment but intricately involved with it, a factor in shaping its own world. The bears in this population reacted to and interacted with the other animal populations of the Yellowstone ecosystem, and all life forms, plant and animal, were in varying degrees interdependent. For example, a sizable proportion of the grizzly bear diet consisted of the carcasses of animals dying off from various large mammal populations: bison, elk, moose, black bear, deer, and antelope. In death, these animals furnished food for the grizzlies. By dismembering carcasses with their powerful jaws, ripping the tough hides, or baring and opening the rib cages, the bears in turn made it possible for less well-equipped carnivorous scavengers — coyotes, for example — to obtain food.

Normally the grizzlies detected decomposing bodies through their keen sense of smell, but at least one incident suggested a different explanation. From closely occurring sightings we learned that Number 94 moved eight and a half airline miles directly to a carcass. The wind was favorable, but it seems improbable that he scented the carcass at such a distance. We often noted the presence at a carcass of ravens and magpies which fed when the bears' appetites were satisfied, and quite regularly the ravens were on the scene even before it was discovered by the grizzlies. They would circle above it, then land, and the first to approach would consume the eyes, which were easily available. After this it was nearly impossible for the ravens to get more sustenance until the carcass was torn open. At one elk carcass within Marian's home range, the first raven to spot it took off, and before long there was a growing assemblage of the large black birds. Some circled overhead, others perched in nearby trees, and still others landed and cautiously approached the food on foot. It seemed that first one raven, then another, had communicated to the raven community that food was available. I have observed free-flying pet ravens apparently do this again and again. I am inclined to believe that in some way they also announce the presence of a carcass to both coyotes and bears. This could explain how Number 94 knew to move rapidly eight and a half miles, and another marked grizzly eighteen miles, to feast on a carcass. Upon arrival the grizzlies ripped the carcass open and scattered food so that the ravens feasted too — an interrelationship profitable to both parties.

A more subtle and delayed type of interdependence also results when grizzlies detect a carcass and move in to feed. At such times they defecate in the area, passing tremendous quantities of berries, grass, or the bulbs of grass and other plants. Around one carcass I found seventeen fresh and apparently spontaneous bowel eliminations. The purpose of this act was unclear, but it appeared related to a sudden change of diet, from plant to meat. The bears, being omnivorous feeders, would need to secrete different digestive enzymes for the digestion of carbohydrates — their diet of bulbs, grasses, and berries — and the massive amount of protein they would consume from a carcass. By rapidly eliminating the former food, they were perhaps capable of more fully digesting the tremendous quantities of meat from the carcass. Whatever the reason, the bears' feces contained seeds of numerous plants: huckleberry, whortleberry, mountain ash, and even seeds of the five-needle pines. Practically unaffected by digestion were quantities of the bulbs of the onion grass, *Melica* (there are various species). Such defecations provided seeds and bulbs for the potential germination and growth of all of those plants, and in the case of the onion grass also assured wide distribution of a staple plant food of the grizzly. The grass was also consumed by ground squirrels, pocket gophers, and meadow mice, which in turn would be an important source of food for the grizzlies during spring and fall, particularly during the years when these rodent populations were high.

Two major forces are continually at work on the bear population, as well as on other animals within the community: elk, coyotes, ravens, ground squirrels, mice, and even man. These forces are biotic potential and environmental resistance. The biotic potential represents the reproductive force, the maximum number of bears that potentially can be produced each year by the Yellowstone population—which potential is never actually achieved. Opposing this are the environmental factors that cause death to various individuals in the community, including seasons of food scarcity, severe winters, disease, fights with other bears, conflict with man, and other circumstances. Environmental resistance, then, is the sum of all the physical and biological factors that oppose the growth of the bear population.

The two forces, which are expressed in the population as the rate of birth, or natality, and the rate of death, or mortality, fluctuate but in the long run tend to equalize each other, resulting in a more or less stable population. This equilibrium is a delicate one, however, and a significant change in any one or more environmental factors can shift the balance. Excessive reproduction tends to increase the size of a population; excessive mortality reduces it, and both can change the age structure. Assuming mortality remains significantly unchanged, if the birth rate increases, the population will grow and will consist of more young animals; when it decreases, the proportion of older animals increases and the size of the population declines.

During the period of our most intensive study, from 1959 to 1967, natality and mortality remained more or less in equilibrium. There was little change in the size of the grizzly bear population, indicating that the carrying capacity of the environment for grizzlies, as modified by then current circumstances, had about been reached. In fact, births during this time slightly exceeded deaths, and the population we were censusing grew at an average rate of approximately 2.4 percent per year. More grizzlies were born and were living to become adults than were dying each year. A stable age distribution had also been attained; that is, the relative numbers of young bears to adults remained more or less constant. Unfortunately this happy situation was about to be reversed, and mortalities would soon far outstrip the number of new bears added each year to the population.

9

The Pattern of
Mortality

The term mortality can refer to the death of any individual of a
species and also, as described in the preceding chapter, to the sum of
all the forces of environmental resistance which may, in time, over-
take whole populations and even the entire species. The cave bear,
Ursus speleous, became extinct at the end of the late Pleistocene
period, 500,000 years ago. A living cave bear will never again be
seen. The California grizzly, *Ursus arctos californicus,* became extinct about 1924, and a remnant grizzly population in Mexico appears
to be about to follow the California grizzly. Ecosystem populations
which once roamed large expanses of Colorado exist no more. Once-

viable populations of grizzlies can no longer be found in Idaho, Oregon, Washington, Kansas, the Dakotas, and New Mexico. In these areas, mortality exceeded reproduction, and the result was drastic decline and extermination.

Our research on the protected remnant population in the Yellowstone ecosystem revealed that up to 1967 it had been holding its own, even increasing slightly by about six grizzlies a year. The history of decline that had removed other populations had been checked here. Individual mortalities, of course, continued. Even as we were beginning to mark grizzlies for our study, the population was losing numbers—some marked bears, some not. It was an ongoing process, the fate of each bear being determined by numerous, often unpredictable variables.

The grizzly is a tough, rugged individual adapted to survive from the time he or she is a hairless, eighteen-ounce cub without sight to the age of thirty years or perhaps more, when the aging process itself brings about death. The grizzly bear does not now have, and never has had, many enemies. This means that its ways of dying are somewhat limited. Old age, of course, is one, and malnutrition due to any of a number of causes is another. Trichina, a roundworm, infects some bears and perhaps results in a few deaths; and a heavy infestation of intestinal roundworms (nematodes) and tapeworms, even if not the direct cause of death, results in lowered vitality, thus increasing susceptibility to other causes. Bears also die from infanticide, occasionally from combat wounds, and from anomalous causes such as being gored by a bison or large bull elk the grizzly has tried to bring down. The cause of the majority of deaths in the adult grizzly bear populations, however, is man, the bear's main enemy. Adaptable as it is, the grizzly has not and cannot adapt to modern man's efficient methods of killing.

Before the advent of the white man and his rifle, the number of grizzlies killed by man was probably not a major factor in that animal's mortality rate. Conflicts between bear and man occasionally terminated in the death of one or the other, or both, but these were the exception. For the most part bear and man competed but coexisted, neither having the means of eliminating the other. Meriwether Lewis wrote in his journal in 1805, "It is astonishing to see the wounds they [the grizzlies] will bear before they can be put to death." Lewis's account of the ten shots it took for William Clark and

George Drewyer to kill a grizzly is one of many such stories told and retold by frontiersmen. Another, revealing the other side of the coin, is the incredible saga of trapper Hugh Glass, who was mauled by a wounded grizzly and left for dead by his companions but somehow survived to make his way back through wild country to civilization. We had no wish to contribute to the record of violent confrontations with grizzlies and took all possible precautions to avoid both bear and human mortalities.

In the first year of our study, we were seeking optimum drug dosages for immobilizing bears and we experimented with minimum dosages so as not to lose bears. On August 11, 1959, in spite of our caution, we brought about our first casualty when we captured grizzly Number 24. He was a male cub weighing seventy pounds and had been given the minimum dose of the immobilizing drug. But with his mother threatening us nearby we had to transport him to a safer location for tagging and weighing. Meanwhile he revived enough to begin wrestling with Maurice and me. Had the struggle been simply muscle pitted against muscle it might have been an even match, but his sharp teeth and ice pick-like claws gave him a decided advantage. To subdue him, we had no choice but to give him another shot of the drug. Almost immediately the cub's respiration faltered; then the heart stopped and he was dead. Evidently a multiple dose of sucostrin, even when the second one was very small, could be lethal to a grizzly. We were a wiser crew but also saddened and depressed, as we went on to immobilize a grizzly captured in another trap that same night. The same dismay hung over us on each of the rare occasions when we lost a bear (less than 2 percent of all the bears handled in the study) to the effect of drugs. This most often occurred in campgrounds, where concern for human beings dictated that a potentially dangerous bear be immobilized quickly and surely, requiring a slightly higher dose than we would otherwise have used. The death of that first cub, though, led us to purchase a respirator for possible future emergencies.

Marked female Number 3 passed out of the population in 1959 when she had to be shot by rangers, and Number 11, at age one, met the same fate that year. Both bears were considered a threat to visiting campers. One-eye, Number 22, an adult male trapped and released on August 12, was shot by a hunter just southwest of Cooke City in October. The known grizzly bear deaths during 1959 in and around Yellowstone National Park were twelve—seven males, three females, and two whose sex we were unable to learn. Twenty-six new cubs were born in 1959.

In 1960 thirty-five cubs were added to the population of bears that we were censusing in Yellowstone, but bears born in former years were also dying off—many being killed by man. In early April, male grizzly Number 19 was shot in the town of Gardiner. In late May, rangers found it necessary to shoot a grizzly at Tower Junction; a troublesome adult male was also trapped and shot at Pelican Creek. Sylvia, grizzly sow Number 31, was trapped and sent to a zoo. Another adult female was shot by the deputy sheriff in Gardiner, and a cub was also gunned down in Gardiner in October. Just outside the western boundary of the park, near Bacon Rind, a mother grizzly was shot—her death remained unconfirmed—and her two cubs killed.

On the happier side, it was also in 1960 that Marian and her littermate were weaned as two-year-olds by an unmarked grizzly mother and went their independent ways as members of the bear population. They had made it through the most precarious years of a grizzly's life, the period from birth to the age of one and a half, during which an average of nearly thirty-nine percent of all recorded deaths occurred over eight years of study. (Forty percent occurred between one and a half and four and a half, and 21 percent through adult life to old age.) Differences between our cub counts one year and yearling counts a year later—interpreted as mortality occurring between the ages of six months and one and a half years—were 34 percent. Still another method of computation using marked bears showed only a 36 percent mortality. Roughly one-third of the bears in the youngest age class—that is, up to one and a half years—can be expected to die each year.

When we began keeping mortality records in 1959, we expected to find that only a small percentage of any generation survives to reproduce, and the results after several years bore out this speculation. Six years after we began our research, 95 percent of the 1959 cohort of nineteen marked animals had died. The bears that we could recognize in the 1960 generation, fourteen animals in all, were all gone, a 100 percent mortality, within five years. However, the females of the population—its vital reproductive nucleus—have a long reproductive life. A relatively few long-lived productive females, it appeared, were sufficient to maintain the population. This was reassuring; but dependence on a few productive sows could jeopardize the population if anything happened to drastically increase the death rate. At this early stage we had no particular forebodings but were well aware of the possibility. It had recently occurred in Colorado, where it was now doubtful that any grizzlies still existed.

The foregoing summary of our methods and the mortality-related events of the first two years of our study is a more or less accurate picture of grizzly mortality for the years up to 1968. With the help of others — rangers, fish and game department personnel, hunters, outfitters, and stockmen — we were able to obtain each year good statistics of grizzly mortalities in the Yellowstone ecosystem, which we could then relate to the census data we were accumulating at the same time. The data from each current year, added to that of those past, revealed where, when, and how members of the bear population met their deaths — and most important, how many died in relation to the numbers annually produced. Using three different computations, we determined that the average annual recorded mortality was just under 10 percent of the total censused population.

In addition to known deaths, however, there was a varying number of unrecorded deaths each year. Most were probably natural mortalities, but it is likely that some man-caused deaths were also unreported. Through annual counts of our marked bears and our ever-increasing knowledge of the size and age structure of the population, we were able to estimate that unrecorded deaths averaged about 10 percent of the censused population each year. Thus the total annual grizzly mortality was about 20 percent. The following table summarizes the results of our record-keeping for the years 1959–67 and breaks down mortalities by cause of death.

In the first nine years of our study, as the figures show, two factors — hunting and control — accounted for the bulk of the recorded adult mortality in the grizzly population. Forty-four percent of the grizzly deaths were caused by shootings outside the boundaries of Yellowstone. Control measures within the park were responsible for 30 percent and all other causes for 25 percent. The last, "cause unknown," category is larger than it should be; we did know the cause of some of these deaths, but certain records of mortality details were lost in a recent fire.

Sometimes grizzly deaths were reported to us by hunters, guides, or outfitters. At other times we heard rumors of a grizzly being shot

Table 1. Recorded Deaths of Grizzly Bears in the Yellowstone Ecosystem, 1959-1967

Cause of death	1959	1960	1961	1962	1963	1964	1965	1966	1967	1959-67 totals	Percent of total recorded deaths
Hunting	4	12	8	5	6	4	7	4	27	77	45%
Control											
1. Problem bears killed	4	9	5	5	2	2	2	6	6	41	30%
2. Bears removed from ecosystem to zoos	1	1	2		4				2	10	
Human-caused accidental deaths	3	1	1	1	1	1	2	1		11	25%
Bear–bear deaths (infanticide or combat)				1		1				2	
Natural deaths (disease or age)							1			1	
All other deaths (cause unknown)		1		3	2	4	3	2	8	28	
Total known deaths	12	24	21	15	15	12	15	13	43	170	9.6%

The grizzly bear's face **top left** is typically "dished" or saucerlike, with a shorter snout than that of the black bear **top right. Bottom:** This black bear peering out of her den near Old Faithful was the first we were able to successfully immobilize inside a den (in 1963).

Top: *Elk carcass partially buried by a grizzly.* **Bottom:** *John Craighead in the Canyon base station, plotting a radio fix to delineate a grizzly's home range.*

Instrumenting the large boar Bruno, Number 14, at night.

Frank Craighead and Charlie Ridenour radio-tracking Bruno in the Absaroka Range.

Marian and her yearling, Number 188, extended their home range in 1965 by swimming across the Yellowstone River.

Attaching numbered ear tags, a key aspect of the grizzly population census.

Top: *John Craighead and Maurice Hornocker making a mold of a grizzly's jaw, a technique for aging grizzlies.* **Bottom:** *A grizzly just recovering from the effects of drugging, about to get to its feet.*

Marian, in Hayden Valley.

and got in touch with the hunter. Such information was particularly useful when it specified the locations of grizzly kills, especially those involving marked bears — though fortunately for our study very few of our twenty-three radio-instrumented bears met violent death at the hand of man while we were working with them. In 1965 seven bears were shot by hunters outside the park. The locations — Crow Creek, Lava Creek, Brown's Meadow, Dime Creek, all in Wyoming — were widely dispersed, yet each grizzly had been marked at about the geographical center of Yellowstone National park. Plotting these kill statistics gave us information on movement and ranges and helped fill in the picture we were forming of wide dispersal of bears moving beyond the borders of Yellowstone in the fall. (See map on page 159.)

The first mortality in 1963 was grizzly Number 37, Beep, the second bear that we radio-collared. From him we had recently been learning just how a young grizzly became a troublemaker, and his career as our instructor was predictably short. He was shot by a Jackson, Wyoming, hunter along Polecat Creek about one and a half miles south of the Yellowstone border.

The same year, Number 80, dubbed the Bug-crew Bear, learned some fatal habits from a crew of young men (a "bug crew") hired for the summer to eradicate *Ribes,* or wild currant, on which forms the blister rust that kills the whitebark pine. The bug crew had been working along Carnelian Creek, which drains the watershed north of Dunraven Peak, and was eating lunch when the young grizzly approached. Although alarmed, they tossed food to him. The bear had already learned that buried remains of their lunches were tasty. Number 80 appeared the next day and the next, becoming bolder each time he was fed. Finally, he made bluffing charges that put the crew up trees while he looked around for more food, rifling packs and lunch containers. When he left this area he passed close to our Canyon laboratory on the way to Hayden Valley. We immobilized, marked, and released him. From Trout Creek he wandered on to Shoshone Lake and there his ramblings ceased. He was killed by a seasonal ranger whose cabin he had entered and torn up.

In August of 1961 the yearlings Number 53 and Number 114 of the Rip-nosed Sow had to be killed, having learned that they could get food in campgrounds. An autopsy of these two animals revealed that their intestines were heavily impacted with nematodes. Hunger caused by this infestation had forced the young bears to repeatedly seek food in the vicinity of man. In this case a natural cause, the nematode infestation, had brought about the need for control measures.

Infanticide, while not particularly common among grizzlies, was responsible for a death in Marian's first family. In 1964, at the age of six, Marian appeared in Hayden Valley with two cubs, the result of her first known mating in June of the previous year. One of the cubs, a male, we later captured and numbered 188.

One day in June Marian was busily digging plant tubers near the timbered southern border of Hayden Valley. One cub was impatiently sitting nearby while his small brother, unnoticed by the diligent but inexperienced mother, had strayed to the edge of the timber. Approaching upwind through the trees, unknown to Marian or her cub, was a large boar. He was almost on top of the tiny cub when the youngster spotted him and in terror started to run. In an instant the boar lunged, caught the cub in his powerful jaws, and dropped him to the ground. A few spasmodic twitches and the cub was one of the 1964 mortalities — his skull punctured by the boar's canines. Marian, who rushed to protect her cub as the boar ran off, was left standing bewildered over her dead young.

Just what prompted this killing is hard to say. Boars occasionally kill cubs, but why? In this case, the boar probably smelled the cub but, unable to see well, lunged instinctively at the running object, mistaking it for prey. The boar, playing no role in family life, has no instinct to protect the young or act in any way like a father. Such a relationship may allow the boar, in times of overpopulation, to be part of the species' built-in control mechanisms. Infanticide then would be a way of keeping numbers down when food is scarce, space at a premium, and survival is more difficult for bears as well as for other forms of life.

The year 1966 saw a known loss of thirteen grizzlies from the Yellowstone ecosystem population, and five of these were marked bears. Numbers 51, 154, and 174 were shot during the hunting season at Hawk's Rest, Sunlight Temple Creek Divide and Cinnibar Ranch. As in 1965 those that fell to hunters outside the park were widely distributed. Number 198 was killed by a drug dose at Old Faithful when rangers decided he must go. At Otter Creek an automobile struck Number 203, a two-and-one-half-year-old male, as he tried to cross the highway. (The automobile, one of the major killers of people, was also a cause of grizzly mortality which would undoubtedly increase as park visitation grew.) Marian whelped two cubs that year, and her older offspring, Number 188, was doing fine. Though he was now apparently completely divorced from any family ties, his chances of reaching adulthood seemed good.

Our statistics on mortalities due to natural causes were scanty because we usually had no way of knowing where or when the deaths took place, but we were on the lookout in the field for indications of such deaths. In the fall of 1966 Old Mose's gait was slow. I did not observe him to run that year, and an uphill climb seemed to be an effort. When he entered his den for the winter, he was not overly adipose but was carrying sufficient fat to take him through the winter. When he left his den in spring, he moved stiffly and each time he broke through the snow crust it was a struggle to plough along until he reached crusted snow that would support his great weight. Old Mose was tired and undoubtedly ailing. He eventually reached the bare soil around Mud Volcano, where his long white front claws stood out in marked contrast to the black soil. These unusual claws that at times flashed in the sunlight like the polished antlers of a bull elk were one of a number of characteristics that enabled us to identify this aging boar. They were apparently a mark of age, but we had observed light-colored to white claws on a few young bears, though none to compare with those of Old Mose.

Near the Mud Volcano, Old Mose found shoots of sedges and fresh green grass, but even they did not restore his energy. His tracks in the mud showed that he had wandered over to the large pool. It was surrounded by the ghostly remains of dead trees, and in the chill of early morning or late afternoon there was usually an ethereal fog drifting in the convection currents above the bubbling warm water. When filtered sunlight struck it right, both water and fog took on a blue tinge broken only by dark dead trees. It was a truly beautiful scene, yet eerie and desolate, too—a netherworld of potholes, geysers, and pools of viscous, coal-black mud in constant motion, where no green vegetation could live. And from this moving, bubbling, spraying blackness came the rumble of forces beneath the earth's surface.

I moved away to the west, investigating both grizzly and bison tracks, and reached the periphery of the thermal area of heat and sulphurous water and air. In the scanty vegetation leading on toward stunted trees, I saw a shapeless mound that nearly matched the dark soil. By the time I realized it was a grizzly, I was too close to retreat, but it was obvious in an instant that the bear was dead. Both sight and smell reinforced this conclusion. The shaggy coat, matted with mud, was dull and colorless. The one small eye that I could see was sunken. I moved closer and to one side, where a protruding front paw appeared, flashing the unmistakable ivory-colored claws of Old Mose. The bear's frame and his coloring were right. There was no doubt, Old Mose was dead. He was the first and only large, aged bear whose death we could attribute to just plain old age.

Ordinarily we would have made a museum specimen of the skin, but the hair was slipping badly from Old Mose's decaying hide. We could and did save the skull. It was our policy, whenever possible, to preserve all parts of a recently deceased bear that we felt might be usefully studied at a later date. Skulls and teeth would help us age the animals. Female reproductive organs would throw light on the interesting phenomenon of delayed implantation. From hearts, blood vessels, sections of stomach, intestine, liver, kidney, lungs, bones, and muscle tissue came information that would help us better understand the morphology and physiology of the grizzly. Much of this material, as well as blood samples for chemical analysis, was sent to our friend and collaborator, Dr. Morgan Berthong. We also sent on request some of the huge muscular hearts to the Armed Forces Institute for study. We hated to see any of the great beasts killed, but if violent death was inevitable, we were determined that it would not be wasteful or in vain.

We could save little of Old Mose, but he would provide meals for the coyotes and, after the carcass had deteriorated to a certain point, for other grizzlies. The grizzly is in a sense a cannibal; perhaps at this stage the flesh of its own kind represents only meat.

Up to 1967, the number of known grizzly deaths averaged sixteen each year. In 1967 the recorded death toll more than doubled. This was largely due to the announcement that the Wyoming hunting season would be closed in 1968. Grizzly hunting increased greatly and an unprecedented twenty-one legal bears were killed that fall, raising the total known mortalities that year to forty-three. None of these was reported as a marked grizzly, but as a result of death from other causes and shipment to zoos, we scratched off seven more of our marked bears.

Among these was our radio bear Number 202, who had been instrumented as a yearling and in 1965 had established a home range of ninety-seven square miles that encompassed Canyon Village and campground. We had already noted that his winter dens were dug on the steep slopes of the Yellowstone Canyon. In the spring of 1966 he left his winter den, swam the Yellowstone River, climbed to the north rim of the canyon, and moved into Canyon campground at night. Here he was retrapped, reinstrumented with a new transmitter, and radio-tracked for 118 days, during which he expanded his home range to embrace an area of 125 square miles, with the Canyon developed area near the center of his range. He caused no trouble that year, but in the fall he visited construction camps, received handouts, and learned the fatal association of man with food. The next spring he left his comfortable den (dug only three hundred feet from the previous year's den) and returned to his old fall haunts near Canyon campground. Although Number 202 was not an aggressive bear and had caused no injury or property damage, he had lost his native caution and respect for man and become a potential threat to park visitors. He was providing us with data on how problem bears developed—information that could well prevent future maulings and save lives—but the risk was judged by rangers to be too great and he was shot to prevent possible human injury.

In summary, during the 1959–67 research period the 170 mortalities we recorded amounted to slightly more than half of the total deaths that occurred. This averaged nineteen bears per year for a known mortality of 10.5 percent in a censused population averaging 178 animals. The overall mortality, as we saw, was in the neighborhood of 20 percent. From among the 170 recorded deaths, 68 were bears that we had trapped, marked, and studied, 74 were unmarked, and the status of 28 was unknown. The deaths of males exceeded females 77 to 51, and there were 42 whose sex we could not learn. As would be expected, more young bears died than adults: 83 and 46, respectively. The ages of 41 bears were unknown. Four of the marked animals were radio bears, though so far Marian was not among them.

We had reinstrumented her for seven consecutive years and had high hopes of continuing to do so. Among her companion radio bears, Numbers 6 (First Cub), 37 (Beep), 75, and 202 had passed away.

We did not realize it at the time, but the close of 1967 was to be a turning point in our study. Changes in park policy would drastically affect the grizzly bear population and our research. Our population statistics, including the nine years of data on grizzly bear mortality, would now provide a basis for assessing the population changes resulting from a complete alteration in bear management policy in the park.

In the years of our study prior to 1967, annual grizzly mortality, though much of it was caused by man, was still not exceeding annual gains to the population. In the six years from 1968 through 1973, 189 known deaths occurred, an average of 31.5 bears per year with maximum deaths of 53 and 48 grizzlies in 1970 and 1971, respectively (See Table 2). Park administrators, not knowing or not understanding the biology of bears and their low reproductive rate, would be eliminating more bears than could be annually replaced; mature females, the crucial nucleus of the population, were to be high among the casualties.

At the end of 1967, however, all this was still to come. Up to this point we had been studying a viable, well-adjusted grizzly bear population averaging 229 animals living comfortably in Yellowstone National Park and the surrounding forest areas. Although the grizzlies were being hunted in forest areas in Montana and Wyoming surrounding the park, and were still being killed as predators in adjoining Idaho, the population was holding its own and was doing well. Grizzly bear management, though uncoordinated and haphazard, was

Table 2.
Recorded Grizzly Bear Deaths
in the Yellowstone Ecosystem, 1968-1973

1968	1969	1970	1971	1972	1973	1968-73
21	23	53	48	27	17	189

Known deaths during this period averaged 31.5 bears per year, compared with an average of 18.9 for the period 1959-67.

adequate. Up to this time the human animal was providing sufficient protection to the grizzly to enable it to survive. This was largely due to the refuge provided by Yellowstone National Park and a realistic approach to hunting by the Wyoming Game and Fish Department. Our studies were revealing how grizzly numbers might be increased, their range expanded, and annual mortalities reduced — if this seemed desirable — and we were trying to encourage cooperative management based on the results of our research. Our studies were not completed, some of our data still unanalyzed, even after nine years of intensive field research, but we were formulating ideas and recommendations based on our findings that we felt would contribute to and improve grizzly bear management.

10

Bureaucracy
and Bear:
The Grizzly
Controversy

The year 1967, as I have indicated, was a watershed both for the grizzly bear in Yellowstone and for our ongoing field study. Events in that year were to significantly affect both the bears' future and that of our research—unfortunately, in both cases for the worse. Ironically, none of these events was the work of the Yellowstone grizzlies themselves.

In August of 1967, in faraway Glacier National Park in northern Montana, two young women were killed by grizzly bears in widely separated locations, though, by a bizarre coincidence, on the same night.* The facts surrounding this double tragedy would be investigated and debated for years to come, and the true cause or causes of the attacks still remain partly in doubt. Predictably, these deaths caused a sensation, with the result that the National Park Service was publicly criticized on the grounds that better bear management might have prevented the attacks.[2] The adverse media attention, and the reluctance or inability of the Park Service to give a straightforward response, created pressures and suspicions which would in a short time be felt at Yellowstone and have a negative impact on bear management policy there.

Another event, while far less dramatic than the Glacier killings, was to have more profound effects on the Yellowstone bear community. This was the Park Service's decision to go forward with a proposal of some long standing: to close down the earth-filled dumps scattered throughout the park and used as foraging areas by grizzlies. They would be replaced by incinerators, which were considered less of a health hazard and would also completely isolate this food source from bears. It was felt that this would be a step toward rehabilitating grizzlies to a completely wild condition.[3]

We had been aware for some time that this plan was under consideration, and we had serious reservations about it. We were not opposed to the idea in principle; indeed, we favored eliminating the unsightly and potentially unsanitary dumps if it could be done without seriously disrupting life in the bear community. We thought it could. But we differed with the Park Service over the question of how best to achieve this goal. The Park Service had made known its intention to shut down the dumps quickly, over a matter of only a couple of years. We considered this "cold turkey" approach to be misguided and dangerous, and advised that the dumps be phased out over a longer period and in conjunction with a plan to monitor the movement of the bears and to provide supplemental food sources during the period of adjustment.

---

*To put these deaths in perspective, it should be noted that in ninety-four years previous to these incidents only three persons had been killed by grizzly bears in the national parks of North America.[1]

Our reasoning was based on our painstakingly acquired knowledge of the grizzly's feeding and movement patterns — patterns which could not (and need not) be abruptly altered to conform to the policies of park administrators. The deaths in Glacier had generated considerable pressure to avoid similar incidents in Yellowstone at all costs. Yet conditions at Yellowstone were quite different. The grizzlies had been using the Yellowstone dumps as a source of easily obtained supplemental food for eighty years, but food foraged from the dumps was not associated directly with man, as were the handouts they received at Glacier. As we had seen again and again, a man-conditioned grizzly is a dangerous grizzly.

The silvertip bears have always congregated where there is food — along salmon streams, around Indian hunting grounds, where whale carcasses are beached, in clover fields, berry patches, oil exploration camps, garbage dumps — and they don't differentiate between so-called "natural" and "unnatural" food sources. Even before the dumps existed, the grizzlies of the Yellowstone ecosystem had appeared each spring in the lush meadows of Hayden Valley and vicinity; it is not really a coincidence that both bears and people found this part of Yellowstone attractive, if for different reasons. The additional food obtained at the dumps only served to make it more desirable from a grizzly's point of view. As park visitation increased, so did the amount of refuse food and in turn the number of bears that gravitated to it. Over the years they came in ever-increasing numbers from farther and farther away, until the early summer influx became an annual migration.

To repeat, we did not favor the perpetuation of this situation or advocate, as has sometimes been stated, "bear garbage dumps." But everything we had learned about grizzlies led us to the conviction that the dumps did, in fact, separate grizzlies from people. We knew that the bears would continue to return to the areas where they had formerly found food. If the dumps were closed abruptly and supplemental food such as elk carcasses were not provided* to draw the

---

*We had experimented with the use of baits over a period of years and found the procedure very effective in drawing bears from distant and diverse habitats, and congregating them in a small localized area. In one instance we attracted twenty-four grizzlies to a single carcass. It was a proven and effective management tool for separating grizzlies and visitors, a function that had been performed by the dumps.

grizzlies away from campgrounds, they would continue foraging and in doing so would inevitably make their way into the nearby campgrounds. This could only result in more grizzly incidents, increased danger to visitors, and an opportunity for many more bears to learn to associate food with the presence of man.

These warnings were set forth in some detail—indeed, constituted one of the crucial recommendations—in a 113-page report titled "Management of Bears in Yellowstone National Park," which we submitted to the Park Service in draft in the spring of 1967 at its request. This report was based on the findings of our largely independently financed research—that is, it had not been initiated or significantly funded by the Park Service—and it contained numerous suggestions for improving bear management policy in Yellowstone to the greater benefit of administrators, bears, and visitors. John S. McLaughlin, who served as superintendent for a brief period following the transfer of Lemuel Garrison and was the first to receive the report, said that he was glad to have it because it contained a great deal of information that would be of help to the park.[4] (The report was never published in its original form, but many of its recommendations were later incorporated into publications authored by John Craighead and myself. Some of these are listed in the Bibliography, and most of the salient points of the report are covered in the Appendix, "Management of the Yellowstone Grizzly.")

The wording of our report with respect to the potential hazard of rapid dump closures was explicit: "The net result could be tragic personal injury, costly damages, and a drastic reduction in the number of grizzlies." The draft report was made available to the Park Service about a year in advance of the first scheduled closing of a dump, with the intent of helping the Service with the problem of changing the established feeding patterns of the grizzly bears. We made in good faith what we considered to be reasonable recommendations, citing extensive research data to support our views. Six months passed, however, with no response from the Park Service to our request for any comments or suggestions they had. At first we were puzzled, but before long it was to become clear that, as outsiders questioning a policy and procedures already approved at high levels in the Park Service, we had unwittingly touched off a storm in what had become an increasingly charged atmosphere. Slowly at first, then more rapidly, we would be pulled into a bureaucratic hurricane.

This manmade storm would not blow over quickly — indeed, it was to grow in intensity from the end of 1967 onward — and it soon became obvious that both our research effort and the grizzly bear population in Yellowstone were considered ultimately expendable by the Park Service bureaucracy when its own power and prestige were at stake. We, as independent researchers, and the scientific knowledge we had gathered, came to be viewed as a threat to the policy-making establishment, as is invariably the case when policy is being made in response to political and administrative expedience rather than on the basis of informed and impartial judgment.

It is difficult to try to pinpoint just what brought about this drastic change in climate, at first bewildering to us after many years of close and relatively amicable cooperation with the Park Service. No doubt various factors were involved (including repercussions from the Glacier deaths). However, it is evident in retrospect that the circumstance most directly responsible for the deterioration of relations was the change that took place in Yellowstone Park administration late in 1967, when Jack Anderson became superintendent and Glen F. Cole his supervisory research biologist. Within a remarkably short time, the rapport that had been established and fostered during the preceding years vanished, and the working relationship came to be characterized by mistrust, suspicion, and what we could only interpret as hostility. Our research programs on grizzlies and other animals began to be subverted or appropriated by Park Service personnel, with no explanation offered or discussion permitted; we were harassed in a variety of ways in our efforts to continue our work; the results of our research were consistently disparaged and misrepresented to the public; and our recommendations on management were completely disregarded.

This chapter will trace our deteriorating relationship with the Park Service through the end of our study and beyond. However, my chief purpose remains to show how policy changes in Yellowstone after 1967 affected the grizzly community. Incidents involving ourselves will be used only when necessary to reflect these policy changes. The point I intend to clearly establish is that the policies and actions of the Park Service during this post-1967 period and the ensuing controversy over management, research, and bureaucratic prerogatives, in the end served neither the grizzlies, the cause of science, nor the people who visit this national park.

In 1968 the Park Service moved to implement its decision to close the dumps rapidly, the first act being to drastically reduce the volume of refuse food at the Trout Creek dump, located within eight miles of the Canyon, Lake, and Fishing Bridge campgrounds. Throughout that summer grizzlies were seen in campgrounds in unprecedented numbers, as attested to by many rangers (some of whom confided to us that our predictions had been right on the nose). As many as eight or nine grizzlies were seen in Canyon campground on a single night. The number of "bear actions" (trapping, transplanting, or eliminating) and incidents involving humans and grizzlies in the Lake campground, as recorded in the official bear logs, increased from thirty-three known incidents in 1966 and nine in 1967 to eighty-four in 1968. The number of grizzlies captured in campgrounds during 1968 rose to about four times the average for the previous nine years.

Most of these incidents involved bears that had lost their normal caution of humans through successful foraging in campgrounds, where they had found available food or even received handouts. It must be emphasized that this kind of conditioning could not be acquired at relatively isolated dumps but could only occur where man had been repeatedly encountered in connection with a food source. Though such man-conditioned animals may coexist with people for some time, there is a tendency for the bears to approach ever closer, and if startled or provoked by a human at close range to attack.

We documented most of the serious bear–man confrontations in 1968, some of which were close calls for the people involved and nearly all of which led to the death of a grizzly. In some of these cases the bear's death had probably become necessary, but most such incidents could have been prevented. They were directly attributable to a policy that forced hungry grizzlies into campgrounds. Equally serious, the public was not receiving adequate warning of these dangerous conditions at the time. Given these circumstances, we considered it little short of miraculous that more serious and tragic encounters had not occurred.

The events of 1968 clearly signaled that both scientists and grizzlies were on a collision course with bureaucracy. For the bears, who could not foresee the changes that would be forced on them, it was becoming a life-and-death matter; according to rangers sympathetic to the bears' plight, the unofficial policy of the park superintendent was: Get rid of the bears, just don't let the superintendent know. In the words of one ranger: " 'Take care of your problem bears at the local level in your own way; we don't need to hear about it at park headquarters.' "[5] We at least were aware of what was happening. The Park Service seemed blindly committed to a bear management policy based not on the available scientific information but on wishful thinking and expedience. Jack Anderson and Glen Cole made the decisions as they saw fit, and these, in the bureaucratic tradition of closing ranks, went unquestioned by those at higher levels. Anderson and Cole ignored our suggestions; indeed, they seemed to view any attempt on our part to influence policy as a personal attack on themselves. They also brought pressure on us to publicly support their policy, which was worse. We did not feel they were obliged to accept our assessment of the situation or to act on the basis of our findings, but we could not tolerate the public misrepresentation of our work and our positions. It was this last that escalated a disagreement in views into a Controversy.

On July 9, 1968, Glen Cole visited the research team at our Canyon laboratory. According to my notebook, written at the time:

> *Glen Cole dropped by the laboratory, said he thought we wanted to cooperate and then said we were doing all we could to clobber the Park Service and give them a bad public image. He mentioned a recent article in the Great Falls, Montana, newspaper and quotes from John. Neither of us knew about or had even seen the article.*

> *A predator-control agent of the federal government was setting grizzly bear snares in the Canyon Campground. I mentioned this use of snares [dangerous to visitors] and he [Cole] said they had no intention of telling us everything they did—this after saying he wanted to cooperate. We suggested it might help both them and us to consult ahead on some things and he said the Park Service has no intention of consulting with us, but would do what they wanted. We discussed the Glacier incident [death of two girls by grizzly bears] and he admitted the report was a whitewash, due to the fact that both the Park Service and concessioneers were at fault and could be sued under the Tort-Claims Act. He said the true situation would probably only be known if cases came to court. I said it seemed to me that this approach would hurt them in court. I indicated that the coverup*

in the past, and now, just meant that more people would be harmed before a solution based on fact was finally sought.

At the same discussion, Cole insisted that we were to give out the information in the official Glacier Report when questioned by the public. And he went further to state that if we did not do this they would see that we were pushed out of Yellowstone.[6] I told Cole that we had no intention of causing trouble for the Park Service, but that I would not give out information that he himself admitted was false. I said that when questioned by the public at meetings and lectures I would give out information based on our research on the grizzly bear in Yellowstone National Park.

Jay Sumner, a research assistant, was present at this discussion, and I asked him to write up the conversation in detail. His notes support mine recorded here.[7]

At a meeting early in 1968 to discuss our "Management of Bears" report, Superintendent Jack Anderson expressed a similarly hostile attitude but took a somewhat different approach, first claiming that we were withholding information from the Park Service and then making it clear that he was not interested in any information we had to offer. Again, from my notes made at the time:

Jack Anderson brought up the subject which he liked to harp on and which was apparently pressed by Glen Cole; that is, that we were not giving the Park any information needed for management and that we were not getting out papers and publications. I told Anderson that this was not the truth, that there was a whole stack of quarterly and annual reports on our grizzly research, all sent to the Park, that there were other papers and publications that we had published and that had been provided to Park personnel. [At this time they had had the draft of the 113-page "Management of Bears" report for about one year.] I also told him that in any long-range ecological study it was necessary to carry out some aspects of the work for six to eight, even ten years before compiling the data and drawing conclusions. I said that this type of data could not always be immediately available. I then pushed two new publications, progress reports published by the National Geographic Society,

*across his desk and asked Anderson if he had seen them. I said
that we'd sent them to Park Service personnel. He said no, he
hadn't seen them, and I said, "Why don't you take them then?"
He pushed them right back at me and said, "I don't want
them."*

At some point Anderson (presumably with the tacit or overt support of his superiors in Washington) decided that our research study
was more trouble than it was worth — that our findings and conclusions could not be controlled — and obstacles began appearing in the
way of our work. Early in the fall of 1968 the old wooden mess hall,
which was the property of the Yellowstone Park Company and had
been serving as the laboratory in our Canyon headquarters, was
bulldozed and burned by the Park Service, ostensibly as part of its
cleanup in preparation for the Yellowstone National Park Centennial
celebration scheduled for 1972.* Replacement of this facility would
cost at least $100,000. There were vacant buildings elsewhere in the
park but we were denied their use for laboratory work and housing.
In order to continue working we moved our equipment and personnel
into our own house trailer, which we were next pressured to move to
the town of West Yellowstone, a three-hour round trip by car from
our main area of operations.

Beginning in 1968, too, we were no longer permitted to handle or
relocate any of the problem bears as we had formerly done on a
routine basis at the request of park personnel; nor could we give advice or instructions on drugging procedures and techniques, which
were new to most rangers because of frequent transfers of park personnel. We were also refused access to Park Service records concerning bear captures, attacks, and control measures; later we were offered summaries, but these were of little or no value to us. Even
officials from the Atomic Energy Commission, an agency supporting
some aspects of our radio-tracking research, were denied permission
to go to Trout Creek for the purpose of reviewing our work.[8]

Grizzly casualties continued to mount at a dismaying rate due to
intentional (drugs as well as bullets were used to dispatch bears) and
accidental overdosing and other control actions. From 1968 through

---

*Under our agreement of understanding, the Park Service was to provide us with
physical facilities and housing.

1970 the average number of grizzlies dispatched in control actions was three times the average for the preceding nine years. The Park Service's reaction to criticism of these accumulating deaths was to state that they were eliminating troublesome and incorrigible bears — "garbage bears" — with the aim of preserving only a wild, free-roaming population.[9] These assurances were based on the convenient but totally unsubstantiated hypothesis that there were two separate grizzly populations in the Yellowstone ecosystem: one that regularly fed at the dumps, and a second "backcountry" population whose members did not visit the dumps and thus were rarely seen. When the opportunity arose, which was not often, we pointed out that all of our data on the movements of the bears indicated that there was but a single population exhibiting one set of behavioral traits when around the dumps and another when in wilderness country. Practically all of the silvertip bears in the huge Yellowstone ecosystem moved into the dump areas to feed, either for short or extended periods, at some time in their lives. They would continue to do so, we were sure, for years after the dumps were removed. Thus a policy that attempted to eliminate only the "problem" bears must eventually decimate the entire Yellowstone population, and this was the cause of our gravest concern.

Conditions in 1969 continued to deteriorate, with grizzly bear incidents and bear–man confrontations increasing. In early June, Daphne Jacks, a five-year-old child, was mauled by a grizzly in the Fishing Bridge trailer village. And on July 9 our team received a call from Dale Nuss, District Ranger of the Lake District, informing us that there had been two bear incidents at Fishing Bridge during the night and that two people had been injured. Our research crew documented these incidents in detail. Briefly, David Lou, age 22, of Los Angeles, was sleeping in a tent with his sister and was dragged out of the tent by a bear, apparently a grizzly. There were several deep wounds in his head and his scalp was ripped back. He was taken to the Lake Hospital in a state of shock. Michael Rock, age 23, of Carnegie, Pennsylvania, was bitten on the head but not critically hurt and was soon released from the hospital. Shortly after hearing from Dale Nuss we received another call, this time from the Superintendent, who again informed us of the situation and gave instructions that in both cases we were to give out only information consistent with what the park released.

We discussed the incidents with Nuss, who told us that park personnel were hunting for the bears, and that the plans were to kill all and any that showed up. According to Tom Hough, a reporter for the Jackson Hole *Guide,* Superintendent Anderson told him that they were using tranquilizing guns and carrying firearms only for protection, and that they did not intend to kill the grizzlies. Anderson also indicated to the news media that the people were not seriously hurt and that no food was involved. We learned from an eyewitness that food was, in fact, involved.

At midnight on July 9, grizzly bear Number 183, a five-year-old, was shot and killed by rangers. Jim Claar was informed and our crew went out to take care of the bear specimen. I wrote in my notes:

It appears that the Park Service and Superintendent Anderson are not giving out the correct information, yet they have asked us and practically insisted that we corroborate their statements. This misleading of the public as to the seriousness of the injuries and as to the cause of the bears coming into campgrounds is doing irreparable damage. It is giving the grizzlies a reputation of attacking and coming into the campgrounds for no apparent reason and is also misleading the public into thinking that the incidents are only minor affairs and brushes with the animals involved. One grizzly shot earlier and wounded severely in the shoulder was later killed by drugs, his maddening wound attributed by Park personnel to a fight, yet his condition a deadly threat to anyone who inadvertently came close to him. I do not want to cause the Park Service embarrassment on this issue, but I feel that they have very definitely created the situation. However, I also do not intend to go along with misinformation. On the contrary, I plan to give our the correct information when approached or requested to do so.

One change in park policy on independent research that occurred in 1969 would damage our study more than any other. When we began our field work that year, Superintendent Anderson informed us that we would no longer be permitted to visually mark or radio-instrument any animals within the park, and further, that all existing identification markers would be removed from grizzlies captured and released in control actions. This course of action (which is well documented in the Lake Bear Logs) was rationalized by the claim that the tags were too "conspicuous" and offended visitors, especially photographers. Again, the upcoming park centennial was cited in this justification. With regard to biotelemetry, Anderson claimed that this activity could be satisfactorily conducted outside the park, though the amount of radio tracking that had led us outside park boundaries had always been minimal.[10]

Visual marking had served from the beginning as our principal method for positively identifying bears; our ability to systematically gather reliable data on grizzly movement, population, and mortality depended on it. We had consistently emphasized its importance, and the previous park administrations, under Superintendent Garrison and briefly John McLaughlin, had concurred and cooperated.*

Our strong objections to the new policy concerned not only the fact that it would effectively disrupt our own long-range record-keeping but that it must also make it impossible for the Park Service to evaluate accurately the effects of their new management policies, including the dump closings, on the grizzly population. As later worded by John in a 1971 letter to Jack Anderson: "By removing our tags and the very inconspicuous color markers you will prevent us from obtaining age-specific mortality data, information vital to future management of the grizzly population. Data on family histories, longevity, and movement will also be impossible to obtain. Since one objective of your present management program is to disperse grizzlies to the backcountry, it is essential to retain marked animals so they can be observed and identified in the field."[11]

In announcing the ban on further marking and the intent to remove existing markers, Anderson told us that the decision had come down from the Natural Sciences Advisory Committee of the National Park Service. Somewhat later, we were to learn that this was not the case.

---

*Other animals were marked for study purposes, specifically black bears and elk. Over 1500 elk, in fact, had been marked by park personnel and John's staff beginning in 1964, and the subsequent work of gathering information had been conducted by John and his University of Montana research unit at the Park Service's request. The Park Service had also approved the marking of black bears by the researchers, and these were seen along the park roads far more frequently and conspicuously than grizzlies.

By the close of the summer of 1969 the Yellowstone National Park administration realized that their grizzly bear management program was in trouble. Though the public was assured that all was going well, it was privately acknowledged that conditions were literally out of control and that some review of current policy had to be undertaken. A meeting was scheduled for September 6, 1969, at Mammoth, in Yellowstone National Park. This Bear Management Meeting was initiated by National Park Service personnel from Washington, and there is little reason to doubt that one of its purposes was to get Yellowstone officials off the hook. The Washington people knew only what Yellowstone officials had told them about the situation, a biased interpretation at best, and most of the others asked to attend were even less well informed. John and I hoped to present another side, and planned to make available copies of progress reports, published papers, and our draft "Management of Bears" report.

A few weeks before the meeting I had two long telephone conversations with Dr. Robert Linn, Director of the Office of Natural Sciences of the National Park Service, in the course of which he agreed to broaden the scope of the subject of the September meeting to "grizzly bear management and research." He also agreed to tape-record the entire meeting so that everything discussed would be a part of the official record,[12] but in the end no recording was made.

On August 16, I met with Senator Gale McGee of Wyoming to discuss grizzly management in Yellowstone and the trend of independent research. I asked Senator McGee what he thought about holding a public hearing; he responded that they would first have to lay the groundwork for this, but that he, like I, hoped that the September meeting might resolve some of these questions and thus make a public hearing or further meetings unnecessary.

Among those who attended the meeting were three members of the Park Service's Natural Sciences Advisory Committee: Dr. A. Starker Leopold (University of California), Dr. Stanley A. Cain (University of Michigan), and Dr. Charles E. Olmsted (University of Chicago). Another group consisted of special consultants, including John (University of Montana), myself (State University of New York), Dr. Frederick C. Dean (University of Alaska), and Dr. Albert Erickson (University of Minnesota). Representing the Park Service would be Park Service Director George B. Hartzog, Jr., Dr. Robert Linn, Jim Reed, Lowell Sumner, Dr. Douglas B. Houston, William J. Barmore,

Margaret M. Meagher, Jack Anderson, Glen Cole, Neil J. Reid, and Clifford J. Martinka.

At the September 6 meeting I sat beside Dr. Stanley Cain and at one point asked him on what basis the Natural Sciences Advisory Committee had decided to prohibit further marking of animals in Yellowstone. Dr. Cain was surprised at my question, and responded that he knew nothing at all about it. I informed him that this was now official policy and that Anderson had told us that the decision had come from the Advisory Committee. Later in the meeting Cain asked Anderson for an explanation, and the latter, apparently flustered by the unexpected question, finally admitted that he had made the decision himself.[13]

As the meeting went on, over a two-day period, there emerged from the discussions certain management objectives which were considered valid by all parties. All seemed to agree that the chief goal of management should be to maintain an optimum population level of a threatened species in a natural condition, with man as an integral part of bear ecology. It was on the question of how to achieve this that our ideas on management and those of the current park administration diverged. The park's policy was based on Glen Cole's contention that there were two distinct populations of bears: "backcountry bears" and "non-backcountry bears." Although he had no scientific data to support his argument, Cole held to the position that the dumps should be closed abruptly, claiming that the grizzly population would regulate itself and that elimination of troublesome bears would make room for other, "backcountry," bears.

John countered with data showing that almost all the grizzlies in the Yellowstone ecosystem visited the dumps at some time in their lives — to show that there was no distinct "dump" population — and proposed various methods of determining the number of grizzlies that actually did utilize the backcountry in August, when the concentration at the dumps was heaviest. We reiterated our earlier recommendation that the dumps be phased out slowly to give the bears time to adjust their social and feeding behavior to this change, suggested that alternate food sources be supplied for the interim period, and offered an updated analysis of population trends and altered distribution patterns under the recent management policies. Our current census data strongly indicated that if grizzly mortalities continued at the increased rates tabulated in 1968 and 1969, the stable bear population that everyone claimed to favor would soon cease to be a possibility.

One product of the September 1969 meeting was a report issued by A. Starker Leopold, Chairman of the Natural Sciences Advisory Committee.[14] This report was published and distributed without our having been permitted to review it and without any mention of our contributions and publications, even though John and I had provided the bulk of the information for this meeting. Weeks of work went into our preparation of the material we presented, including charts, tables, and much earnest discussion, yet in the report we were unjustly criticized for not providing information. At our insistence Linn and Leopold eventually and reluctantly agreed to amend the statement "the bulk of the data on grizzly biology accumulated in this study is unavailable for the use of public agencies administering grizzly populations" to read "a number of publications and reports, including a 113-page report, 'Management of Bears in Yellowstone National Park,' have been made available to the National Park Service and other agencies administering grizzly populations. Much data on grizzly bear biology accumulated in this study are as yet unpublished due to the long-term nature of the research. Early publication is urged." By that time, however, the original Leopold Report had been sent out and it was the earlier version which was widely distributed.

The Leopold Report was a National Park Service-oriented appraisal of the management problem. Although it did include the suggestions and ideas of both sides in the controversy, the Park Service argument was treated as "policy" while our arguments were only "suggestions." Despite the fact that these "suggestions" were based on sound research, the Superintendent could and did choose to ignore them.

The early part of 1970 saw the first attempts to deal with the heightened bear–people conflict in the Yellowstone ecosystem through wider participation on the part of all concerned. In January 1969 John had sent a memorandum to Frank Dunkle, Director of the Montana Fish and Game Department, suggesting a meeting to explore the cooperative management of grizzlies.[15] The suggestion was favorably received, and a year later, on January 15 and 16, 1970, a state-sponsored meeting called by Frank Dunkle did take place in the town of West Yellowstone, with about thirty-five participants from four federal and four state agencies, including the superintendents of Glacier and Yellowstone and the directors of the fish and game departments of Wyoming, Montana, Idaho, and Colorado.

The first day John and I presented a rundown of our grizzly bear studies and made management recommendations. The entire second day was spent in presentations, comments, and discussion by personnel representing federal and state agencies. An interesting question related to grizzly attacks was put to William Briggle, Superintendent of Glacier National Park: why the 1967 attacks on the two young women in Glacier had been blamed in part on the women's menstrual cycles. Dr. William H. Sippel, an M.D. from Bozeman, Montana, criticized the National Park Service for releasing this kind of information, saying, "Many of my patients are afraid to hike in the backcountry when they are menstruating." He went on to say that "whether the NPS realizes it or not, women have been menstruating for thousands of years and have been on the trails in this condition. Why weren't they attacked before?"[16] Harry Woodward, Director of the Colorado Fish and Game Department, appointed a committee to evaluate the Leopold Report and keep him informed on the management of grizzlies in Yellowstone. He also warned the National Park Service that the time has passed when the Park Service could manage its (our) resources without consulting with other concerned agencies and people.

Not long after this, on July 7, 1970, a more formal meeting of the Special Grizzly Bear Committee of the International Association of Fish and Game Commissioners was held at Macks Inn, Idaho, in which representatives of three states (Wyoming, Montana, and Idaho) and three federal agencies (the National Park Service, the U.S. Forest Service, and the Bureau of Land Management) took part. Again efforts were made to determine the status of the grizzly, research needs, transplanting possibilities, cooperative management, closing of park dumps, etc. A few people were trying to figure out how to share a small part of their planet with another creature, and some progress was being made; but as in the past they were unable to put existing knowledge to use effectively in agreeing on a management program that would satisfy all the agencies involved.

From 1969 through 1971 grizzlies continued to move in unprecedented numbers into campgrounds, where they were either killed or trapped and transported to distant parts of the park or beyond. Most of those in the latter category eventually became mortalities as well: killed by drugs, killed by hunters, campers, or ranchers when they were released outside the park, or eliminated by rangers when they returned to their point of capture. It was inevitable that most of those that were not killed upon release would eventually return. The grizzly's strong homing instinct was by now familiar to us, as it was to park officials, too. In 1970 the Rabbit Creek dump was closed, followed in 1971 by the complete closure of the Trout Creek dump, encouraging the movement of grizzlies from these areas into campgrounds and also into the vicinity of West Yellowstone, Montana, just outside the boundaries of Yellowstone National Park.

Ten marked bears were casualties of control measures and hunting in 1970. Among these were two radio bears, both killed by hunters outside the park. Female Number 164, Lucky, the first grizzly we had tracked to a winter den, was shot in upper Slough Creek north of the park, well over fifty airline miles from Old Faithful, where we had instrumented her. Female Number 96 was shot along Broadwater Creek. Her hibernation site had been in the northeastern part of the park. Both of these grizzlies had responded to the abrupt cutoff in food by foraging further afield, unfortunately straying outside the park, where they were fair game. They had never had cause to learn about hunters and guns, and like many other bears during this time their first learning experience was their last. Yellowstone National Park was no longer functioning as a refuge to wildlife, even for increasingly rare species like the grizzly. Inside they were being killed for acting like bears; forced out, they faced the guns of hunters and ranchers.

Shortly before the 1971 summer season the open dump near the little town of West Yellowstone, practically on the western boundary of the park, was eliminated and relocated nearby as a bear-proof enclosure surrounded by chain-link fence inside an electrified three-wire fence. This abrupt relocation, according to Montana Fish and Game officials, resulted in an expected increase in grizzly bear complaints, and a control program was required. One of the directors for the state agency said that he knew they were going to have a problem when they closed the West Yellowstone dump.[17] They also knew that forty-four grizzlies were in the area, largely bears from neighboring

Yellowstone, many of whom had moved into the area since the earlier closing of dumps within the park. Under a three-agency agreement, nineteen of these bears captured in West Yellowstone were trapped and transported elsewhere. They were taken first to Mammoth, within Yellowstone Park, from which park biologists flew them by helicopter to national forest areas north of the park, where they could be hunted. By late fall of 1971, eleven of the nineteen had been killed in one way or another; by spring the following year all but one were dead. In the West Yellowstone area alone there were twelve known grizzly mortalities and four probable mortalities, for a total of sixteen in 1971. In the ecosystem as a whole, forty-three grizzlies (including eighteen marked bears) died in 1971, and in the Lake campground alone 101 incidents involving grizzlies were reported — and this was the year the Park Service claimed all was well in the campgrounds and the grizzlies were back on natural food.[18]

It was also during 1971 that our already reduced research team left Yellowstone National Park for good. We had seen this coming for several years, of course, but the formal break occurred when it came time to renew the memorandum of understanding between our study team and the Park Service under which we had been working since 1959. In practice, the "understanding" as set forth in the original agreement had long since ceased to exist, and the new agreement offered by the Park Service was not one that we could in conscience accept. Among the clauses introduced in the revised memorandum of August 4, 1971, was one stipulating that any material we intended to publish should henceforth be screened and approved by a federal agency: "All oral and written statements, including but not limited to progress reports, popular and scientific articles and other publications, talks, and press releases prepared by the Montana Cooperative Wildlife Research Unit (and collaborators) concerning grizzly bear research within Yellowstone National Park shall be submitted to the Director, Bureau of Sport Fisheries and Wildlife, for approval prior to publication or otherwise disseminated [*sic*] to the public."[19] (John, as mentioned previously, was the leader of the Montana Cooperative Wildlife Research Unit, and I and others were his collaborators.)

John, in a later interview, recalled: "I showed that agreement to some of my professional colleagues at the University of Montana. They said, in effect, 'John, if you accept that you can no longer call yourself a scientist.' " Nothing in our recent experience encouraged us to believe that the prerogative of censorship contained in the memorandum would not be exercised, and we both refused to sign the new agreement.

Although we could no longer directly study the Yellowstone grizzlies after 1971, we could still make use of previously gathered data in our continuing efforts on their behalf. The rapid decline in bear numbers due to control measures and hunting led John, Joel Varney, and associates at the University of Montana in 1972 to program our accumulated population statistics through an IBM 620 computer. This was done by comparing population data for the 1959–67 period against the 1968–71 period of revised management.

The population data that we had gathered in Yellowstone through yearly field work permitted John and Joel to construct a model that would predict actual population changes. (These predictions would be as accurate as our techniques for gathering field data would allow. Data compiled through systematized procedures and averaged after a number of years ensured greater accuracy than would have been the case had we used annual statistics. This, of course, is why we could not publish some information as rapidly as our Park Service critics wished.) Into the computer went the kind of information discussed in earlier chapters: such population characteristics as age structure, sex ratios, reproductive rates, mortality and survivorship rates, and longevity. These data were incorporated into a program which calculated the changes occurring in the population and were the basis for a mathematical model. The model was then used to determine the effects on the population of changes in various biological parameters. Since we were no longer taking field censuses, this was the only way to predict grizzly bear population trends after 1970. We had by then concluded that prior to the change in management starting under Superintendent Anderson in 1968 the grizzly bear population inhabiting the Yellowstone ecosystem had exhibited a slow growth rate and was not threatened or endangered. Using the increased mortality for the period 1969–71, however, a rapid decline in population could be projected. John presented these results at a Bear Management Meeting in Mammoth on September 19, 1972.

In September 1972 we had known of 91 grizzly bear mortalities in two years' time. By the end of the year we had recorded 120. In the years 1968 through 1972 there was a total of 160 known deaths, an average of 32.0 bears per year with highs of 46 and 45 in 1970 and 1971, respectively. The total of known deaths after 1968 was in itself dangerously high, and there was no way to determine the number of unknown deaths after our research group was prohibited from continuing censuses in the park. Unknown deaths as computed from the age structure of the population for 1959 to 1967 had averaged 15 per year. The latter represented mostly natural deaths: young bears dying from the rigors of their first winter and old bears succumbing to disease, old age, etc. There were also the unreported killings of bears outside the park by stockmen, hunters, and poachers, and, in apparently greater numbers from 1968 on, the unreported killings by rangers.[20]

Using a hypothetically large grizzly population, John and Joel's initial computer analysis revealed that the allowable known mortality rate for a stable population was approximately 10 percent (assuming a constant unknown mortality of about 10 percent). In 1970 known mortalities amounted to 18 percent of this assumed larger population; in 1971, 20 percent; and in 1972, 14 percent. If the population decline was to be halted in 1973, total known mortalities must not exceed twelve animals if the reproductive rate remained as low as it was. This figure was, in fact, exceeded (see Table 2).

The causes of mortalities, as before, were control measures, hunting, and natural deaths. Nothing could be done to lower natural deaths. And control deaths, the exact number of which will never be known, were determined by Park Service policy; however, some improvements were made in the number of hunting deaths. Idaho had had a moratorium on grizzly hunting since 1946 (though bears causing depredations could still be killed), and Wyoming had reduced the number of licenses issued for the taking of grizzlies.

John and his colleagues went on to further perfect the mathematical model of the population, and it was then used to ascertain the overall population trend since 1970. The results of the analysis through 1974, published in a paper, "A Population Analysis of the Yellowstone Grizzly Bear,"[21] indicated that the grizzly bear population in the Yellowstone ecosystem had rapidly declined after 1968 and had continued to decline with the mortality that occurred in 1970–73.

Under normal conditions, an excessive adult mortality should in most animal populations be offset by an increase in reproductive rate and greater survival of the young. This would permit a declining population to stabilize and to grow. Such compensatory processes take time, however, and we found no field evidence that this had begun in the grizzly bear population. Because the grizzly population we were studying had had a low man-caused mortality rate until recent times, it could be expected to respond very slowly, if at all, in compensating for population declines caused primarily by man.

When mortality increased or additional data indicated an altered reproductive rate, adjustments were made to the computer model so that it would simulate as closely as possible the actual population trends. To test the model's accuracy in predicting population changes, trial runs were made against known census data for the 1959–67 period. Using the average observed reproductive rate for the 1959–67 period (0.651), for example, the model predicted a 2.3 percent growth rate, which was quite close to the 2.4 percent actual rate obtained from the accumulated census data. The biological parameters that we fed into the computer varied from year to year as new environmental changes and physiological stresses (such as those caused by the abrupt closing of the dumps) were encountered. No allowance could yet be made for a compensatory rise in the reproductive rate.

When the model was checked and rechecked and perfected as much as possible, simulation runs were made to examine past, present, and future grizzly bear population levels in the entire Yellowstone ecosystem. The runs were made for the years 1959 through 1974. Our projections showed that the reproductive rate, which had reached a high of 0.735 in 1967, had dropped to 0.544 in 1974. The most probable case showed the ecosystem population increasing from 222 animals in 1959 to 245 in 1967, then declining to 136 animals in 1974 (a decline of 44.5 percent) and continuing to decline thereafter. In our September 19, 1972, warning to the Park Service we had stated that should known mortalities after 1972 drop to ten or twelve grizzlies per year and the reproductive rate stay depressed, the grizzly population could not increase but would remain essentially static. Our final 1974 computer analysis verified this statement.

Our grave concerns for the future of the Yellowstone grizzly population under post-1967 management policies were only heightened by the results of the computer analyses in 1972 and 1974.

But this was only one side of the coin, for we had long feared that the substantial increase in man–bear incidents from 1968 on must inevitably result in a human tragedy like that which had occurred in Glacier National Park in 1967. On June 25, 1972, these fears were realized when a young camper named Harry Walker was killed by a grizzly in Yellowstone. Walker, who was twenty-five years old, and his friend Phillip Bradberry, had hitchhiked to the Old Faithful area, where there was no longer a campground, and were camped about 250 yards from a boardwalk near Grand Geyser and Purple Pool. They had been told by a girl they met — though not by park officials — that they were camping illegally and that bears were around. The attack on Walker took place as he was returning to camp at about midnight, carrying a flashlight. A large, toothless grizzly hauled him off and crushed his larynx, not even breaking the skin. Thirty-six hours later the suspect bear was caught in a snare and shot.[22]

Walker's death is the more tragic in that it might perhaps have been avoided had park personnel been more diligent in investigating an incident that had occurred nearly two years earlier. There is some evidence to link the bear that killed Harry Walker with another possible, though unpublicized, fatality in 1970. The Old Faithful Bear Log for August 23, 1970, contains the following chilling entries:

[Time] 1651 — David Hamilton, Old Faithful, reports that visitors at the upper Firehole Bridge are gazing at a scalp on a blanket.

1736 — Re: 1651 [entry] It is a scalp with pieces of flesh and maggots, pictures taken and pieces collected and [placed] under rear of building.

On September 16, 1970, Dan Bean, of Eugene, Oregon, reported to rangers at the Old Faithful station that an abandoned camp on the Firehole River a half-mile south of the new highway bridge had been ransacked by a bear.[23] It appeared that the bear might have been old and toothless, cans of food having been mouthed but not broken open. An official Park document stated that the camp was damaged by a bear — no sign of occupant. Apparently, no other evidence was found. The camper never showed up, and the camp was removed by rangers. Rangers Herbster, Cherry, Connelly, Argill, and Williamson inspected the site on September 16 and took all items to the Old Faithful ranger station. They estimated the camp had been there at least five days to one week. Seventeen items were found, including a tent with accessories, clothing, a fishnet, a swimming facemask and fins — and a duffel bag which bore the name Herbert Muller and the number 37790176. Was this the name of the camper who had disappeared?

The first time I had access to the meager records on this incident was in a Federal District Court in Los Angeles in 1975, where the National Park Service was being sued for negligence by the estate of Harry Walker. No evidence in the logs suggested that any attempt was made to locate relatives of the victim, if there was one. I found no evidence that any warnings were issued to the public that there had been a man–grizzly incident perhaps resulting in a fatality.[24] The Park Service's handling of this situation so disturbed Ranger Jerry Schroeder that when an opportunity arose, on October 10, 1972, he introduced himself and told me about it. In doing so he knowingly risked his job and perhaps future employment. His job was "eliminated" the following year, he claimed later, and he left the park.

A month after the torn-up camp was located in 1970, an old, partially toothless bear was trapped near the Camper Cabins Cafe at Old Faithful, less than a mile from the camp, and tagged with NPS tag number 1792. The bear had been seen in this developed area four or five times before it was trapped, but apparently no association between the presence in the area of this old bear and the destruction of the nearby camp and disappearance of its occupant was considered. Bear 1792 was transplanted only eighteen miles away, a distance easily traveled by a bear in a single day.

The bear that killed Harry Walker was positively identified as number 1792, and the attack took place only a few miles from the site of the earlier incident. This fact was never noted in the hue and cry that immediately surrounded Walker's death. In fact, the overall reaction of the Park Service to the attack left much to be desired. A key function of this government agency is to provide the public with professional services in the areas under its jurisdiction, including information affecting visitor safety. In failing to remove to a safe distance from a heavily visited area a bear that ought to have been presumed hazardous, and in neglecting to alert visitors to the presence of such a bear or bears in the vicinity, the Park Service certainly did not perform this function. Now, rather than immediately taking steps to prevent further incidents and to alert the public, the agency first undertook to protect its own image. Denying the possibility of its own negligence, the Park Service attempted to shift the blame onto the Walker and Bradberry boys, giving out the impression that they had a dirty camp and were camping illegally, thus inviting a confrontation with a bear.[25] Careful investigation in federal court later showed that the boys were not at fault, that they in fact camped well and conducted themselves in a manner above reproach. One of Judge Andrew Hauk's findings of fact was that "the decedent was not contributorily negligent, and did not directly or indirectly contribute to the cause of his own death."[26]

Judge Hauk, with long experience on the bench, asked key and penetrating questions. In his findings of fact he found the Park Service negligent in that it willfully and intentionally failed to provide warnings and place signs of danger from grizzlies, and that it was negligent to discontinue radio and visual monitoring of bears at the time it undertook the extra hazard of closing down the garbage dumps. He found that the defendant (Park Service) had failed to exercise due care toward decedent in five respects, and concluded: "As a sole, direct, and proximate result of each of the negligent acts and omissions of defendant, taken individually and together, including and as a direct and proximate result of the activity of abrupt closing of garbage dumps, and as a direct and proximate result of defendant's failure to avert an attack on the decedent by prudent control action on the grizzly bear which killed decedent, and as a direct and proximate result of the failure of the defendant and its employees to warn decedent of danger known to them but unknown to him, to wit, the danger of grizzly bears in Yellowstone National Park, and particularly in the Old Faithful Subdistrict and Old Faithful Village area of Yellowstone National Park, Harry Eugene Walker's death was caused."

Partly because of the uproar created by Walker's death, and also at the urging of Harry Woodward, Director of the Colorado Fish and Game Department, Assistant Secretary of the Interior Nathaniel Reed called yet another meeting on grizzly bears. This took place on September 19, 1972, at Mammoth. In many ways it paralleled the meeting of September 1969. Originally, there were to be two separate meetings: in the morning Nat Reed and Starker Leopold were to meet with federal and state representatives; in the afternoon, they would meet with John Craighead and his colleagues. John and I felt strongly that there should be a single, open meeting with the opportunity for questions from all parties; we tried all channels in the attempt to effect this and succeeded up to a point. My first request, that the press be present, was denied. We then requested that Dr. Lawrence M. Gould, former President of the American Association for the Advancement of Science, be permitted to attend. This too was rejected. Mrs. Martha Shell, a freelance writer doing a book on bears and the Park Service, had unsuccessfully sought access through her Congressman. Finally, just prior to the meeting, I released word to the press that it was to be a closed meeting, and I also sent copies to a number of concerned people of a directive of President Nixon which was in force at the time. Appearing in the August 4, 1972, issue of *Science*, the directive stated "that all Scientific Advisory Meetings were to be open to the public."[27] These tactics, plus some political pressure that reached clear to the White House, at last forced an open meeting.

Our success was less than gratifying, however, since the decision to open the meeting was made only on the morning of the day it was held. Many who were interested could not attend. The room was completely full by the time John and I and our colleagues, Jay Sumner and Dr. Frank Sogandares, were told we could attend; I had to turn a waste paper can upside down to use as a seat for the entire meeting.

Papers were presented in the morning by several Park Service people, in addition to Cole, Cliff Martinka from Glacier, and Ken Greer of the Montana Fish and Game Department. After lunch John gave his briefing on the grizzly situation, the first presentation of the initial results of the computer analysis of the grizzly bear population we had done with Joel Varney.[28] The purpose of the briefing was to alert all concerned to the dangerous downward trend in the grizzly population and to once again warn the Park Service that its present course could very likely end in eliminating the grizzly from the ecosystem.

John said, "If we assume that the known mortality remains at the 1972 level and the reproductive rate of 0.7 continues over a ten-year period, the population declines sharply, reaching twenty-three, plus or minus five animals, by 1983." He also pointed out that for the grizzly population to grow at the same rate as during the 1959–67 study period, it could sustain only ten known deaths during 1973 and would have to exhibit a reproductive rate of 1.0. Based on the continuing high mortality of ninety-one recorded grizzly bear deaths in 1971 and 1972, John told the meeting that "the present National Park Service management program, if continued, will very probably exterminate or nearly exterminate the Yellowstone grizzly bear population in about twenty to twenty-five years."

John's briefing urged that the most responsible approach to future planning and management would be for all agencies concerned about the welfare and preservation of Yellowstone grizzlies to work together cooperatively and to use our worst-case population estimate for determining allowable annual mortality. This would leave some margin for error. Glen Cole had walked out and was not present to hear John's presentation.

I was not asked, or permitted, to deliver a statement, though I had a paper prepared.[29] I did raise some questions, one of which concerned the death of the Walker boy. When Ken Greer commented that there had been little adverse reaction to this particular grizzly bear killing, I stood up and inquired whether this might not be due to the image projected of the boys as dirty hippies. Nat Reed reacted to this by saying something like, "Surely you don't mean that." Either he did not know all the facts or he approved of the Park Service's handling of the incident. If the former, I hoped by opening Nat Reed's eyes to spark an investigation into the actions of the Park Service following the Walker boy's death, and possibly even lead to an exposé of what did happen or might have happened to the missing camper on the Firehole River. I was trying to give Nat Reed a tip in the hope of obtaining an opportunity to discuss the whole management–research controversy with him. It was imperative that he be given information on both sides of the issue in order to make proper and unbiased decisions, if indeed he was interested in doing so. I was beginning to doubt it. Reed did not seem to be able to differentiate between the type of information Cole was giving him and the systematically gathered data based on years of research that John had just presented. Still, John and I hoped he would reconsider his stand and make some changes. We left copies of John's paper on a table in the middle of the room and invited all present to take them.

Bob Linn, head of the Park Service Office of Natural Sciences, attended the meeting but made no comments. Although he had heard all of John's presentation and had seen the copies placed out for distribution on the table in front of him, he later stated in an official letter to Senator Lee Metcalf of Montana, "The afternoon session consisted of a presentation by Dr. John Craighead of several graphs and charts intended to show a rapid decline in the grizzly population until sometime between 1986 and 2006, when no grizzlies would remain in the Yellowstone population. No written statement, unfortunately, is available from Dr. Craighead which presents the information given by him."[30]

Reed and Cole apparently released statements to the press a few days after the meeting. The gist of Reed's comments was that there were plenty of grizzlies in Yellowstone, in fact, too many — that the park was supporting more grizzlies than it ought to.[31] Cole, for his part, used the opportunity to disparage our techniques for population analysis, remarking: "If you put garbage dump data in the computer, you'll get garbage dump data out."[32] After this, we relinquished any remaining hopes that they might modify their stand and began to explore other avenues of getting our message across. John and I published an article, "Tuning In On the Grizzly," in the World Book Encyclopedia's *Science Year 1973*, and in December 1972 I presented a lecture to the Environmental Protection Agency in Denver that included information on the grizzly controversy and a proposed eight-point management program.[33] I wanted to try everything possible short of confrontation in the press.

On September 25, 1973, I missed a plane connection from Denver to Jackson, Wyoming, and as a consequence inadvertently ran into Nat Reed and a group on their way to a grizzly bear meeting to be held in Yellowstone. While waiting in the airport terminal I asked Reed and Dr. Charlie Loveless, of the U.S. Fish and Wildlife Service, if John had been asked to attend the meeting. Both hemmed and hawed briefly, then Reed indicated that he had not. I inquired why neither John nor I was invited to participate, and was told that other subjects besides grizzlies were to be discussed and our presence would therefore be inappropriate — which I interpreted as a polite way of telling us that they did not care to hear what we had to say. All the same I was determined to see whether I could profit from this unique opportunity to express my views to a captive audience. When we all boarded the next plane to Jackson, I seated myself next to Charlie

Loveless and proceeded to argue my case. I began with my estimation of the critical situation facing the grizzlies, and went on to express concern about the repressive climate in Yellowstone with regard to independent research: the various forms of harassment and the strictures against our releasing any information that didn't mesh with existing policy.

Loveless suggested that I talk with Nat Reed, and arranged it. This was what I had hoped for. Reed and I sat in the back of the plane and talked for most of the trip, the topics ranging from the very particular to the fundamental. I emphasized to Reed that he wasn't getting correct information on the grizzly bear situation, that he was seeing only one side of the whole controversy. I suggested, among other things, that he request a description of methods being used by the Park Service to arrive at its claims of a high grizzly population. I pointed out that there were systematic, scientific methods for gathering such information, and that to my knowledge the Park Service had not followed these accepted techniques.

As we flew over the Wind River Range, once grizzly bear habitat, I made clear to Reed that regardless of the outcome of this latest bear meeting, or of the bear situation as a whole, I intended to make an issue of the freedom to use public lands for independent research and the need to protect such research from unwarranted interference by government agencies. I also said that I wanted to see a Congressional investigation into the condition of the grizzly in Yellowstone, in which all the people concerned would be required to testify under oath.

As our conversation moved on I sensed that Reed had pretty well made up his mind and was too committed to his position to consider altering it. His principal argument was that most of what I was saying concerned events which had occurred in the past. Also, he said he didn't want to get involved in what he saw as a personal battle, to which I responded by suggesting that this was exactly how his subordinates — our opposition — wanted him to see it. He also objected to the publicity battle of sorts that we had been waging in the press and elsewhere; I replied that I had published and lectured only to refute misinformation released by the Park Service. Just before we prepared to return to our seats I asked Reed if he had seen John's computer analysis. Reed said that he had seen an abstract of it and questioned the validity of parts of it. It seemed apparent that he had been shown only certain parts, and had received, at best, a questionable interpretation of them. I thought it would be difficult for him to evaluate the accuracy of the interpretation. When I asked him if John would be permitted to release the analysis, Reed wouldn't give an affirmative answer.

Toward the end of the discussion, Reed diplomatically asked me what should be done to preserve and manage the grizzly. I repeated that every effort should now be made to minimize grizzly mortality, particularly among mature females of reproductive age; that Montana and Wyoming should declare a moratorium on hunting; and that during the current period of adjustment, carcasses should be used as supplemental food to concentrate grizzlies in areas well away from campgrounds and people. Reed said that this baiting had already been tried. I expressed my doubts about this and said I would like to see concrete evidence, as past experiences did not encourage me to believe much of what Yellowstone personnel told me.

By the end of our discussion I had the feeling that Reed was considering the whole subject more seriously. I concluded by advising him that if he wanted good bear management the sensible approach would be to accept the findings of our computer analysis and proceed on the assumption that the bears were in trouble rather than to accept the optimistic population information supplied by Park Service people and assume that all was well.

If I had hoped that this informal chance meeting with Reed might produce results where formal attempts had failed, I was to be disappointed. But another development, earlier in 1973, offered a yet stronger hope. In response to pressure from several sources, the Department of the Interior had commissioned the National Academy of Sciences to study the controversy over grizzly bear management.[34] For some years, I, colleagues, and concerned friends and scientists such as Dr. Lawrence Gould had made oral and written requests for either a Congressional investigation of the Yellowstone situation or a review by a committee of the American Association for the Advancement of Science or the National Academy of Sciences. I had had encouraging feedback on the possibility in correspondence and discussion with several legislators, including U.S. Senator Gale McGee and Congressman Teno Roncalio of Wyoming. On January 11, 1973, Jim White, Director of the Wyoming Game and Fish Department, made a formal written request for an investigation by the National Academy of Sciences, and this request was expedited by the Wyoming Congressional representatives.[35] In February 1973 the Committee on the Yellowstone Grizzlies was established to "study and evaluate data on the population dynamics of the grizzly bears in Yellowstone National Park and to make recommendations concerning the scientific and technical implications of those data."[*][36] This committee was in the potentially uncomfortable position of having been selected by the Department of the Interior to investigate a problem involving an Interior bureau. This obviously was a drawback, but at least scientists were involved. Would they not be more objective than politically oriented administrators? We hoped for the best.

John and I, with some of John's University of Montana colleagues, met with the committee only once, on October 31, 1973, at Missoula, Montana. (Though we were assured there would be other meetings, none materialized.) The chairman, Dr. Cowan, opened the Missoula meeting by noting that the committee would concern itself only with biological problems relative to the surviving population of grizzlies in the lower forty-eight states. He emphasized that, although an examination would be made of all available grizzly bear data, including the current status, population trends, and management of the grizzlies, the study would not take up questions of federal or state policy or the sociopolitical aspects of the issue. Hearing this I commented on the difficulty of separating political and policy issues from biological ones. I feared that the scope and jurisdiction of the study had been so narrowed as to prevent exactly the type of investigation which was needed. Farther along in the meeting John gave a presentation outlining the methods, findings, and conclusions of our research project. Additional data requested by the committee were furnished later by John's research unit in correspondence.

Early in the second year of its existence the Committee on the Yellowstone Grizzlies received a long letter addressing many of the

---

*Its six members were all respected scientists: Dr. Ian McTaggart Cowan, chairman, Dean, Faculty of Graduate Studies, University of British Columbia; Dr. Douglas G. Chapman, Dean, College of Fisheries, University of Washington; Dr. Robert S. Hoffmann, Museum of Natural History, University of Kansas; Dr. Dale R. McCullough, Associate Professor, Resource Ecology Program, University of Michigan; Dr. Gustav A. Swanson, Department of Fishing and Wildlife Biology, Colorado State University; and Dr. Robert B. Weeden, Professor of Wildlife Management, Department of Wildlife and Fisheries, University of Alaska.

specifics of the bear management issue from former ranger Harry Reynolds, Jr. Reynolds had been involved with the situation in one way or another for perhaps longer than any other individual. He had been a National Park Service ranger for thirty-four years, sixteen of them (from 1947 to 1963) in Yellowstone. For much of this time he served as South District Ranger and acting District Manager of the central plateau area around Hayden Valley, where the grizzlies congregated in summer, and after 1962 he was detailed to park headquarters at Mammoth as staff officer to the chief ranger. In 1963 he was promoted and transferred to Washington, D.C., as staff park ranger in the Division of Resource Management. He retired from the federal government in the summer of 1967 and actively participated until early spring 1968 in the grizzly study at Yellowstone as a wildlife research assistant in the temporary employ of the University of Montana. "Consequently," he wrote to the committee, "I was in a unique position to acquire an intimate and detailed understanding of the grizzly research study and wildlife management policies and practices of NPS officials throughout the most significant period of activities, 1959–68."

Reynolds' letter, addressed to committee chairman Cowan, summarized and supported a number of our criticisms of post-1967 management policies, particularly with regard to the maintenance of statistical records. As this was among the chief points we were attempting to communicate to the NAS committee, I quote from the letter at some length:

> *To suit his own purposes—the reasons for which remain obscure but may be speculated upon—Mr. [Glen] Cole, with or without the approbation of Superintendent [Jack] Anderson, endorsed or initiated a park practice of underreporting all bear incidents and not recording all "controlled" or otherwise deceased grizzlies. Thus, the files which had been completely and accurately maintained for decades became merely a repository for statistical information which would support his point of view. I discerned clear evidence of these discrepancies and omissions when I reviewed the official NPS bear files at Mammoth during the winter of 1967–68.*
>
> *Too many park rangers, for a variety of reasons, failed to question this change in practice. The elimination of one less piece of*

*paperwork was a welcome relief to a ranger already overbur-
dened with reports. Also, by no longer being accountable for
submitting written dossiers on each grizzly incident, it was not
necessary to always report a bear succumbing to an uninten-
tional overdose of tranquilizing drugs. By this time, bears were
not infrequently killed in this manner by the use of drugs in
inexpert hands. Even marked "study" grizzlies were killed by
rangers within the park when alternative methods of control
were available. Such instances were sometimes not reported,
either in official records or information provided to the
Craigheads.*

*. . . This deterioration of bear management practices was only
possible because administrative and operational controls had
been relaxed, modified, or rescinded. Reports and records compiled since 1967 under the direction and control of Biologist
Cole and the administration of Superintendent Anderson are
consequently considered by some rangers (including myself) to
be inaccurate or incomplete. Records which had been formerly
maintained meticulously for both internal review and public in-
spection have become distorted. Then . . . the park administration marshalled backing at both the National Park Service re-
gional level and at the Washington office. Finally, in keeping
with a trend occurring too often in government activities, a solid
front—political rather than analytical in character—appears
to have been formulated within the Service.*

In conclusion, Reynolds wrote: "I have found it difficult to remain
less specific and nonpartisan under the circumstances. I am available
to give you further assistance, if requested, and I can fully support
the position I have stated in this letter."[37]

The committee referred to Reynolds' letter only once in its final
report. It stated: "It has been alleged (H. V. Reynolds, personal
communication, January 19, 1974) that control actions have not always been recorded. If this allegation is true, such failure jeopardizes
rational research and management programs for grizzly bears within
the National Parks." This "Report of Committee on the Yellowstone
Grizzlies"—a sixty-page typewritten document released in August
1974[38]—had effectively skirted the policy issues.

Acknowledging the value of our research, the report states, "While the grizzly is a difficult species to study, the information assembled in the fifteen years of research by the Craigheads and their colleagues, together with the shorter term efforts of many other workers, is a uniquely rich data bank. It is certainly the best available for a population of grizzly bears."[39] The committee agreed with our criticisms of the Park Service's post-1968 population figures and the manner in which they had been obtained. "Yellowstone Park authorities have stated to us their conviction that grizzlies are so readily recognized individually by their natural characteristics that conspicuous markers are unnecessary for censusing or other research. We question this and believe that the Yellowstone grizzly population estimates since termination of the Craigheads' studies cannot be substantiated."[40] Again, "Estimates of bear numbers for 1971 to 1973 (Cole, 1973, 1974) are based on hypothetical calculations and there are no data to verify them."[41]

Having acknowledged this much, the committee proceeded to straddle the fence in setting forth its own estimate of population decline since 1968, giving Cole's "hypothetical calculations" some slight benefit of the doubt. The committee itself estimated that the ecosystem population of grizzlies had shrunk from about 234 bears in 1968 to 158 in 1973. Our figures for the same years were 231 and 139, respectively. Cole had estimated a population of 350 in both 1971 and 1973,[42] compared with our estimates of 218 in 1970 and 139 in 1973. The committee also made considerable allowances for the possible effects of "compensatory mechanisms" in the population (such as a change in the survival rate of young grizzlies, or an increase in the number of cubs per litter due to greater availability of summer and fall food to the pregnant female). However, the report did not identify any of these as being operative in the population, and as mentioned in the discussion of our computer analysis, we had found no evidence to indicate that they were.

In most other respects the conclusions were almost completely in accord with ours. Some nineteen were set forth in the report, three of which were of particular significance:

No. 17. The Research program carried out by the National Park Service Administration since 1970 has been inadequate to provide data essential for devising sound management policies for the grizzly bears of the Yellowstone ecosystem.

No. 18. There is no convincing evidence that the grizzly bears in the Yellowstone ecosystem are in immediate danger of extinction.

No. 19. We believe that the compensatory processes discussed above have resulted in, or will lead to, replacement of bears that were removed from the ecosystem in 1968–73. However, until there is a more precise estimate of the population total and better information on the changes in population parameters that have resulted from the return of grizzlies to total dependence on natural foods, we believe that a conservative policy on removals is essential.

The committee made several specific recommendations based on these conclusions. Among these recommendations was a limit of ten on the number of bears that could be removed from the ecosystem by man each year (beginning in 1974) without endangering population stability. This limit would include both hunting and control killings. The committee also urged the National Park Service and the U.S. Forest Service to support and encourage independent research on Yellowstone grizzlies. These and the other recommendations accorded with our stand.

We were naturally encouraged by the overall tone of the committee's findings. On the negative side, it must be remembered that the committee's charge was limited to analyzing evidence and formulating recommendations; it had no direct authority to set or change policy. Control killings did drop in the ensuing years, but this can be attributed in large part to the previous drastic decline in the grizzly population and the increasing sensitivity of Yellowstone officials to criticism. Even so, our records show that at least fourteen grizzlies were killed in the ecosystem in 1974, thus still exceeding the committee's recommended limit.

The Park Service, not surprisingly, was not pleased by the committee's findings, and lost little time in countering them. In September 1974 it published the preliminary draft of an Environmental Impact Statement entitled *Grizzly Bear Management Program, Yellowstone National Park, Wyoming, Montana, Idaho.*[43] This EIS was a poorly documented effort to obscure facts which by now were officially established. Consistent with past publications, there was no scientific support for the population estimate it offered. The 1974 population was estimated at 450–550 grizzlies, with no attempt at substantiation. Figures for past years were incorrectly cited as applying currently; for example, the 1968 estimate of 234 grizzlies was used as a basis for most of the proposed management actions. Parts of the National Academy of Sciences report were quoted out of context and, in at least one case, misquoted. In the statement, "The National Academy of Sciences Committee on the Yellowstone Grizzlies (Cowan, 1974) has reviewed all available data and concluded that there is no convincing evidence that this population of grizzly bears is in danger of extinction." The word "immediate" which preceded "danger" in the NAS report was eliminated.

The committee's conclusion that extinction was not imminent was stressed by the Park Service (usually with the word "immediate" omitted) in its press releases following publication of the NAS report. Someone had assumed, correctly, that most people wouldn't bother to read the full report and compare it with the EIS. An October 17, 1974, editorial titled "Bad Manipulation" in the Jackson Hole *News* criticized the Park Service for this sort of misrepresentation:

> *We in the newspaper business tend to forget how easy it is to manage the news until we run into someone or agency trying to control the information we get. We encountered just such a case recently.*
>
> *For the past month we have received a number of releases from the National Park Service and the Department of the Interior on a recently completed study of the grizzly bear in Yellowstone National Park. Because of the controversy between independent researchers and the Park Service over the current population and management of the Yellowstone grizzly, the National Academy of Sciences was commissioned to study all data and evaluate the situation.*
>
> *When the study was released late in August, Park Service releases began arriving. The Academy, it said, had concluded "There is no convincing evidence that the grizzly bears in the Yellowstone ecosystem are in immediate danger of extinction."*

Anyone reading this would rightfully conclude, "Well, the park must be right." The problem is that park releases ignored that the study chastised them for having insufficient data on which to base a management plan, generally supported the research data supplied by Drs. Frank and John Craighead, and recommends prompt and adequate funding of a comprehensive research study on the grizzly by qualified independent scientists.

All of which sounds considerably different than the simple conclusion that all is well in grizzly land. In fact, it would appear that considerably more research is needed before the park totally commits itself to any particular course of action. Withholding or attempting to manipulate the news as the Park Service appears to have done in this case can do nothing but destroy the credibility of its position.

The grizzly might not be in "immediate" danger of extinction in the Yellowstone ecosystem, but the extremely high mortality rate from 1967 to 1973 had left very little margin for error. If control and hunting deaths continued to exceed the recommended limit, or if one of the many variables affecting the composition of the population were to shift (for example, if mortalities should be concentrated among reproductive females in a given year), the decline in population could reach a point where it would be irreversible.

Sow Number 101, the bear that in 1967 had foster-mothered Marian's yearlings, thus enabling Marian to breed a year earlier than was otherwise probable, was reported killed in Yellowstone in 1974. In earlier years we had tracked Number 101 by radio. Now sixteen and one half years old, she had insisted on returning home after having been transplanted several times. The Casper, Wyoming, *Star Tribune* of November 16, 1974, quotes Glen Cole as saying: "This particular bear was almost beating us back to the capture area after being transplanted. This meant she was not ever going to stay out in the wild." Cole also speculated that the aging grizzly may have been forced out of wild areas by younger bears. Our experience with the cooperative feeding of grizzlies, their lack of territoriality, and the sharing of home ranges and food supplies gives no credence to such an interpretation. Number 101, accustomed now to campgrounds, had simply acquired habits not readily broken.

Another long-lived grizzly sow, and a former radio bear as well, was shot illegally in the fall of 1974 by a hunter who coveted a bearskin rug. He also shot one of her two cubs, but apparently fearing arrest should he take the hides, left the dead animals to rot. He told someone about the shooting, however, and word eventually made its way to me via a local State Conservation Officer. I was told that the sow had a square tag numbered N-1583 on her left ear, which identified her as grizzly Number 120. She had managed to survive the traumatic period from 1969 to 1973 by avoiding campgrounds, but the search for new food sources had led her beyond the southern boundary of Yellowstone. She and her cubs were feeding within sight of the Turpin Meadows ranch buildings when she was killed.

I obtained the remains of sow Number 120's skull, which I shipped to John at Missoula for aging. The tooth cementum layers revealed that grizzly Number 120 was twenty-six and one half years old at the time of death. At this advanced age she had two cubs, her third known litter. Prior to this the oldest live grizzly that we had captured and aged was twenty-five and one half years old, and the oldest productive female twenty-two and one half years old. I wondered how much of such valuable information on reproductive vitality and longevity had been missed since the termination of our field research. I wondered, too, how many such illegal kills went unrecorded; only luck had brought this one to the attention of law enforcement officials. The unrecorded losses of mature females would tend to make even our projected population estimates optimistic.

In 1973, the various grizzly bear meetings — West Yellowstone, Macks Inn, Bozeman — the activities of the NAS committee, our warnings, public criticism of grizzly control killings, and the Park Service's concern over increased danger to visitors finally led to the creation of the Interagency Grizzly Bear Study Team. It consisted of research biologists from the National Park Service, the U.S. Fish and Wildlife Service, and the U.S. Forest Service cooperating closely with biologists from the states of Wyoming, Montana, and Idaho. The current team leader is Dr. Richard Knight of the National Park Service (this choice in contradiction to the NAS recommendation that the coordinating body be chaired by a neutral individual).[44] Broad objectives of the team are to determine the status and trends of the grizzly bear population and to study the use of habitats by bears and the relationship of land management activities to the welfare of the bear population. No independent researchers were included or were permitted to study the grizzly. An abstract of the 1975 report from this group states that unduplicated sightings of bears are down compared to previous years In 1975, only four sows with cubs and three sows with yearlings were sighted.[45] The report claims that the bears spent much more time in timber cover than in previous years and thus grizzly sightings and signs observed by various agency personnel were down about one-third from the previous year. The lush vegetation resulting from a wet spring and summer was believed to be responsible for this decline in sightings. It also stated that "observation did not indicate a shift in areas occupied by bears."[46]

The vegetation of the Yellowstone ecosystem consists predominantly of coniferous forests. Such forests do not respond to a single season of rain with growth lush enough to attract grizzlies entirely out of the open. They might feed somewhat more in the timbered areas during wet years, but grizzlies are by preference open-land foragers. Sagebrush–grass areas and alpine meadows would to some extent respond to a single season of rain and so would some understory vegetation, but it is inconceivable that this would, from one year to another, have any measurable effect on sighting and counting grizzlies, which tower over open land vegetation. No doubt the team members by now had second thoughts that the grizzly population might be alarmingly low and still declining, as our data indicated, but the 1975 report made no mention of such a possibility.

The report of the Interagency team for 1976 still did not indicate an increase in the decimated population.[47] An unduplicated sample of 102 individual bears was identified from all sources of observation including sixty-two airplane flights totalling 213 hours. The great mobility of the grizzlies and the lack of readily identifiable markers throws doubt on the reliability of this count. The report goes on to say, "The portion of the study area enclosing the unduplicated sample was about half of the entire area but did enclose that portion containing the bulk of the population."[48] The area actually included nearly all of Yellowstone National Park and forest areas in the vicinity of municipal dumps at Cooke City and West Yellowstone. In this heartland of the grizzly the figure 102, even if unduplicated, does not indicate a growing population and is decidedly lower than our figure of 136 in 1974 for a slightly larger area. The team nevertheless concluded that it is probable the grizzly bear population in the study area is growing or at least stable.

The plight of the grizzlies and the growing awareness of their population decline resulted in demands for their protection under the Endangered Species Act of 1973. A species may be listed as "threatened" under the Act if biological data indicate that it is not on the brink of extinction ("endangered") but is likely to become so if certain environmental conditions or human practices are not modified. The purposes of the Endangered Species Act are to provide a means whereby the ecosystem upon which endangered and threatened species depend may be conserved and also to provide a program for the conservation of endangered and threatened species. In February 1974, the Secretary of the Interior was petitioned by the Fund for Animals to list the grizzly bear in the lower forty-eight states as an endangered species. On May 25, 1975, after investigation by the Department of the Interior, the grizzly bear was classified as threatened. Section 7 of the Endangered Species Act makes it mandatory that critical habitat of threatened species be delineated and evaluated. Complying with this has brought about jurisdictional jealousies and disputes among the state and federal agencies involved with the grizzly. It has engendered concern and open hostility among outfitters, dude ranchers, stockmen, and others whose livelihood depends on forest, park, and wilderness lands and resources that may be considered critical habitat. They are apprehensive that their activities in these areas could conceivably be curtailed by the U.S. Fish and Wildlife Service after appropriate consultation with the affected states. The end result to date has been to intensify and expand the bear controversy and to delay the taking of responsible measures on behalf of the grizzly population.[49]

The states of Wyoming and Montana seem unanimous in their determination not to have the grizzly declared an endangered species. They are working to remove it from the threatened species listing, thus returning management of the grizzly outside of Yellowstone Park to the states. On the basis of federal grizzly bear management in Yellowstone National Park in the recent past, their claim that they can do a better job may be valid.

At present, the grizzlies and black bears of Yellowstone are infrequently seen — either along the roads or foraging in the backcountry meadows. They have not gone into hiding, they are simply not there. Even under the most enlightened management and favorable circumstances, it will be a long, long time before the Yellowstone grizzly bears recover to their former numbers — if they ever do.

Alive, the grizzly is a symbol of freedom and understanding — a sign that man *can* learn to conserve what is left of the earth. Extinct, it will be another fading testimony to things man should have learned more about but was too preoccupied with himself to notice. In its beleaguered condition, it is above all a symbol of what man is doing to the entire planet. If we can learn from these experiences, and learn rationally, both the grizzly and man may have a chance to survive.

Epilogue

Throughout her lifetime, the bear Marian had wandered, foraged, met most of the grizzlies in the Yellowstone ecosystem, mated, raised families and had come into contact with man, learning some of his ways. All of her activities in the early years of our study had taken place within an area of about thirty square miles — not a large expanse for a grizzly to roam. Marian's home range provided all her needs and there was no reason to expand it. Supplemental food was available from the Trout Creek dump and from natural sources in the surrounding forests and meadows. When the Trout Creek dump was abruptly closed, Marian, like hundreds of other grizzlies that had learned to seek food here, found none. This food was not essential, but habits die slowly, and the grizzlies returned again and again expecting to find food on the next visit as they had in the past. Finding none, they ranged out ever farther from the dump area. Coinciding with the abrupt elimination of refuse food at the Trout Creek open pit dump, Marian's home range expanded during 1968. She had to travel farther to obtain the same amount of food. Marian and the other grizzlies that concentrated in Hayden Valley were forced to look elsewhere. Many entered nearby campgrounds and some, such as grizzlies Number 130 and Number 239, were killed while doing so. It was inevitable that Marian too would locate and enter a campground, though up to this year of her life she had never been in one.

In the late fall of 1968 we had left Marian curled in a self-dug den with her three cubs of the year sleepy and lethargic beside her. The rising grizzly mortalities of that year had made us anxious to follow Marian to her den, fearing that it might be the last den we would locate by radio tracking. And as I trudged away from the den I also had the foreboding that this litter might be Marian's final family. The changes that were taking place and their effect on the behavior of the bears were evident; they clearly threatened the population and each and every individual.

Marian and her three active and demanding yearlings made it through the tourist season of 1969, when bear–man encounters were becoming ever more frequent and the toll in bear deaths was rising. With the dramatic reduction in park visitors after Labor Day, the major threat should have been over. But there was a shortage of berries and a dearth of pine nuts that fall, and Marian's continued foraging took her into the Lake utility and campground area. She was first observed there on Friday, October 10. Two of her yearlings, numbers 241 and 256, were trapped there and transplanted. They would later return. On Monday, October 13, at 7:30 A.M., the Lake Subdistrict Ranger saw Marian and a yearling near a trap. He partially immobilized the yearling with a drug-laden dart and, knowing that the sow was lurking nearby, he moved in to finish the job with another dart. Unfortunately, in doing so he placed himself in a position where he would have to shoot in self-defense if the mother tried to protect her struggling yearling. As might have been expected, Marian came out of the woods at full charge. Just short of the ranger she turned toward her yearling, then pivoted back, as though uncertain of her next move. The ranger did not hesitate. He shot Marian between the eyes with his .44 magnum. As she turned he shot two more quick rounds, followed by two more to assure that she was dead. The Lake Bear Log for October 13 reads: "0730 — 2 bears hanging around trap by sign cache in utility area. . . . When #1 was trapped . . . tranquilized one of the two-year-olds . . . about 180 lbs." Then, "Mother charged . . . had to shoot her . . . mature sow 300 lbs. . . ."

With Marian dead and family ties fragmented, her young dispersed to fend for themselves in a pattern that was being repeated throughout the population as death struck more and more grizzly mothers. Number 256 traveled south. He crossed the southern border of Yellowstone and left the park in the vicinity of Flagg Ranch. Here he sought food into November, trying to accumulate enough reserves for the winter at a time when it took ever more energy to forage. On November 8, he fell victim to a poacher's rifle. His littermate, Number 241, slept safely through the winter but wandered westward, out of the park and beyond the town of West Yellowstone, where he was under the jurisdiction of the state of Montana. Hunting was permitted. He was dropped with one bullet that crushed through his rib cage and shredded his heart. He was only two and one half years old. The trio making up Marian's last litter were all dead by 1972. Number 188, from an earlier litter, has not yet shown up on our mortality list. Perhaps he is still alive. Perhaps he has sired a litter that will carry on within the bear population some of the characteristics of the bear Marian, a grizzly that had adjusted to man perhaps as well as a wild grizzly ever ill.

No es to Chapter 10

1. Stephen Herrero, "Human Injury Inflicted by Grizzly Bears," *Science* 170(1970):593 – 598.

2. Jack Olsen, *Night of the Grizzlies* (New York: Putnam, 1969).

3. A. Starker Leopold et al., *A Bear Management Policy and Program for Yellowstone National Park* (revised), results of meetings September 6 and 7, 1969.

4. John S. McLaughlin to John Craighead, September 29, 1967.

5. Quoted in a letter from Harry V. Reynolds, Jr., a former ranger, to Ian McTaggart Cowan, chairman, Committee on the Yellowstone Grizzlies, National Academy of Sciences, January 18, 1974.

6. From the author's notes of a conversation with Glen Cole and Jay Sumner, July 9, 1968.

7. Jay Sumner's notes of the same conversation.

8. John Craighead's notes of a conversation with Jack Anderson, August 7, 1968.

9. "Grizzlies Will Control Themselves," Jackson Hole *Guide,* August 28, 1969.

10. Jack Anderson to John Craighead, April 7, 1969, and August 13, 1970.

11. John Craighead to Jack Anderson, July 13, 1971.

12. The author's memorandum of a telephone conversation with Dr. Linn, August 15, 1969.

13. From the author's notes of this meeting.

14. Leopold et al., *Bear Management Policy and Program.*

15. John Craighead to Frank Dunkle, January 17, 1969.

16. From Jay Sumner's notes of this meeting, January 15 and 16, 1970.

17. Kenneth R. Greer, "Managing Montana's Grizzlies for the Grizzlies," in *Bears —Their Biology and Management* (Morges, Switzerland: In-

ternational Union for the Conservation of Nature and Natural Resources, 1976), pp. 177–189.

18. The Park Service claims were presented in testimony in U.S. District Court, Central District of California, Dennis G. Martin, as Administrator of the Estate of Harry Eugene Walker, deceased, v. United States, case no. 72-3044-AAH, 1975.

19. Proposed "Memorandum of Understanding Between the National Park Service and the Bureau of Sports Fisheries and Wildlife Providing for Research on the Grizzly Bear, Ursus arctos, in Yellowstone National Park by the Montana Cooperative Wildlife Research Unit," August 14, 1971.

20. Reynolds to Cowan, January 18, 1974.

21. John J. Craighead, Joel R. Varney, and Frank C. Craighead, Jr., *A Population Analysis of the Yellowstone Grizzly Bears*, Bulletin 40, University of Montana, School of Forestry, Montana Forest and Conservation Experiment Station, 1974.

22. Estate of Harry Eugene Walker v. United States, Brochure of Demand, October 10, 1973.

23. "Old Faithful Camp Incident," official Park Service document presented at the Walker trial, 1972.

24. Ibid.

25. Transcript of testimony, Estate of Harry Eugene Walker v. United States.

26. A. Andrew Hauk, United States District Judge, Final Findings of Fact and Conclusions of Law and Order for Judgment, Estate of Harry Eugene Walker v. United States, March 26, 1975.

27. Barbara J. Culliton, "Advisory Meetings: Confidentiality Dropped, Public Is Invited," *Science* 177 (1972):412.

28. John J. Craighead, "A Briefing of the Grizzly Bear Situation in Yellowstone," Mammoth, Yellowstone National Park, September 19, 1972.

29. Frank C. Craighead, Jr., "Grizzly Bear and Black Bear Management, Yellowstone National Park," unpublished paper prepared for September 19, 1972, meeting.

30. Robert Linn to Senator Lee Metcalf, November 3, 1972.

31. "Grizzly Bears Secure, but a Bit Too Prolific," Casper *Star Tribune*, September 29, 1972.

32. Missoula, Montana, *Missoulian*, September 1972.

33. Frank C. Craighead, Jr., "Suggested Solution to Grizzly Bear Problem," abstract of "Grizzly Bear and Black Bear Management," prepared for Grizzly Bear Management Meeting, September 19, 1972, but not presented. Presented to EPA staff, Denver, Colorado, December 1972.

34. Ian McTaggart Cowan to John Craighead, September 16, 1973.

35. James B. White to Senator Gale McGee, January 11, 1973.

36. Ian McTaggart Cowan et al., Report of Committee on the Yellowstone Grizzlies, Division of Biological Sciences, National Research Council, National Academy of Sciences, 1974.

37. Reynolds to Cowan, January 18, 1974.

38. Cowan et al., Report of Committee on the Yellowstone Grizzlies.

39. Ibid., p. 9.

40. Ibid., p. 7.

41. Ibid., p. 15.

42. Glen F. Cole, "Management Involving Grizzly Bears in Yellowstone National Park, 1970–1972, Natural Resources Report no. 7, U.S. Department of the Interior, National Park Service, .

43. Draft Environmental Statement, Proposed Grizzly Bear Management Program, Yellowstone National Park, Wyoming, U.S. Department of the Interior, National Park Service, September 18, 1974.

44. Cowan et al., Report of Committee on the Yellowstone Grizzlies, p. 39.

45. Report of the Interagency Grizzly Bear Study Team, 1975, pp. ii, 15.

46. Interagency Grizzly Bear Study Team, *Grizzly Bear Newsletter,* no. 1, October, 1975, p. 1

47. Report of the Interagency Grizzly Bear Study Team, 1976, pp. 14, 16.

48. Ibid., p. 16.

49. Hearing before the Senate Committee on Appropriations, Proposed Critical Habitat Area for Grizzly Bears, 94th Cong., 2nd sess., special hearing, November 4, 1976.

Table of Grizzly Bear Numbers and Names

Author's note: Many of the grizzlies marked and numbered for study by the Craighead research team acquired names during the course of our acquaintance with them—in a few cases, more than one name. Others were identified only by number, and some bears that were never marked or numbered were given names that reflected notable physical or behavior traits (Cutlip, Old Mose, Scar Chest, the Rip-nosed Sow, and G.I., or the Disciplinarian, belong to this category). In the text I have generally referred to individuals by number and name when they are first introduced and by name alone thereafter. The following table should help the reader to keep track of the bears' identities.

4	Old Andy	**65**	Grizzled Sow
6	First Cub (also known as Lonesome, offspring of Number 7)	**76**	Pegleg
		78	Ignatz (offspring of Number 31)
7	Sour Creek Sow		
12	Inge	**80**	Bug-crew Bear
14	Bruno (also known as Bigfoot or the Thousand-pound Boar)	**86**	Orphan Runt
		88	Loverboy
		148	Owl-faced Sow
22	One Eye	**150**	Alum Creek Sow
26	Fifty-pound Cub	**164**	Lucky
31	Sylvia	**181**	
37	Beep	**192**	The Four Musketeers
38	Beep's brother	**193**	
40	Marian	**194**	
41	Ivan the Terrible, or Old Ivan	**190**	Fidel

Appendix:

Management of the Yellowstone Grizzly

The best kind of management for the privacy-loving grizzly bear would be no management at all. In today's world, however, this would be possible only if one could somehow isolate from any human presence an entire ecosystem adequate to maintain a viable grizzly population. Whereas in primeval North America a natural balance existed between the grizzly and man as codominant species, modern man and his works — farming, ranching, recreation — have coexisted uneasily with the great bears. The result, as we have seen, has been a drastic decline in grizzly numbers throughout their range and the elimination of all but a few remnant ecosystem populations in the contiguous United States. This trend will certainly continue unless informed and appropriate management programs are enacted.

In considering management it is essential to recognize that nearly all the remaining grizzly habitat in the lower forty-eight states has been modified or affected by the human presence to some extent. Although the Yellowstone ecosystem is approximately twice the size of Yellowstone National Park (see Map 1), the park itself — some 3,412 square miles — is the heartland of the grizzly population. And while the park does contain wild and pristine areas still lightly impacted by man, it is by and large greatly modified by the two million visitors a year, their automobiles, busy highways, gas stations, shopping centers, marinas and motorboats, lodging and administrative buildings, and the vast quantities of food required for the seasonal influx of people, some of whom spread out afoot or on horseback to the more remote areas. In any single day's activity during the summer months, some grizzlies will come into contact with humans, even if it be only crossing a highway at night or catching the scent of a meal cooking on a backcountry fire.

Assuming that we do wish to preserve a viable population of grizzlies in Yellowstone and in other remaining ecosystems — and such is clearly the will of the majority of Americans, as expressed through Congress in the protection of grizzlies under the Endangered Species Act — the multiple use of grizzly habitat dictates management. The overall aim of management must be to minimize the possibility of conflict between bears and humans wherever they make use of the same habitat. The unfortunate and occasionally tragic results of this conflict have been thoroughly documented here and elsewhere: (1) direct man–bear confrontations may lead to maulings, injuries, and human deaths but more often to the dispatch of the offending grizzly; (2) conditioning of grizzlies to humans through foraging in campgrounds almost inevitably leads to direct confrontation and thus to the death of the bear; (3) there is competition for habitat where human interests such as stock-raising and land development are at stake; and (4) critical habitat has been eliminated through development both inside and outside Yellowstone National Park. All of these are major factors in the decline in grizzly numbers, either through mortalities or a decrease in the reproductive potential; indeed, the only important mortality factor which is not in some way an expression of conflict over habitat is hunting.

To be fully effective, management must accomplish several specific things, all closely interconnected. It must prevent the loss or deterioration of critical habitat; resolve conflicts over the use of habitat insofar as is possible; lessen the danger of injury to humans by grizzlies; and reduce grizzly mortalities — particularly among mature reproductive females — in order to halt population decline and prevent eventual extinction. If it is to achieve these goals, management must be tailored to the biology and life history of the grizzly, based on all available scientific knowledge, and must also take careful account of the social, political, and economic context in which it operates. Effort here is needed on both the public and the private levels. The professional managers — government agencies and bear biologists — have the larger coordinating and educational role. Individual visitors to parks and wilderness areas have a responsibility to conduct themselves in such a way as to reduce the possibility of conflict with bears. Finally, management must be flexible enough to adapt to rapidly changing conditions without bureaucratic foot-dragging.

The author, John Craighead, and other colleagues have previously presented to the public and the government agencies involved detailed management recommendations for the grizzly bear in manuscripts, reports, presentations at meetings, memos, and scientific publications. The suggestions which follow are not offered as a comprehensive or definitive management program but rather will attempt to outline the most significant steps that can and should be taken to effectively manage the grizzly bear in the Yellowstone ecosystem.

1. Official recognition of the grizzly as a threatened species (in the lower forty-eight states) under the Endangered Species Act mandates the preservation of its "critical habitat," the character and extent of which is to be determined by the Secretary of the Interior after appropriate consultation with the states involved. Evaluation and delineation of critical grizzly bear habitat is of paramount importance in maintaining a stable population, but to date this issue has not been fully resolved. The habitat made available to the Yellowstone grizzlies must be extensive, for the grizzly requires a variety of conditions for its foraging activities, daytime rest areas, and den sites. Although some home ranges are relatively small (thirty to forty square miles), others embrace a thousand square miles or more, and movements of fifty airline miles from point to point are not uncommon.

The boundaries of the Yellowstone ecosystem, as defined by the Craighead research team in 1974, encompass about five million acres, including all of Yellowstone National Park and a comparably sized zone of surrounding national forest and wilderness areas (see Map 1). These boundaries are based on records of grizzly sightings, kills, and on habitat and land-use inventories, and in our experience this area is of sufficient size to support a viable population. The Secretary of the Interior together with other federal and state agencies having jurisdiction over these lands should take steps to reach a formal agreement to consider the entire ecosystem, thus defined, as critical habitat for the grizzly and manage it accordingly.

2. The Yellowstone ecosystem as defined above should be expanded only after careful consideration and for substantial reason. Grizzlies will naturally continue to range outside the boundaries of any man-designated area, and the greater the population density, the more likely they are to wander. However, little stands to be gained by increasing the size of the total habitat on account of such sporadic movement, and the sociopolitical problems arising from attempted habitat expansion could easily outweigh any benefits to the grizzly. The technique of transplanting grizzlies to expand habitat is one which should be worked out in the event it is needed, but this, too, requires considerable advance study.

3. The characteristics of preferred grizzly habitat — open country interspersed with timbered sanctuaries and openings within more extensively timbered areas — may at times be encouraged or maintained through habitat manipulation. Controlled natural burns, for example, can be permitted to provide open areas and their accompanying plant foods. Selective logging or small-scale clearcutting can likewise be beneficial. However, the possibilities for such manipulation are limited in national parks and wilderness areas, and in any case should be conducted in critical grizzly habitat only with great restraint and in consultation with bear biologists and researchers.

4. Grizzlies need isolation when hibernating. Under present conditions the Yellowstone ecosystem provides isolated denning sites sufficient for a grizzly bear population close to the carrying capacity of the area. Road construction and other development, lumbering, mining, and excessive fall and winter recreational use could alter this situation. The probable effect of any such activity on grizzly hibernation should be evaluated before approval is given. Known denning sites and timbered north slopes between seven and nine thousand feet elevation should be protected from habitat changes or manipulation, including otherwise permissible burns due to natural causes.

5. A concerted effort should be made toward a fully cooperative program of grizzly bear research and management among the managing agencies: the National Park Service, the U.S. Fish and Wildlife Service, the U.S. Forest Service, the Bureau of Land Management, and the fish and game departments of Wyoming, Montana, and Idaho. As early as 1963, a report of the Scientific

Advisory Committee to the National Park Service stated: "Research by the National Park Service has lacked continuity, coordination, and depth. It has been marked by expediency rather than by long-term considerations. It has in general lacked direction, has been fragmented between divisions and branches, has been applied piecemeal, has suffered because of a failure to recognize the distinction between research and administrative decision-making, and has failed to insure the implementation of the results of research in operational management."

6. Independent research on the grizzly should be reestablished in the Yellowstone ecosystem, and particularly within the park, as a source of unbiased data and accurate interpretation of the facts. The Committee on Yellowstone Grizzlies of the National Academy of Sciences stated in its 1974 report, "We recommend that the National Park Service and the U.S. Forest Service pursue a policy of supporting and encouraging independent research on Yellowstone grizzlies. The freedom of scientists to conduct research throughout the Yellowstone ecosystem is imperative if the data essential to successful management of Yellowstone grizzlies are to be obtained; the presence of independent investigators will enhance and invigorate study programs undertaken by land-management agencies."

In particular, both independent and agency researchers should be permitted to mark grizzlies, including radio-tagging, within the park. Only through some system of marking can dependable population statistics, essential to effective and knowledgeable management, be gathered. Marking is also required in order to recognize and keep tabs on troublesome or potentially dangerous bears.

7. If the grizzly population is to recover from the drastic reductions it suffered from 1968 to 1973, the agencies responsible for management should work to ensure that the total of man-caused grizzly mortalities or removals of grizzlies from the ecosystem does not exceed the limit of ten per year recommended by the Committee on Yellowstone Grizzlies. In some years this objective has been achieved, in others not; moreover, it is unlikely that all man-caused deaths are reported. Few poachings, for example, go down in the record books, and there is both direct and circumstantial evidence that poaching may be increasing.

There is as yet no evidence from the Interagency Grizzly Bear Study Team that the grizzly population has increased since 1973 or that it has even stabilized. Nor is there evidence that the low reproductive rate on which we suggested that management be based (0.515 to 0.544) has improved. If high attrition continues in the grizzly population, other management steps can be of little value in saving the bears.

8. Hunting of grizzly bears has largely been curtailed in the three states that comprise the Yellowstone habitat. There has been a moritorium on the hunting of grizzly bears in the state of Idaho from 1946 to the present (1978). In Wyoming, no permits have been issued for the hunting of grizzlies since July 28, 1975, when the U.S. Department of the Interior designated the grizzly a threatened species. (Prior to 1968 a Wyoming big game license also permitted the hunting of both black and grizzly bears. Wyoming declared a moritorium on hunting grizzlies from 1968 to 1970, then went to a special permit system in 1971, issuing 24 permits that year, followed by 16 in 1972 and 12 in 1973–1974.)

Montana has closed the season on grizzly bear hunting around Yellowstone National Park but since 1975 has allowed an annual total of 25 grizzlies to be taken from northwestern Montana, the total including those taken by hunters. A special license has been required for hunting grizzlies in Montana since 1967. (The current fee is $5 for residents and $35 for nonresidents. Within ten days after killing a grizzly the hunter is required to purchase a $25 special trophy license.)

If and when the grizzly bear population again increases to 1959–1967 levels, hunting outside the Yellowstone National Park sanctuary may be considered. Some form of control will then be necessary, and hunting can be an acceptable and effective control on expanding numbers and widely dispersing grizzlies. State fish and game departments, in collaboration with federal agencies and bear biologists, should formulate regulations annually based on current biological, political, and economic parameters (e.g., population estimates and reproductive rates, effect on outfitters, and losses to stockmen).

9. Formerly, the earth-filled garbage dumps served to "zone" grizzlies away from people during the busy visitor season. Zoning of one kind or another can still do more to reduce bear—man confrontations, injuries, and human death than any other single management procedure, and it would reduce the need for control activities which so often result in grizzly mortality. Baiting, the strategic placement of animal carcasses to attract grizzlies, is a tested and workable technique. It might only be needed temporarily, but could also be a continuing management tool. This should not be considered a "supplemental feeding" of grizzlies (which is not needed) but a means of concentrating and keeping grizzlies in areas where there are no people. Due to a lack of natural predation there are usually surpluses of both elk and bison within Yellowstone National Park, and these are periodically reduced by transplanting or by shooting (by the ranger staff). Elk carcasses have in the past been given to Indian tribes, but could instead be frozen and later distributed for consumption by grizzlies in summer and early fall. This would accomplish another Park Service objective: to recycle rather than eliminate nutrients within the ecosystem.

If baiting and other management procedures do not reduce the number of maulings and injuries to humans, and if annual man-caused grizzly mortalities continue to exceed the level permissible to maintain the population, consideration should be given to once again zoning grizzly bears away from people by establishing one or more feeding sites in isolated areas using elk carcasses and pellets as food attractants. Under modern conditions this may be the only truly effective method of maintaining the Yellowstone grizzlies. Possible locations for this project that should be considered are the upper reaches of Nez Percé and Trout creeks as well as upper Pelican Valley.

10. Vigorous efforts on the part of both the Park Service and visitors to thoroughly "sanitize" campgrounds would do much to reduce conflict. Table scraps, the contents of ice chests, waste food deposited at garbage dumps or burned in incinerators, and even cooking odors, attract bears as effectively as natural food sources, and once a bear has obtained food in a given area it will return there—perhaps for years, if reinforcement is continued. Return visits may even be timed to coincide with former successful foraging visits.

From a practical standpoint food cannot be eliminated, but food available to foraging bears can and should be minimized in areas such as campgrounds, where grizzlies are a threat to man. A program to do this is currently in effect, but continued improvements should be sought. The use of bear-proof garbage cans and daily garbage pickups are methods that should be strictly adhered to. Such a program obviously has its limitations, since people require food, and the odor itself is sufficient to attract grizzlies. However, unrewarded grizzlies will not linger and are less likely to return.

11. Whenever grizzlies are known to be entering campgrounds or prowling around developed areas, the visiting public should be alerted by signs, broadcasts, and ranger patrols. Maulings and injuries should be announced publicly to warn others who might unknowingly place themselves in danger.

12. Every human injury or death should be thoroughly investigated and its probable cause determined. This should be done by independent investigators. One of the surest ways to reduce grizzly bear injuries in the long run is to conscientiously investigate each incident, determine a pattern of cause, and take steps to correct the situation that precipitated it. This has not yet been done.

13. Problem bears that are repeatedly trapped in campgrounds should, as is currently being done, be transported to distant release points. The release areas should be carefully selected to meet the grizzly's requirements and to minimize conflict or contact with man. Food, preferably an animal carcass, should be placed in the vicinity of the released bear to help insure that it will remain. Recreationists and others in the area of release should be informed, if at all possible; those camping in the capture area (to which the bear may return) should also be warned of the situation and a course of action suggested. Frequent and well-timed warnings will reduce the chance of human injury and save the lives of bears as well.

14. Visitors should be informed when hiking, backpacking, or camping in the Yellowstone backcountry of a few precautions that will minimize confrontations with grizzlies. (Scare-type information and signs should be avoided.) Factual information can be handed out to visitors as they enter the park, and more specific information given on request and when issuing backcountry fire or camping permits.

Grizzlies may attack when they are injured, startled, or cornered and at rare times without any apparent provocation. The temperaments of individual grizzlies differ, likewise the temperament of the same individual from time to time depending on age, mood, and physical condition. A hungry or injured grizzly may attack more readily than a healthy, well-fed one. Females weaning their young are often irritable and hence dangerous. Females with cubs are often nervous and defensive and quick to attack if they feel threatened.

When hiking in the backcountry, your aim is to keep from surprising the grizzly; you want him to know you are approaching. Where sightings or signs reveal the presence of grizzlies, it is well to whistle or talk to companions while hiking through dense timber or windfall. If possible, avoid those areas, as grizzlies rest or sleep in such retreats. If you sight a grizzly, do not try to approach the bear but give it a wide berth, *especially a sow with cubs.* Often a good procedure is to move so that air currents carry your scent to the bear. When alerted in this way, most grizzlies will take off at a run. Often the bear's behavior depends on the distance separating bear and human at the moment of confrontation. The critical distance, that within which the bear is most likely to attack, is usually about 300 feet in open country and less in timbered areas.

When close to a grizzly, or if the bear is approaching, look for a tree you can climb and go up it. The grizzly doesn't climb. You can't outrun a grizzly, so don't run unless the grizzly is far enough away that you are sure you can make it to a tree. If you have started to run and reaching a tree seems doubtful, drop your pack to delay the grizzly and to facilitate climbing. At close range, stand still, face the bear, and talk quietly until the bear retreats, which it probably will. If the bear does attack, you may reduce your injuries and speed the bear's departure by playing dead and offering no resistance (advice that is harder to follow than to give).

When camping where the presence of grizzlies is suspected, sleep close to a tree you can climb and place your food at least 100 feet (preferably more) away from the sleeping area. At night all food should be enclosed in bags or a pack and either suspended from a tree limb by a rope or covered with a tarp to reduce odors. Don't go off for the day leaving food in your tent. Leave your camp clean and burn or carry out all trash. Don't bury it. Under no circumstances should you feed a grizzly. This endangers you, the bear, and other people the bear might encounter in the future.

Don't take chances with grizzlies, and do remember that in most cases, they want to avoid you. Give them an opportunity to do so.

15. People who enter onto and use public lands such as parks, national forests, and wilderness areas or rivers should expect to do so at their own risk. However, under the Tort-Claims Act an injured party can sue the government and receive damages if government negligence such as failure to warn the public of a known danger—for example, a rogue grizzly or grizzlies prowling campgrounds—can be proven. Unfortunately, rather than deterring negligence this sometimes leads to *post facto* attempts to misrepresent or cover up the facts (as in the case of the death of Harry Walker; see Chapter 10). Because of this, a program of private insurance against injury by wild animals in national parks should be seriously explored. The premium would be low, possibly no more than fifty cents, and all visitors could buy such insurance when entering a park. This should help to eliminate the tendency to misrepresent incidents that might result in financial loss to the government, and it could reduce litigation that is costly to both the plaintiff and the taxpayer regardless of the court's decision.

16. Many of foregoing suggestions also apply to the black bear; conversely, the presence of this species in the same ecosystem must be taken into account in managing the grizzly. Many park visitors as well as park personnel do not distinguish between blacks and grizzlies, and to do so is vital. Black bears are far less aggressive than grizzlies and thus do not pose the same threat of injury or death. However, they are dangerous and an attack (usually provoked) can prove fatal. They can climb trees, an ability the grizzly lacks; they are or used to be seen much more frequently than grizzlies along park roads and near developed areas; and the problem of food handouts from tourists has been more evident with black bears. These are the so-called roadside bums and beggars. When overabundant, black bears can and do cause excessive property damage to cars and camps, and minor injuries to tourists who foolishly feed or approach them. The Park Service's warnings against feeding have not proven fully effective.

While black bear numbers should be regulated and troublesome individuals removed or relocated, this does not imply wholesale extermination. In recent years the number of black bears seen along Yellowstone's roads has declined from as many as fifty or sixty in a single day to practically none in a period of weeks — a great disappointment to many tourists. It seems probable that the black bear, like the grizzly, has been heavily controlled in the last decade, and the Park Service's theory that the bears have dispersed into the backcountry to forage on their own cannot be verified by evidence. It is more likely that this once-abundant species has been severely decimated.

Black bears are perhaps the chief tourist attraction in Yellowstone National Park, and visitors who enjoy seeing them are not well served by heavy-handed control measures. One possible way to keep blacks around but out of trouble would be to construct turnouts with parking areas at strategic sites along the roads, where bears could be attracted so tourists could observe and photograph them. Visitors would have to be educated about how to behave around the bears, but this procedure would at least keep the animals off the highways and still accessible to view.

Bibliography

Introduction

Couturier, Marcel A. J. *L'ours Brun, Ursus Arctos.* Grenoble, France, 1954.

De Voto, Bernard. *The Journals of Lewis and Clark.* Boston: Houghton Mifflin, 1953.

Erickson, Albert W., et al. *The Black Bear in Michigan.* East Lansing: Michigan State University, Agricultural Experiment Station, 1964.

Hittell, Theodore H. *The Adventures of James Capen Adams.* New York: Arnold Press, 1972. Reprint of 1911 ed.

Jonkel, Charles J., and Cowan, Ian McT. "The Black Bear in the Spruce-Fir Forest." *Wildlife Monographs* 27. Washington, D.C.: The Wildlife Society, 1971.

Kelsey, Henry. *The Kelsey Papers.* Introduction by A. G. Doughty and C. Martin. Published by the Public Archives of Canada and the Public Record Office of Northern Ireland. Ottawa: F. A. Acland, printer, 1929.

McCracken, Harold. *The Beast that Walks Like a Man.* Boston: Houghton Mifflin, 1955.

Myers, John J. *Saga of Hugh Glass, Pirate, Pawnee and Mountain Man.* Lincoln: University of Nebraska Press, 1976.

Mills, Enos A. *The Grizzly: Our Greatest Wild Animal.* Boston and New York: Houghton Mifflin, 1919.

Murie, Olaus J. "The Last of the Big Bears." *Audubon Magazine,* July–August, 1958, pp. 156–89.

Rausch, Robert L. "Geographic Variation in Size in North American Brown Bears, *Ursus arctos L.,* as Indicated by Condylobasal Length." *Canadian Journal of Zoology* 41 (1963):33–45.

Russel, Andy. *Grizzly Country.* New York: Alfred A. Knopf, 1968.

Schneider, Bill. *Where the Grizzly Walks.* Missoula, Mont.: Mountain Press Publishing, 1977.

Storer, T. I. and **Tevis,** L. P., Jr. *California Grizzly.* Berkeley and Los Angeles: University of California Press, 1955.

White, Thomas. "The Possibility of Grizzly Bears Still Existing in Saskatchewan." *The Blue Jay,* September, 1965, pp. 136–40.

Wright, W. H. *The Grizzly Bear: The Narrative of a Hunter–Naturalist.* New York: Chas. Scribner's Sons, 1909.

Chapter 1

Craighead, Frank C., et al. "Radio-Tracking of Grizzly Bears." In Lloyd E. Slater, ed., *Bio-Telemetry: the Use of Telemetry in Animal Behavior and Physiology in Relation to Ecological Problems.* New York: Pergamon Press, 1963.

Craighead, Frank C., Jr., and Craighead, John J. "Knocking Out Grizzly Bears for their Own Good." *National Geographic* 118(1960):276–91.

———. "Tracking Grizzly Bears." *BioScience* 15(1965):88–92.

———. "Trailing Yellowstone's Grizzlies by Radio." *National Geographic* 130(1966):252–67.

———. "Grizzly Bears." In *Science Year 1973: the World Book Science Annual.* Chicago: Field Enterprises Educational Corp., 1973.

Curry-Lindahl, Kai. "The Brown Bear (Ursus arctos) in Europe: Decline, Present Distribution, Biology, and Ecology." In *Bears—Their Biology and Management.* Morges, Switzerland: International Union for the Conservation of Nature and Natural Resources (IUCN), 1972, pp. 74–80.

Kurtén, Björn. *Pleistocene Mammals of Europe.* London: Weidenfeld and Nicolson, 1968.

National Geographic Society, *Research Reports,* 1961–1962 Projects through 1969 Projects. Washington, D.C., 1968–1978.

Varney, Joel R. "A Tracking and Telemetry System for Wildlife Research." In *NTC* (National Telemetering Conference) *Record.* New York: Institute of Electrical and Electronics Engineers, 1971, pp. 247–52.

Chapter 2

Craighead, John J., et al. "Trapping, Immobilizing and Color-Marking Grizzly Bears." Transactions. 25th North American Wildlife and Natural Resources Conference. Washington, D.C.: American Wildlife Institute, 1960.

Hornocker, M. G. "Population Characteristics and Social and Reproductive

Behavior of the Grizzly Bear in Yellowstone National Park." M.S. thesis, University of Montana, 1962.

Stonorov, Derek, and Stokes, A. W. "Social Behavior of the Alaska Brown Bear." In *Bears—Their Biology and Management,* IUCN, 1972, pp. 232–42.

Chapter 3

Craighead, John J.; **Craighead,** Frank C., Jr.; and **Summer,** Jay, "Reproductive Cycles and Rates in the Grizzly Bear, Ursus arctos horribilis, of the Yellowstone Ecosystem." In *Bears—Their Biology and Management,* IUCN, 1976, pp. 337–56.

Craighead, John J.; **Hornocker,** M. G.; and **Craighead,** Frank C., Jr. "Reproductive Biology of Young Female Grizzly Bears." *Journal of Reproduction and Fertility,* Suppl. 6(1969): 447–75.

Erickson, Albert W., et al. "The Breeding Biology of the Male Brown Bear (Ursus arctos)." *Zoologica, Scientific Contributions of the New York Zoological Society* 53(1968):85–105.

Chapter 4

Craighead, Frank C., Jr. "Radiotracking of Grizzly Bears in Yellowstone National Park, Wyoming," *National Geographic Society Research Reports, 1963 Projects.* Washington, D.C., 1968, pp. 59–67.

_____. "Biotelemetry Research with Grizzly Bears and Elk in Yellowstone National Park, Wyoming, 1965." *National Geographic Society Research Reports, 1965 Projects.* Washington, D.C., 1971, pp. 49–62.

Craighead, Frank C., Jr., and **Craighead,** John J. "Radiotracking of Grizzly Bears in Yellowstone National Park, Wyoming, 1962." *National Geographic Society Research Reports, 1961–1962 Projects.* Washington, D.C., 1970, pp. 63–71.

_____. "Grizzly Bear Prehibernation and Denning Activities as Determined by Radiotracking." *Wildlife Monographs* 32. Washington, D.C.: The Wildlife Society, 1972.

_____. "Radiotracking of Grizzly Bears and Elk in Yellowstone National Park, Wyoming, 1966." *National Geographic Society Research Reports, 1966 Projects.* Washington, D.C., 1973, pp. 33–48.

Craighead, John J., et al. "Telemetry Experiments with a Hibernating

Black Bear." In *Bears — Their Biology and Management*, IUCN, 1976, pp. 357–71.

Chapter 5

Craighead, John J., and **Craighead,** Frank C., Jr. *Hawks, Owls and Wildlife*. 2d ed. New York: Dover Publications, 1969.

Green, J. A., and **Dunn,** F. "Correlation of Naturally Occurring Infrasonics and Selected Human Behavior." *Journal of the Acoustical Society of America* 44(1968):1456–57.

Jenness, Robert; **Erickson,** Albert W.; and **Craighead,** John J. "Some Comparative Aspects of Milk from Four Species of Bears." *Journal of Mammalogy* 53(1972):34–47.

Kistchinski, A. A., and **Uspenski,** S. M. "Immobilization and Tagging of Polar Bears in Maternity Dens." In *Bears — Their Biology and Management*, IUCN, 1972, pp. 172–80.

Reynolds, Harry V. "Denning Ecology of Grizzly Bears in Northeastern Alaska." In *Bears — Their Biology and Management*, IUCN, 1976, pp. 403–9.

Uspenski, S.M., and **Kistchinski,** A.A. "New Data on the Winter Ecology of the Polar Bear (Ursus maritimus Phipps) on Wrangel Island." In *Bears — Their Biology and Management*, IUCN, 1972, pp. 181–97

Chapter 6

Bray, Olin E. "A Population Study of the Black Bear in Yellowstone National Park." M.S. thesis, Colorado State University, 1967.

Craighead, Frank C., Jr. "Radiotelemetry Research on Large Western Mammals in Yellowstone National Park, Wyoming, 1967." *National Geographic Society Research Reports, 1967 Projects*. Washington, D.C., 1974, pp. 35–51.

Craighead, Frank C., Jr., and **Craighead,** John J. "Studying Wildlife by Satellite." *National Geographic* 143(1973):120–23.

Craighead, Frank C., Jr., et al. "Satellite Tracking of Elk, Jackson Hole, Wyoming." *National Geographic Society Research Reports, 1969 Projects*. Washington, D.C., 1978, pp. 73–88.

Craighead, John J., et al. "Satellite Monitoring of Black Bears." *BioScience* 21(1971):1206–11.

——————. "Telemetry Experiments with a Hibernating Black Bear." In *Bears—Their Biology and Management*, IUCN, 1976, pp. 357–71.

Erickson, Albert W., et al. *The Black Bear in Michigan.* East Lansing: Michigan State University, Agricultural Experiment Station, 1964.

Folk, Edgar G. "Physiology of Hibernating Bears." In *Bears — Their Biology and Management*, IUCN, 1976, pp. 373–80.

Hock, R. J. "Mammalian Hibernation. VIII. Seasonal Variations in Physiologic Functions of Arctic Ground Squirrels and Black Bears." *Bulletin of the Museum of Comparative Zoology, Harvard University* 124 (1960):155–71.

——————. "Heart Rate of Black Bears in Relation to Age." *Journal of Mammalogy* 47(1966):328–29.

Johansson, Bengt. "Mammalian Hibernation. XII. Brown Fat and Its Possible Significance for Hibernation." *Bulletin of the Museum of Comparative Zoology* 124 (1960):233–48.

Kayser, Charles. *The Physiology of Natural Hibernation.* New York: Pergamon Press, 1961.

Morrison, Peter. "Mammalian Hibernation. IV. Some Interrelations between Weight and Hibernation Function." *Bulletin of the Museum of Comparative Zoology* 124(1960):75–91.

Nelson, Ralph A. "Winter Sleep in the Black Bear, a Physiologic and Metabolic Marvel." *Mayo Clinic Proceedings* 48(1973):733–37.

——————. "Nitrogen Metabolism in Bears: Urea Metabolism in Summer Starvation and in Winter Sleep and Role of Urinary Bladder in Water and Nitrogen Conservation." *Mayo Clinic Proceedings* 50(1975):141–46.

Nelson, Ralph A., et al. "Metabolism of Bears Before, During and After Winter Sleep." *American Journal of Physiology* 224(1973):491–96.

Chapter 7

Beeman, Larry E., and **Pelton,** Michael R. "Homing of Black Bears in the Great Smoky Mountains National Park." In *Bears—Their Biology and Management*, IUCN, 1976, pp. 87–95.

Berns, V. D., and **Hensel,** R. J. "Radiotracking Brown Bears on Kodiak Island." In *Bears—Their Biology and Management*, IUCN, 1972, pp. 19–25.

Burt, W. H. "Territoriality and Home Range Concepts as Applied to Mammals." *Journal of Mammalogy* 24(1943):346–52.

Craighead, Frank C., Jr. "Radiotracking of Grizzly Bears in Yellowstone National Park, Wyoming." *National Geographic Society Research Reports, 1963 Projects.* Washington, D.C., 1968, pp. 59–67.

————. "Grizzly Bear Ranges and Movement as Determined by Radiotracking." In *Bears—Their Biology and Management,* IUCN, 1976, pp. 97–109.

Craighead, John J., and **Craighead,** Frank C., Jr. "Grizzly Bear–Man Relationships in Yellowstone National Park." In *Bears—Their Biology and Management,* IUCN, 1972, pp. 304–32.

Murie, Adolph. "Cattle on Grizzly Bear Range." *Journal of Wildlife Management* 12( ):57–72.

Chapter 8

Cole, Glen F. "Preservation and Management of Grizzly Bears in Yellowstone National Park." In *Bears—Their Biology and Management,* IUCN, 1972, pp. 274–88.

Craighead, John J.; **Craighead,** Frank C., Jr.; and McCutchen, Henry E. "Age Determination of Grizzly Bears from Fourth Premolar Tooth Sections." *Journal of Wildlife Management* 34(1970):353–63.

Craighead, John J.; **Varney,** Joel R.; and **Craighead,** Frank C., Jr. "A Population Analysis of the Yellowstone Grizzly Bears." Bulletin 40. Montana Forest and Conservation Station, School of Forestry, University of Montana, 1974.

Sauer, Peggy R. "Determining Sex of Black Bears from the Size of the Lower Canine Tooth." *New York Fish and Game Journal* 13(1966):140–45.

Sauer, Peggy R., et al. "Age Determination in Black Bears from Canine Tooth Sections." *New York Fish and Game Journal* 13(1966):125–39.

Chapter 9

Craighead, Frank C., Jr. "They're Killing Yellowstone's Grizzlies." *National Wildlife,* October 1973, pp. 4–9.

Regenstein, Lewis. *The Politics of Extinction.* New York: Macmillan, 1972.

U.S. Congress. Senate Committee on Appropriations. Hearings on Proposed Critical Habitat Area for Grizzly Bears. 94th Cong., 2nd sess., special hearing, November 4, 1976, pp. 85–158.

Chapter 10

Cowan, Ian McTaggart, et al. Report of Committee on the Yellowstone Grizzlies, Division of Biological Sciences, National Research Council, National Academy of Sciences, 1974.

Craighead, John J.; **Varney,** Joel R.; and **Craighead,** Frank C., Jr. "A Population Analysis of the Yellowstone Grizzly Bears." Bulletin 40. Montana Forest and Conservation Experiment Station, School of Forestry, University of Montana, 1974.

Culliton, Barbara J. "Advisory Meetings: Confidentiality Dropped, Public Is Invited." *Science* 177(1972):412.

Hauk, A. Andrew (United States District Judge). Final Findings of Fact and Conclusions of Law and Order for Judgement. Dennis G. Martin, as Administrator of the Estate of Harry Eugene Walker, deceased, v. United States. U.S. District Court, Central District of California, case no. 72-3044-AAH, March 26, 1975.

Herrero, Stephen. "Man and the Grizzly Bear, Past, Present, but Future?" *BioScience* 20(1970):1148–53.

Leopold, A. Starker, et al. *A Bear Management Policy and Program for Yellowstone National Park.* Report to the Director by the Natural Science Advisory Committee of the National Park Service, as a result of meetings in Yellowstone National Park, September 6 and 7, 1969.

Olsen, Jack. *Night of the Grizzlies.* New York: Putnam, 1969.

Transcript of Testimony. Estate of Harry Eugene Walker, deceased, v. United States. U.S. District Court, Central District of California, 1975.

Index